# SOUTH AFRICA:
# THE BATTLE OVER THE CONSTITUTION

# South Africa:
# The Battle over the Constitution

SIRI GLOPPEN
*Department of Comparative Politics,*
*University of Bergen*

**Ashgate**
DARTMOUTH
Aldershot • Brookfield USA • Singapore • Sydney

Published by
Dartmouth Publishing Company Limited
Ashgate Publishing Limited
Gower House
Croft Road
Aldershot
Hants GU11 3HR
England

Ashgate Publishing Company
Old Post Road
Brookfield
Vermont 05036
USA

Coventry University

**British Library Cataloguing in Publication Data**
Gloppen, Siri
    South Africa : the battle over the constitution. - (Law,
    social change and development)
    1.South Africa - Constitutional law
    I.Title
    342.6'8

**Library of Congress Cataloging-in-Publication Data**
Gloppen, Siri.
     South Africa : the battle over the Constitution / Siri Gloppen.
       p.    cm. – (Law, social change, and development)
    Originally presented as the author's thesis (doctoral–University of Bergen, 1993).
    Includes bibliographical references and index.
    ISBN 1-85521-922-0 (hc)
     1. Constitutional law–South Africa. 2. Constitutional history-
-South Africa. 3. South Africa–Politics and government–1989-
I. Title. II. Series.
KTL2070.G59    1997
342.68'02–dc21                                  97-24962
                                                     CIP

ISBN 1 85521 922 0

Printed in Great Britain by Galliard (Printers) Ltd, Great Yarmouth

# Contents

# List of Figures

# List of Tables

# List of Abbreviations

| | |
|---|---|
| ACDP | African Christian Democratic Party |
| ANC | African National Congress |
| AT | Amended text of the 'final' Constitution of the Republic of South Africa (amended on 11 October 1996). |
| CA | Constitutional Assembly |
| Codesa | Convention for a Democratic South Africa |
| COSAG | Concerned South African Group. A conservative alliance led by the IFP and the Conservative Party (1993) |
| Cosatu | Congress of South African Trade Unions |
| CCT | Constitutional Court |
| CP | Constitutional Principle (34 fully entrenched constitutional principles are included in the 1993 Interim Constitution) |
| DP | Democratic Party |
| NT | The text of the 'final' Constitution of the Republic of South Africa as adopted on 8 May 1996 |
| FF | Freedom Front |
| GNU | Government of National Unity |
| IC | Interim Constitution of the Republic of South Africa (1993) |
| IFP | Inkatha Freedom Party |
| JSE | Judicial Service Commission |
| MP | Member of Parliament |
| NCoP | National Council of Provinces |
| NGO | Non-governmental Organisation |
| NP | National Party |
| PAC | Pan Africanist Congress |
| PR | Proportional representation |

# Preface

The Battle of the South African Constitution has been long, fierce, and conducted on several arenas, political, academic and military. Vast amounts of energy have been devoted to constitution-making, the 'final' post-apartheid constitution that is implemented in 1997 is the outcome of more than five years of constitutional negotiations, with preliminary 'talks about talks' before that. When so much effort by the most able men and women in the country go into a document, it inevitably gives rise to expectations. But do constitutions matter?

Constitutions are intriguing documents. Based on a curious form of authority that somehow seems to wane when critically examined, the constitution is nevertheless acknowledged as the highest norm of most modern democracies. In some countries the constitution exerts a long-standing and profound influence and effectively regulates the political life of the country. In other cases constitutions have proved largely irrelevant.

The theoretical starting point of this book is a preoccupation with questions of how constitutions operate. What makes the difference between a paper tiger and a constitution that actually regulates the political life of a country? Can anything be done to make this difference happen? Does constitutionalism and democratic consolidation depend on the 'right' type of society, for instance a particular civic culture (Putnam, 1993)? Or is it a matter of finding the 'right' constitution to match the context? And, presuming that the latter is important, what is the 'right' constitution for South Africa?

What fascinated me most when I started to study this in 1991 was how the rivalling constitutional positions on the South African scene could be understood not only in terms of political expediency, but as coherent normative structures. And how each seemed 'right' for South Africa according to its own interpretation of the conflicts of South African society.

As the analysis — and the negotiations — proceeded it became more and more clear how difficult it was, theoretically, to reconcile the two into a well-functioning constitutional structure. At the same time it became obvious that, politically, a compromise was the only workable solution.

This understanding of the disparate logic of the rivalling positions, made the process more transparent. It facilitated an understanding of why the negotiations took the form that they did, and why certain outcomes resulted. This perspective also exposed weaknesses in the 1993 Interim Constitution as well as in the 'Final' Constitution of May 1996, weaknesses that could potentially affect the prospects for constitutionalism and consolidation of democracy. The focus on the constitutional models as coherent normative structures also brings the relevance of legitimacy for constitutionalism into focus. If a compromise, and the process that brings this about, broadens the legitimacy of the constitution, to what extent does this compensate for inconsistencies and 'defects' in the structure?

To study the South African constitution-making process has been extremely fascinating also because of the political dynamics. The political achievements have at times been awe-inspiring — particularly given the context: centuries of distrust and hostility, extreme inequality and poverty, ethnic divisions, violence and rampant crime. At other times trivialities threaten to cause havoc. It is said of South Africa that it is a country where miracles seem easy and the possible beyond reach, and this characterisation keeps coming to mind. It highlights the tension so central to constitutionalism and democratic consolidation, that between the institutional and legal framework on the one hand and statesmanship on the other.

# Acknowledgements

This book has been in the process for quite a while. It originated as a thesis delivered in 1993 as part of the requirements for the Cand.Polit (M.A.) degree at the Department of Comparative Politics at the University of Bergen. Whilst working on the thesis I was very fortunate to be affiliated to the Chr. Michelsen Institute (CMI) in Bergen. I want to express my thanks to both of these institutions for generous support, including financial support to make further development of the manuscript possible.

Special thanks to Elling Njål Tjønneland of the CMI who was an excellent supervisor in all respects, and who has continued to be a source of inspiration and support. Likewise, thanks to my supervisor Frank Aarebrot of the Department of Comparative Politics who with his knowledge and creativity provided invaluable comments.

The work on the thesis inspired a further interest in the phenomenon of constitutionalism more generally and the South African constitution-making process in particular. Fortunately, my present position as a doctorate scholar at the Department of Comparative Politics has given me the opportunity to pursue these interests and to improve my understanding of them.

From February to July 1995 I was with the Centre for Political Studies at the University of the Western Cape (UWC). I want to thank the staff, and Professor Willem van Vuuren in particular, for making this stay both pleasant and useful. During this period I had the opportunity to follow the proceedings in the Constitutional Assembly and talk to people involved in the process both politically and administratively. This gave a valuable first-hand impression of the process. I also had the chance to examine submissions from the public and to talk to representatives of civil society involved in the writing of submissions.

A number of people have commented on drafts and presentations, inspired ideas, and provided support at various stages of the process. I would like to thank former and present colleagues at the CMI, at FAFO at the UWC and here at the Department of Comparative Politics. Special thanks are due to Bernt Hagtvet, Lauri Karvonen, Stein Kuhnle, Lise Rakner, Åshild Samnøy, Arne Tostensen and Liv Tørres.

I also want to thank Professor Abebe Zegeye, the editor of this book series, and Dartmouth Publishing Company, for showing an interest in my manuscript, and Sarah Smith for her help with the copy-editing.

Finally, thanks to Ole Frithjof Norheim, my husband and intellectual ally, whose support is invaluable in so many respects.


Bergen, January 1997

Siri Gloppen

# PART I
# RIVALLING REALITIES

# 1 Introduction

## A New Constitution for South Africa

When South Africa's 'final' post-apartheid Constitution was signed into law by President Nelson Mandela in Sharpeville on 10 December 1996, it marked the end of a six year long battle over the constitution where competing visions of the new South Africa, formed during the decades of struggle, clashed through paragraph after paragraph.

This book is an attempt to analyse this battle and the constitution that came out of it, from the perspective of the constitutional models that dominated the negotiations, and the normative conceptions and world views that inform them. The character of the rivalling positions and the dynamic between them is our primary concern, while the actual negotiation process is outlined in broad stokes to indicate how the parties' perspectives informed their bargaining strategies and how this in turn influenced the outcome.

A land-mark in the negotiation process was the adoption of an interim constitution in November 1993. This document prepared the grounds for the April 1994 general elections that brought President Mandela and his African National Congress (ANC) into power. It defined the framework for the subsequent negotiation process and laid down the 'rules of the political game' for a transitional period of five years. A key element of the interim constitution was a set of 34 entrenched constitutional principles binding on the 'final' constitution.

Disagreement on fundamental issues characterised the constitutional negotiations throughout. How much power should be conferred on the central government? How should minority interest be safeguarded? In the days before the deadline for the passing of the 'Constitution of the Republic of South Africa Bill' on 8 May 1996 central issues remained deadlocked. Eventually a deal was struck. With the votes of the ANC, the National Party (NP), the Democratic Party (DP) and the Pan Africanist Congress (PAC), the Bill got the required two-thirds majority.

Adoption Day did not, however, mark the end of the battle over the constitution. According to the 1993 Interim Constitution, the Constitutional Court must certify that the text of the new constitution complies with the 34

3

constitutional principles. After a thorough process where political parties as well as the public were invited to make submissions, the Court ruled that the text could not be certified. In order to comply with the constitutional principles several changes had to be made, most significantly on the controversial issue of provincial powers. The Constitutional Assembly reconvened and on 11 October 1996 passed an amended constitutional text. This was again submitted to the Constitutional Court for certification and on 6 December the constitution was certified.

Is the battle over? The 'final' South African constitution is still a controversial document. The NP, although voting in favour of the constitution, demonstrated its dissatisfaction by resigning from the Government of National Unity (GNU) in May 1996. The Inkatha Freedom Party (IFP), who boycotted the constitutional process,[1] condemned the constitution as a death certificate for pluralism in South Africa.

Why did the Constitution turn out the way it did, and what are its prospects for making a positive contribution to South African politics? These are is the questions that underlie the analyses throughout the book.

## Focus of Analysis

In order to shed light on the potential of the new South African constitution a number of questions need to be addressed.

Firstly, there are general questions concerning what kind of political instrument a constitution is. How does it exert influence? What conditions are favourable to constitutionalism? Constitutions differ on a number of dimensions, both with regard to normative choices and technical mechanisms, how does this affect their role in political life?

Secondly, the character of the new South African constitution must be established. This constitution is best understood from the perspective of the rivalling constitutional positions that stood against each other throughout the process and kneaded the constitution into its present shape. These positions, in turn, answer different interpretations of South African society and different sets of problems, and should be seen against the perceptions of society and the normative traditions that underlie each of them.

The focus of this book is on the two main rivalling positions throughout the process, represented by Arend Lijphart's (1985) work 'Power-Sharing in South Africa', a classic consociational approach, and Albie Sachs' (1990a) *Protecting Human Rights in a New South Africa* which can be seen as an attempt to apply liberal theories of justice to the South African context. The models represent, from an analytical point of view, the main approaches towards democratic constitutional design. Politically they cover the space within which the constitutional negotiations in South Africa have taken place.

The analysis seeks to understand the ways in which constitutions influence democratic performance and stability and to show how various constitutional models provide different answers to problems in South African society.

The analysis takes as a point of departure the major obstacles to democratic consolidation in South Africa as seen by different parties in the constitutional process. Particular attention is given to how the models respond to the problems of socioeconomic inequality and ethnic diversity. The precise effects of constitutional set-ups cannot be determined,[2] but is it possible to show how each institutional framework is directed against a particular set of problems and how it creates incentives for, and impediments against, various forms of political action. This assessment of the models in turn provides a basis for an evaluation of the new constitution, which can be seen as a compromise between the two.

Divergence with regard to institutional solutions is a consequence of conflicting normative concerns and perceptions of South African reality. The methodological and normative differences between the two models of constitutional design stand out against the background of contemporary political philosophy. The analysis explicates the implications of these differences for the acceptability of the models as constitutional frameworks.

The empirical focus is on South Africa, but the analysis is of relevance beyond this context. South Africa is unique in many respects due to the legacy of apartheid. Still, the problem focus of this study — the dynamics between ethnicity, poverty and inequality — is well known and acute throughout the world. 'Ethnicity is at the centre of politics in country after country, a potent source of challenges to the cohesion of states and of international tension' (Horowitz, 1985: xi).

## The Structure of the Argument

The structure of the analysis is as follows. Part I focuses on fundamental problems that South Africa is facing, and for which address has been sought through constitutional design: crime and violence, poverty and inequality, and the potential of ethnic and racial tension. In Part II, the constitutional 'solutions' that have been the main rivals throughout the negotiation process are presented. In Part III the models are analysed, both in terms of their normative and theoretical acceptability, and in terms of their ability to contribute to a solution of the problems discussed in Part I. In Part IV this is used to analyse the constitution of 8 May 1996, and the process leading to its adoption. How is the constitution influenced by the two models? What are the consequences of this particular mix of elements? And what are the prospects for constitutionalism in South Africa?

## Part I: Rivalling Realities

The entire constitution-making process in South Africa has taken place in a context of violence. During the early stages of the process political violence was rife, bordering on civil war. With the exception of the province of KwaZulu-Natal, the levels political violence dropped after the April 1994 elections. This was, however, replaced by a rocketing rate of violent crime. Violence is in itself a serious threat to democratic stability. It is also a symptom of underlying conflicts in society. The nature of these underlying conflicts is contested. Some speak of a culture of violence resulting from the brutality and the manipulation of the previous regime. Others emphasise structural factors as primary causes: persisting unemployment; poverty; inequality. These explanations have been challenged by those who see violence as a symptom of underlying racial and ethnic tension. This conflict of diagnoses goes beyond the issue of violence, it is a general conflict over the interpretation of the cleavage structure of South African society. What represents the greatest obstacle to democratic stability, class or ethnicity? This battle of 'reality' is crucial in understanding the different approaches to constitutional design.

Neither side denies the existence of poverty and vast social and economic inequality in South Africa, or that these are serious problems. Some see them, however, as secondary to ethnic conflict with respect to political stability. When it comes to the problem of ethnicity and ethnic conflict there is more controversy with regard to the 'facts'. While ethnic heterogeneousness is undisputed, the political significance of ethnicity, and the potential for ethnic conflict in the future, is hotly contested.

In order to do justice to the constitutional models that have been set forth they should be seen against their own interpretation of South African reality — only then is their rationale and potential brought out.

*Part II: The Quest for Solutions*

Given the controversy over the interpretation of 'facts' it should come as no surprise that the constitutional solutions brought forward as a means to address the problems has differed. The second part of the book looks at ways in which one has tried to come to grips with the problems of ethnic tension and social and economic inequality by way of constitutional design.

Constitutionalism and constitutional design is discussed in general terms in Chapter 3. The assumptions on the role of constitutions as political instruments that underlie the analysis, is clarified and different conceptions of constitutionalism are discussed, explicating ways in which constitutional constraints operate, and the aims they seek to achieve. Thereafter, a conceptual framework is constructed, delineating dimensions on which constitutions vary.

The strategies for constitutional design presented in Chapters 4 and 5 fall in two categories. The first focuses on the question of justice. The central objective is to construct a constitutional structure which safeguards fundamental human rights for all individuals, and which works towards a just distribution of resources and opportunities.

The second approach, consociation or power-sharing models, focuses on the question of stability, and in particular on containment of ethnic conflict. Central characteristics of this approach are reliance on (ethnic) groups as the main political units; emphasis on proportionality — in legislative and executive bodies and in allocation of vital resources; and insistence on measures that facilitate decisions by consensus (e.g. minority vetoes and grand coalition governments). The models strive to minimise political stakes in the centre through decentralisation of political authority (federalism) by granting autonomy to the various groups. A central idea is that hard decisions should be lifted out of the central political bodies when possible, and the main role of the state should be that of a mediator between groups rather than an autonomous actor.

While the consociational models emphasise and elaborate on the electoral system, the focus of the justice model is on the legal system. The constitution should contain a bill of rights guaranteeing equal civil and political rights to all citizens, as well as provisions to ensure that social and economic rights are attended to — for instance by securing a firm constitutional foundation for affirmative action. A system of councils should be institutionalised for monitoring the enforcement of rights. And while consociational models emphasise the need for decisions by consensus, the justice model relies on majoritarian decision-making procedures, while emphasising the need to create a broad consensus on the basic norms underlying the political institutions. This consensus is to be advanced through establishing structures for civil society participation in the constitution-making process, and through ensuring that the political system has the perceived fairness needed to generate its own support.

In order to move towards distributive justice, the justice model underscores the need for a potent government. The implicit assumption is that a centralised state and extensive reliance on majority decisions is necessary in order to transform South African society into a fairer scheme of cooperation.

The two approaches coincide with the constitutional views of the main parties in the South African constitution-making process. The National Party has throughout the process had consociational and federal models as their preferred constitutional option, while leading sections of the ANC has opted for a majoritarian constitutional structure emphasising social justice.[3]

The two solutions differ not only in their institutional set-ups, but also with respect to ontology and methodological focus. The logic underlying each of the models is seen against a backdrop of normative political philosophy. By reading Sachs' justice model as an application of John Rawls' liberal theory of justice, and by showing how consociational models correspond to ideas of communitarian political philosophy, each model stands as a coherent structure. The normative differences are brought out and their consequences made clear so that they may be evaluated on their own terms.

## Part III: Assessing the Contenders

The constitutional structure is the basic rules of society as legally defined, and regulates most areas of social life. An assumption underlying this book is that the character of the constitutional structure influences political performance, including resource distribution in society, conflict reduction and political stability. Thus, an adequate constitutional structure can be a powerful instrument of conflict regulation, or the transformation of society into a more just or fair scheme of cooperation, while an inadequate constitutional structure can work as a catalyst to exacerbate conflicts.

When assessing the constitutional models that have been recommended for South Africa, it is particularly relevant to assess how they answer the demands posed by poverty, inequality and ethnic diversity. That major latent and manifest conflicts are accommodated within the system, and not forced into extra-legal forms of expression, is crucial for the legitimacy of a democratic regime as well as for political stability.

A constitution's adequacy depends on several factors. Lijphart's consociational proposal and Sachs' justice model are examined against three different sets of criteria. Whether it is valid on methodological grounds; whether it is acceptable according to normative criteria; and whether it is feasible in the light of the problems of South African society.

The first set of criteria concerns the theoretical and *methodological qualities* of the models. Are the models valid as theoretical constructs? Are the circumstances of South Africa such that the conditions for applying the models are satisfied? These questions are addressed in Chapter 6.

The second set of criteria regards the models' *normative qualities*, measured against criteria set by central democratic and human rights norms. The legitimacy of constitutions rests in part on the acceptability of the arrangements in normative terms; the extent to which they are perceived as fair or just; whether they provide protection for fundamental human rights and whether they are perceived to be sufficiently democratic. The normative *acceptability* of the models is considered in Chapter 7.

Normative analysis, bringing out values underlying the constitutional models and submitting them to critical examination, is a central part of the analysis. The normative qualities of the constitution are crucial in light of the assumption that normative acceptability is a precondition for a regime's ability to generate the internal and external legitimacy needed for democratic consolidation and stability.

The assessment of acceptability does not focus only on 'theory-internal' features. The relevant context — the ideological climate and 'circumstances of justice' in South Africa — is taken into consideration, in particular the urgent need for reconciliation and nation-building.

The third set of criteria concerns the *feasibility* of the constitutional models. The technical qualities of a constitutional set-up are important. Are the mechanisms appropriate and sufficiently potent in the light of the problems of inequality and ethnicity? Do the models have the ability to regulate conflict, provide stability, and contribute to an acceptable distribution of resources and opportunities? The technical adequacy of the constitutional structure is of vital importance for the performance of a regime. This in turn is crucial both for the capacity of the regime to gain legitimacy, and for its ability to endure and operate efficiently. The feasibility of consociationalism and the justice model for South Africa is the theme of Chapter 8.

Throughout the assessment of the models it is necessary to bear in mind the interpretations of the South African reality underlying them. The models differ in respect to the identification of the most central problems. This in turn is reflected in their institutional solutions and accounts for important differences between the models. The question of feasibility is most fruitfully addressed by distinguishing, on one hand, whether the models could function as intended within their own interpretation of the situation, and, on the other hand, how the measures they propose would work in the light of the inverse reading of the situation.

Normative arguments based on a certain ontological perspective, and power-politics based on a pragmatic consideration of self-interest, often run parallel. Political rhetoric present the interests of a particular group as 'the common good' of society. Theoretical models corresponding to these interests provide a form of 'objective' justification. Uncovering the interpretation of reality underlying each of the models, and situating it in the context of South African politics, detracts from the models' appearance of objectivity or neutrality. In a concrete political situation no theoretical model can provide a neutral solution, least of all in South Africa. It will always be a more or less well-founded argument, favouring one part or another.

## Part IV: The 'Final' Constitution

In Chapter 9 the new South African constitution is presented according to the conceptual framework developed in Chapter 3, emphasising ways in which it corresponds to the justice model and the consociation model, respectively.

The process leading to the adoption of the constitution is central to this analysis. Particular focus is set on the 1993 interim constitution, which is not only a significant landmark of the constitution-making process, but a major source of influence during the last phase of the constitutional negotiations.

Another aspect of the constitution-making process is the focus of the tenth and last chapter, namely the extensive public participation process. During the last phase of constitution-making, calls for submissions went out to institutions and organisations in civil society and to the public at large. Close to two million submissions and petitions were received, along with oral statements in public hearings. The process closely resembles the justice model's recommendations of 'participatory formulation of rights'. What is the effects of this widespread public participation effort on the constitution as a product, and in terms of legitimacy?

This chapter also addresses the question of constitutionalism. Is the new South African constitution, with its particular combination of elements from profoundly different constitutional models, superior to the models that influenced it, or is it a compromise within which the best qualities of each model are lost? Given the character of this 'final' constitution, what are the prospects for constitutionalism in South Africa?

## Notes

1. The boycott of the Constitutional Assembly was staged in protest against what the IFP saw as a failure to honour a pre-election agreement on international mediation. The IFP continued, however, to participate in Parliament and in the Government of National Unity.
2. It is impossible to *predict* how South Africa would develop under the different models. Prediction in social science is founded on the premise that the future can be determined on the basis of past and present activity. The human capacity for *action* — in the sense of actualising an infinitesimal possibility and thereby bringing something completely new into being — is excluded. As long as people have the capability for *acting*, the future cannot be determined (Arendt, 1958). While it may be possible to foresee short and medium term effects of marginal changes, it is generally impossible to determine long-term effects of radical change.
3. Albie Sachs, as a leading ANC expert on constitutional issues, was central in the first phases of the constitution-making process, until he was appointed as a judge of the Constitutional Court.

# 2 Obstacles to Democratic Consolidation

South African society and its democratically elected regime face severe challenges in terms of crime and violence, poverty, inequality, and racial and ethnic tension. Interpretations vary on which conflicts represent the greatest danger for democratic consolidation and stability, and how they can be mitigated. The contest between rivalling interpretations of 'reality' has been an important aspect of the battle over the constitution.

## Violence

The fear of crime and violence is a shared concern throughout the South African population, and with good reason. South Africa is arguably the most violent country in the world outside a war zone. Almost 19 000 people were murdered in 1995 — an average of 49 per day or one every half hour.[1] The murder rate was estimated at 87.5 per 100 000 people, which is almost ten times that of the United States.[2] An armed robbery was committed every 11 minutes and there was an average of 92 rapes per day.[3]

The murder centre is KwaZulu-Natal. 10 651 people were murdered in the province during 1994 and 1995. Since the mid-1980s more than 14 000 people have been killed in political violence in the province.[4] Unlike the rest of the country, where political violence dropped sharply after the first democratic elections in April 1994, the politically related killings have continued in KwaZulu-Natal.

Violence is one of the most serious challenges of South African society, threatening political and economic stability. It is also a manifestation of underlying conflicts in society. Both the violence itself and the conflict over the nature and causes of the violence, are important parts of the context in which the constitutional negotiations have taken place. The causes of the violence have been, and are still, in dispute. Many explanations centre on the nature of the apartheid state. Direct state complicity is one aspect, another is the deprivation apartheid inflicted on the majority of the population, and the resulting inequality permeating all dimensions of life. Other analyses interpret (at least parts of) the violence as a manifestation of ethnic hatred.

The experience of violence is not new to South Africa. South African society has been violent throughout the 20th century. It is argued that, more than in most other societies, violence is an integral part of South African culture.[5] Rapid industrialisation and modernisation caused disintegration of traditional structures, and social fragmentation. And apartheid with its forced removals and artificial 'homelands' exacerbated the tensions. Political violence is one manifestation. The high and rising crime rates, domestic violence and psychiatric morbidity are other indicators. In magnitude, criminal violence is by far the most widespread, even during the height of political violence in the run-up to the 1994 elections.

Factors such as the country's recent militarised past, leaving a legacy of negative attitudes towards the law, police and justice systems, combined with anger and frustration in poor communities, are clearly relevant. The level of violence cannot be separated from the poverty and inequality prevailing in South African society.

## Political Violence

The political violence, often referred to as 'black-on-black' violence, posed serious threats to a peaceful transition to democracy and is of particular significance as a context for constitutional design. The wave of politically related killings started in Natal in the mid-1980s and escalated in the early 1990s. In the period after the lifting of the ban on the ANC, the violence spread to other areas and the situation became particularly dramatic in the townships on the East Rand. The violence and the competing analyses of the conflict directly affected the negotiations for the interim constitution in 1993; it affected the parties' bargaining strength as well as their constitutional positions. To understand how the violence has been interpreted and used to underpin the parties' positions is crucial for an understanding of the constitutional process and of the constitution itself.

Analysts agree that the political violence is the result of several factors working together. There is no uniform pattern of political violence and local dynamics are important. The structure of the violence is different in Natal than on the East Rand, in townships and rural areas, and they also differ over time (Minnaar, 1994: 389). It is important to bear in mind the complexity of the issue. There are different trends in the interpretations of the character of the violence, with respect to which causal factor that is emphasised as the most decisive.

One line of analysis has focused on political manipulation and placed responsibility for the political violence primarily with the (apartheid) State. It has been regarded as a case of direct government complicity: a secret 'third-force' provoking violence; governmental lack of will to take action to stop the aggressors; and/or lack of ability to control other state agents were, according to this view, the main factors feeding the vicious circle of violence until the elections in April 1994. The conspiracy explanations frequently voiced by the ANC leadership, have in latter years been substantiated, first through the reports of the Goldstone Commission and confessions from ex-members of the security forces, later through the so called third-force trials and the on-going hearings of the Truth Commission.

Despite proofs of political manipulation and covert state violence, there is still the question of how important this factor has been — and whether it still is a factor in the violence in KwaZulu-Natal.[6]

A second trend of analysis supports the interpretation of the political violence given by the Nationalist Party and major sections of the white South African establishment: that ethnic tension between groups within the African population is the dominant factor underlying the violence. This was also the dominant explanation in the international press particularly during the first phase of the constitutional negotiations leading to the adoption of the interim constitution and the April 1994 elections.

With diminishing levels of political violence in South Africa after the elections, and the subsequent rise in criminal violence, ethnicity is less frequently cited as a cause of violence. This does not mean that the fear of ethnic conflict has vanished. Ethnicity continues to be seen as a major source of conflict in KwaZulu-Natal, as a factor in the recurring hostel violence as well as in incidents of violence committed by right-wing Afrikaner groups.

During 1996 the Cape Town metropolitan area, saw the rise of a militant anti-crime movement, also organised along ethnic lines, in the muslim-dominated People Against Gangsterism and Drugs (PAGAD)

Finally, the prospects of ethnic mobilisation through the party system continues to be cited as a major threat to democratic stability. In the rhetoric of the IFP Zulu tradition and identity figure prominently, and their demands are extensive autonomy for KwaZulu-Natal. Right-wing parties, including the Freedom Front, mobilise on the need to protect Afrikaner culture and traditions, with a Volkstat, an Afrikaner homeland, as the ultimate goal. Also in the coloured population there are groups mobilising on a ticket of ethnic and cultural identity. These are small groupings, but they have added to the focus on the dangers of ethnicity and ethnic mobilisation, particularly in the Western Cape province, where 'coloureds' are in majority.

The third line of analysis focuses on structural conditions and ascribes the upsurge of violence first and foremost to the devastating poverty and inequality in South African society. In this context the distinction between political and criminal violence is less emphasised.

A more thorough presentation of the different perspectives is given below, emphasising the links between the different interpretations of violence and various political outlooks. This is not primarily to hint at the opportunistic motives that the various parties and groupings may have for supporting one view or another. The main objective is to demonstrate how the views are conditioned by and related to a broader, underlying issue dividing the parties. What is the primary cleavage of South African society — race/ethnicity/culture or class?

## Conspiracy, Government Negligence and the 'Third Force'

The key element in this line of explanation is the (apartheid) state as the decisive factor fuelling the unrest. According to the conspiracy explanations violence is fuelled by covert state violence coupled with open use of force.[7] The typical argument runs roughly as follows: black provocateurs (Inkatha Zulus) were encouraged and aided by state agents (the South African police and security forces and the KwaZulu Police) to create terror and unrest in ANC dominated black townships and squatter camps. The violence, once started, gained a momentum of its own thus creating conditions for the 'legitimate' use of police and security forces against the angry masses.

At the time, the observed behaviour of police and security forces, and the passivity shown by the government strengthened the claims that state agents were involved in the violence. In later years documentation substantiating such claims has been forthcoming. State funding and training of black groups involved in the violence were documented in 1991 with 'Inkathagate' — the disclosure of secret financial support from the NP-government to Chief Buthelezi's Inkatha Freedom Party. The Goldstone Commission reports documented extensive state activity to smear the ANC. Since the transition from apartheid rule more material has come forth, not least due to the trials against former defence minister General Magnus Malan and Colonel Eugene de Kock, who were both convicted of third-force activities, and through the on-going hearings of the Truth Commission.

The role of the domestic and international press is important to take into account in order to understand why the (apartheid) state would want to set off and fuel this spiral of violence, spreading terror throughout society and risking dire long-term political consequences. The political killings and mass-action were given substantial press coverage both inside and outside South Africa. Depicted as 'black-on-black' violence it strengthened the impression that African groups are divided by primitive ethnic sentiments and loyalties. Images of ethnic warfare were arguments against black majority government, reinforcing the fears of majority rule among white South Africans and the Indian and coloured population. Internationally — and among political scientists — the 'facts' of ethnic violence gave rise to calls for power-sharing arrangements and constitutional protection for minorities. The relative position of the NP regime and the legitimacy of its demands for minority protection were strengthened.

Manipulation by the regime of ethnic and other tensions in the African majority is documented beyond doubt. On the basis of this evidence it is reasonable to assume that direct and indirect government interference played a significant role in fuelling the vicious cycle of violence in South Africa, up to the 1994 elections. Still, its relative importance is not clear. Manipulation and conspiracy by the *ancien régime*, important though it is, is hardly a sufficient explanation of the violence.

To the extent that political manipulation is the driving force of violence, political agreements and actions to put an end to subversive activities by government agents are the most immediate remedies. This does not follow automatically from a change of regime. Restructuring of the police and the armed forces have been priorities for the new government. This has included integration of 'freedom fighters' from Umkhonto we Siswe (the armed wing of the ANC) and APLA (Azanian Peoples' Liberation Army, affiliated with the PAC) in the armed forces as well as integration of the former 'homeland' police units into the national police corps. In addition, programmes of 'community policing' have sought to improve the standing of the police in the eyes of the public, particularly in the townships.

The inauguration of a democratic regime did see a drop in political violence, which is consistent with it being for a large part state-driven, but with the continuation of political violence in KwaZulu-Natal, and the rise in criminal violence throughout the country, indicate that violence is a symptom of fundamental cleavages in South African society. These conflicts may themselves have been created, or at least exacerbated, by regime manipulation, but this does not mean that they are not 'real' or that they cease to exist when the manipulation comes to a halt. The level of violence in South African society is linked to problems and conflicts that are likely to persist, and pose serious threats for democratic stability.

The violence and its causes has continued to be at the forefront throughout the constitution-making process. Some believe the underlying conflicts in South African society are of a basically cultural nature, subsumed under the label 'ethnicity'. Others point to structural factors: poverty and inequality. In both cases constitutional design has been proposed as a strategy for addressing the problems. The problem (ethnicity/inequality) must be given primacy when the constitution is drawn up. In following chapters the two main constitutional 'solutions' are outlined, but first a more thorough examination of the problems is presented.

## Ethnicity

'Ethnicity' frequently figures as the main explanation of violent conflicts, for example in Rwanda and Burundi, in Sudan and Somalia, in the former Yugoslavia and Trans-Caucasus, in Burma and Sri Lanka. This has also been the case in South Africa. The 'black-on-black' violence plaguing South Africa, and particularly KwaZulu-Natal, is frequently interpreted as ethnic. Ethnic mobilisation within the political system is also often cited as the major obstacle to democratic consolidation and stability.

### The 'Fact' of Ethnicity in South Africa

That social 'facts' are neither objective nor indisputable, and that their meaning — or reality — is a matter of interpretation rather than discovery, is widely recognised in the social sciences, at least on the theoretical and intellectual level. In practical research, however, complicated social phenomena, such as ethnicity and ethnic conflict, are readily given the status of 'fact' and scholars concerned with the question of how to prevent ethnic warfare frequently take the existence of ethnic identity, divisions and conflicts as given.

In the South African situation the problems with this attitude become striking. Hardly any social 'fact' is uncontroversial in South Africa, and the 'fact' of ethnicity certainly is not.

That South African society is of a diverse ethnic make-up is generally recognised, but this is about as far as consensus goes. Not only is the political significance of ethnicity disputed, but also the criteria for group-identification. Table 2.1 gives an impression of the multi-ethnic character of South African society.

**Table 2.1 South African population by race and home language**

|  | Estimated size (million) | Percentage of total population |
|---|---|---|
| Total population | 40.7 | |
| African | 31.1 | 76.4 |
| Coloured | 3.5 | 8.4 |
| Asian | 1.0 | 2.5 |
| White | 5.7 | 14.0 |
| Language groups | | |
| Zulu | 9.1 | 22.4 |
| Xhosa | 7.4 | 18.3 |
| Afrikaans | 5.9 | 14.5 |
| North Sotho | 3.7 | 9.1 |
| English | 3.4 | 8.4 |
| Tswana | 3.2 | 7.7 |
| South Sotho | 2.6 | 6.4 |
| Tsonga | 1.5 | 3.7 |
| Siswati | 1.3 | 3.1 |
| Venda | 0.7 | 1.7 |
| Ndebele | 0.3 | 0.7 |
| Other | 1.6 | 4.0 |

*Source:* Race Relations Survey 1994/95: 9, 12.

In this table groups are identified by language and race. These criteria are empirically problematic and politically sensitive, but they are hard to avoid. The social differences created by the apartheid classification system persist, and even under the new dispensation these labels mark off what are often seen as distinct population groups. Boundaries between groups are not always sharp and sub-group identification may also be important. However, for the purpose of our discussion this table gives a sufficient illustration of the ethnic variety of the South African population. But are these groups or categories 'ethnic groups' or 'minorities' in a politically relevant sense?

*Ethnicity and Nationalism: Conceptual Clarifications*

What makes *ethnic groups* distinct from other sub-units of society is, according to Max Weber, that they are united by a 'subjective belief in common descent ... whether or not an objective blood relationship exists' (Weber, 1968: 339). Ethnic groups may be differentiated by colour, language or religion. In most cases it is a mix of attributes that denotes group differences. *Racial groups* are a special category of ethnic groups where physical attributes, most notably skin colour, are the criteria of demarcation (Horowitz, 1985). Although objective differences often appear important, they are only relevant to the extent that they are used to distinguish one ethnic group from another. 'It is not the attribute that makes the group, but the group and the group differences that make the attribute important' (Horowitz, 1985: 50). *Subjective identification* is the strongest cohesive element, while objective differences work as a catalyst.

Ethnicity is always linked to a notion of ascription, however diluted. The ascriptive character of ethnic identification imports to ethnic conflict an intense and permeative quality, that poses special difficulties for democratic politics; inter-ethnic compromise is difficult because those who practice compromise are running the risk of being treated with 'the bitter contempt reserved for brothers who betray a cause'.[8]

The key element is subjective belief in common descent. This sets ethnic groups apart from other social groupings, and also explains the particularly explosive potential of ethnicity. That the groups outlined in Table 2.1 are ethnic groups in this sense, implying a strong subjective identification, is not self-evident. Particularly within the ANC, the prevailing conception has been that in South Africa, racial and ethnic groups are legal categories imposed from above, rather than a matter of subjective identification (Taylor, 1991a).

'*Nation*' and '*nationalism*' are recurring terms in discussions of ethnicity. Special difficulties are posed by these concepts because they have several, even contradictory, usages. 'Nation' denotes the population of a legally defined state. It is also used as a synonym for *ethnos* or ethnic group. 'Nationalism' is the ideology of congruence of culture and political power, of people and state (Degenaar, 1991: 2). It may be used to describe both efforts to create common loyalties and a common culture between citizens of a state — and the centrifugal ideology underlying ethnic groups' struggle for exclusive control of the state, or for secession. It is important to keep in mind the dual meaning of the concepts. For our discussion of ethnicity in South Africa, the definition of a nation as 'a politically conscious ethnic group' and nationalism as 'politicised ethnicity' is particularly relevant.[9] Nationalism in the sense of 'building a common nation onto societal plurality', is important in ANC ideology — and an aim underlying Sachs' constitutional models, presented in Chapter 4.

## The Myth of Ethnicity

Critics argue that if ethnic conflict appears to be a significant social phenomenon in South Africa it is due to the imposition of ethnic categories by the apartheid system, and manipulation of ethnic tension by the previous regime.

> For apartheid, drawing on the work of anthropologists and organic notions of 'national' communities derived from German Romanticism, created a view that South Africa is a multi-national country composed of discrete ethnic groups, such as Zulus and Xhosas, each having a sense of common unity stemming from common origin, each possessing immutable cultural and psychological attributes. Through the 'homeland' system, these ethnic identities have been implanted and constantly reinforced to serve political ends. (Taylor, 1991a: 8)

It is argued that the ethnic character of the conflict is illusory. Seemingly ethnic conflicts are rooted in socioeconomic conditions. The real basis of the conflict is obfuscated by focusing on divisions drawn according to the Population Registration Act of 1950, divisions which were never acknowledged by the people on whom they were imposed.

According to this view ethnicity is not a relevant fact in South African politics. It is neither relevant to explain the conflict prior to the fall of the apartheid regime, nor the subsequent conflicts in KwaZulu-Natal or the wider political mobilisation. Hence, provisions to accommodate ethnic groups have no place in the constitution. The best way to handle the situation — even assuming that ethnicity has taken on some reality — is, according to this line of analysis, to avoid reinforcing ethnic identities and ethnic conflicts by emphasising them. Insistence on the importance of ethnic identity and its corollary, devices for protection of the rights of minorities, is a continuation of apartheid politics. The phenomena should be ignored in the democratic South Africa, rather than built into the constitutional framework.

Even the legitimacy of interpreting the conflicts in terms of ethnicity is questioned: 'ethnicity' is seen to be an invention of the oppressor. When conflicts and cleavages are interpreted in terms of ethnicity, it covers up the conflicts that really matter; class, inequality and power. And it traps South Africans in the "imagined' mentality of thinking itself an ethnically divided society. It is this mentality which, quite obviously, underpins the need to specially accommodate minority interests in the new South Africa' (Taylor, 1991: 8). Reluctance to acknowledge ethnicity as a 'real' problem is understandable in the light of the apartheid legacy. On the other hand, those arguing for the importance of ethnic elements in South African politics, also have points worth considering.

## The Primacy of Ethnic Divisions

'Ethnicity is a fundamental fact of social and political life in South Africa and is a decisive factor underlying political violence. Ethnic groups and ethnic conflicts are likely to play a major — and potentially dangerous — political role in a democratic South Africa.' These were dominant views and predictions prior to the transition from apartheid rule. They were voiced by the NP regime, large sections of the domestic and international press, as well as by influential international scholars, such as Arend Lijphart and Donald L. Horowitz (Lijphart, 1985; Horowitz, 1991). From this perspective ethnic identities are constants which ought to be *accommodated* rather than social problems that the state should attempt to *'solve'*. Ethnicity is regarded as the most important social phenomenon to be taken into consideration when the constitutional structure is designed.

Two arguments were set forth to justify the claim that ethnicity was — and still is — the most important problem to be addressed in South Africa. One departs from an interpretation of the political landscape in South Africa as ethnically defined, and the political violence as ethnic warfare. The second argument is based on experience from other countries with ethnically heterogeneous populations.

## Is Ethnic Conflict Manifest in South Africa?

Prior to the 1994 elections there was a widespread perception of a Xhosa dominated ANC fighting the Zulus, alias the Inkatha Freedom Party (IFP). The 'black-on-black' violence was taken as proof of the significance of old tribal identities in South African society. While this interpretation is too simplistic, the conflict had, and still has, ethnic elements. This is also true of the political mobilisation of various parties.

The IFP leader, Chief Mangosuthu Buthelezi, quite successfully invokes Zulu tradition to rally support. His rhetoric has gradually turned more traditionalistic,[10] arousing strong currents of ethnic sentiments and chauvinism. The heritage of Shaka, the Zulu king conquering the tribes of Southern Africa; the golden age of the Zulu nation, culminating with the Zulu army inflicting on the British army 'the most grievous defeat that modern troops have ever suffered at the hands of aborigines' (Sparks, 1990: 97). He uses greatness of the past as well as traditional symbols, costumes and weapons to kindle a sense of ethnic pride in underprivileged people. His political objective is maximum autonomy for the province of KwaZulu-Natal — or rather the Kingdom of KwaZulu-Natal — within a loose South African federation or confederation.

The 1994 elections confirmed the notion of the IFP as an ethnically based party. The party drew 85 per cent of its support from Zulu-speakers (Mattes, 1995: 24). This, as we shall see shortly, does not mean that the IFP is supported by the majority of Zulus.

The ANC, despite their explicit ideology of non-racialism and non-tribalism, have a Xhosa dominance in their leadership. The notion of the ANC as a Xhosa organisation is, however, not supported if we look at the composition of its support base. The ANC draws support almost equally from three distinct linguistic/tribal groups (Xhosa 24 per cent, Tswana 23 per cent and Zulu 22 per cent) (Mattes, 1995: 25). Contrary to the conventional view, a majority of Zulu speakers support the ANC. Surveys indicate that at the time of the 1994 elections, more than half of all Zulu speakers in South Africa identified with the ANC, while 20 per cent identified with the IFP. Only in the rural areas of KwaZulu-Natal does the IFP hold a majority of

Zulu support (Mattes, 1995: 27). The image of the ANC-IFP conflict as a conflict between Xhosas and Zulus has a very limited empirical base.

This is also the case when we look at the 'black-on-black' violence. The wave of political violence started in KwaZulu-Natal in the mid-1980s, where it was mainly a matter of Zulus fighting other Zulus. The conflict ran along rural/urban and traditional/modern lines, rather than ethnic affiliation. It has the character of political rivalry between (older, male, rurally based) Zulus supporting Inkatha and (younger, urban) Zulus supporting the ANC.[11] It was only when the violence spread to the Vaal triangle (Gauteng) that it could reasonably be interpreted as a Zulu/Xhosa conflict (Minnaar, 1994). At this stage the violence started to draw the attention of the international media, and the impression of ethnic violence gained ground.

Social conditions can also account for the violence. The township violence, in KwaZulu-Natal as well as in Gauteng, has often been related to the hostels (see Minnaar, 1993a). The hostels are a product of the systems of influx control and labour migration. Rurally based people could not move to the cities with their families and settle in the townships. They were only allowed to stay in single-sex hostels for as long as their contracts lasted.[12] There is a wide gap in terms of social conditions between the lives of ordinary township dwellers and the extreme conditions of hostel inhabitants. Differences in social conditions combined with geographical proximity, are bound to create feelings of relative deprivation. Incidences of aggression and fighting between hostel inhabitants and township people have occurred since the start of the system of labour migration. Currently unemployment among migrant workers is high and increasing, and the social conditions in the hostels clearly add to the conflicts.

On the other hand, ethnicity has also for decades been part of the conflict between migrant workers and township dwellers.[13] As far back as the 1930s there are examples of ethnically organised gangs (Guy, 1989: 166). Hostels have often been segregated between ethnic groups and for migrant workers their ethnic identity was — and is — a double-edged sword. Ethnicity has been important in order to organise and protect workers in a lawless and dangerous milieu — at the same time it has played into the hands of the apartheid state, and aided their strategy of divide and rule.

Ethnicity is difficult to distinguish from other sources of social tension. It is hard to identify and define the specifically ethnic element in the political violence in South Africa, or determine its relative strength, just as it is difficult to draw the distinction between political and criminal violence. Due to breakdown of apartheid structures, rapid changes have taken place in South

Africa over the last decade. Major influx to the cities and social differentiation within the African population have created strong social tensions. Gangsterism, urban-rural differences, tension between established township communities and 'outsiders' such as migrants and squatters are important factors that are difficult to distinguish from ethnicity.

With respect to voting patterns it is also difficult to distinguish class and race/ethnicity as underlying factors. If we look at the results from the first democratic elections in April 1994,[14] we see that white and black South Africans gave their support overwhelmingly to traditionally white and black parties. Surveys indicate that less than 2 per cent of Africans support traditionally white parties, while some 4 per cent of whites support traditionally black parties, mainly the IFP (Mattes, 1995: 26).

Most political parties drew their support largely from one specific group. The ANC and the PAC both drew 94 per cent of their support from the African population (across all linguistic groups). The remaining support for the ANC came mostly from the coloured population. Only 0.2 per cent of the ANC support came from whites. The IFP drew 88 per cent of their support from Africans, almost exclusively Zulus, with the rest coming primarily from English-speaking whites. The Freedom Front has an exclusively white, and almost exclusively (83 per cent) Afrikaans speaking support-base, while the DP draws almost 70 per cent of their support from English-speakers and the remaining from the Afrikaans speaking population. The NP has the most diverse support base. 52 per cent of NP supporters are white, 31 per cent coloured, 9 per cent Indian and 8 per cent African. In terms of language the NP is predominantly a party for (white and coloured) Afrikaans-speakers (60 per cent). The remaining are mainly English-speaking (Mattes, 1995: 23–25).

Based on this pattern, some commentators judged the election as an 'ethnic census' where voters registered their (racial and ethnic) identities rather than voted according to interests and preferences (see Schlemmer, 1994: 162). This is, however, not the only possible interpretation. The election results also support hypotheses of class-based voting patterns. As a consequence of the policies pursued during the apartheid years class coincides overwhelmingly with race. Controlling for race we see continuing effects of income on party support. 'As monthly household income decreases, support for the ANC increases steadily' (Mattes, 1995: 27). For the NP there is the opposite tendency. It is thus also possible to interpret this as class-based voting on the basis of interests.

*Ethnicity in Comparative Perspective*

While the political importance of ethnicity is contested, South Africa is indisputably a multi-cultural society. Its white elite is divided by language as well as religion. There are people of European, Asian and African origins and there is a multitude of African languages. Objective differences to mark groups off from one-another are ample.

This is the point of departure for the other argument for giving priority to ethnic divisions in the constitution: the experience of other countries with ethnically mixed populations.

Country after country — in Eastern Europe, in the former Soviet Union, in Asia and in Africa — have seen an upsurge of ethnic conflict as the grips of authoritarian governments are loosened. Democratisation processes, allowing political organisation and expression, seem to exacerbate ethnic conflicts. Time and again ethnic sentiments are successfully mobilised. Difficult economic and social conditions seem to increase temptations to exploit ethnic sentiments in the struggle for political power.

Although the significance of ethnicity is disputed in most cases, it seems unwise to dismiss off-hand the relevance for South Africa of the comparative evidence pointing at the salience of ethnic conflict.

## Structural Conditions

The third line of explanation of violence in South Africa regards the ethnic element as illusory, or at least secondary to structural factors.

> (T)he structural conditions in South Africa are such (economic inequality, atrocious housing conditions, inadequate education facilities, rampant poverty and hunger, unemployment, totally inadequate channels for political expression or civic administration, deep feelings of relative deprivation etc. etc.) that many forms of violence are not only possible, but it would be surprising if, under such conducive circumstances they did not occur. (Van Zyl Slabbert, 1990: 71)

Poverty and inequality are seen to be the most fundamental problems in South Africa and the main cause of social conflict and violence. According to this structural explanation poverty and inequality are the problems that need to be at the forefront when the constitution is designed.

*Poverty, Inequality and Race*

South Africa experienced high and rapidly rising urbanisation after the gradual breakdown, and eventual abolition of the pass laws in June 1986. Millions of people are living in shacks and informal housing and the slums and squatter camps are expanding rapidly, both due to population growth and urbanisation. In the established black townships the infrastructure (electricity, water, roads, hospitals etc.) is over-loaded and of poor quality, and such facilities are close to non-existent in the informal settlements.

Poverty is widespread and rampant. A third of all households, with around half the total population, can be classified as poor (Pillay, 1996: 45). Poverty is related to race, gender and age. Some 60 per cent of the poor are women, and nearly half of the ultra-poor live in female-headed families. An estimated 61 per cent of South African children live in poverty. Among African children the poverty rate is more than 70 per cent (Pillay, 1996: 42). The infant mortality rate for blacks is ten times that for whites.

Unemployment is one of the most important indicators of poverty. The unemployment rate is estimated at 30 per cent across all groups, but only 43 per cent of the working age population is actively employed. Again, there are significant race and gender inequalities. Employment levels are lowest among Africans (46 per cent of men and 27 per cent of women) and highest among whites (82 per cent of men and 60 per cent of women). There are also great disparities between provinces (Pillay, 1996: 32).

The unemployment problems are likely to increase as, even with optimistic forecasts, the labour absorption capacity of the formal economy is lower than the annual additions to the labour market. Adding to the problems, and detracting from the possibility of rapid improvement of the situation, is the fact that many labour market entries lack even proper primary education. Six out of every ten black South Africans are functionally illiterate. Of African males between 15 and 24 years of age, 12 per cent have no education at all and an additional 34 per cent have not completed primary school (Tjønneland, 1992: 27).

Unemployment problems, unemployed youth in particular, has a direct influence on the level of crime and violence. The number of gangs has exploded with the rapid social changes in the last decades, drawing more and more young people into a culture of crime and violence.

The relationship between violence and other aspects of poverty is more difficult to determine. The fact that large sections of the South African population experience poverty, even right-out hunger, may in itself provoke unrest. Still, in absolute terms the social and economic living conditions for the black population in South Africa is comparable to that of the population in neighbouring countries such as Botswana, Lesotho, Namibia, Swaziland and Zimbabwe, and better than in e.g. Tanzania or Zambia (Tjønneland, 1992: 138). These are countries with lower levels of violent crime and little or no politically directed violence on the part of the poor. Poverty in itself may as readily lead to apathy as to action.

What sets South Africa apart from other African countries is not poverty, this is a common characteristic. But in very few other countries is the stark poverty of the majority contrasted with affluence as in South Africa. A standard of living among the highest in the world is enjoyed by a substantial — and highly visible — section of the population.

In 1991 the income earned by the poorest 40 per cent of households was less than 4 per cent of total income while the richest 10 per cent earned more than 51 per cent of total income. Available statistics suggest that the gap between rich and poor has been growing over the past decades. 'From 1975 to 1991, 80 per cent of the African households experienced a decrease in their income; half of them experienced as much as a 40 per cent drop' (Tjønneland, 1996: 3). Vast social and economic inequalities exist in virtually all spheres of South African society, and the distributions of income are the most unequal of any country for which statistics are available.[15] The richest 5 per cent of the population also account for 88 per cent of all personally owned wealth. (McGrath, 1990: 96).

This enormous inequality is probably a more potent source of aggression than poverty itself. Adding to the appalling nature of inequality in South Africa is the fact that the 'haves' are overwhelmingly white, the 'have-nots' almost exclusively black. Nearly all South Africa's poor (95 per cent) are Africans, the rest are mainly 'coloured'. Africans have a poverty rate of nearly 65 per cent, while the poverty rate of 'coloureds' is 33 per cent. For Indians and whites it is 2.7 per cent and 0.7 per cent respectively (Pillay, 1996: 41).

While race and income continue to be closely linked, the income gap within the racial groups, and particular in the African population, is increasing. From 1975 to 1991 the richest 20 per cent of the African households enjoyed faster income growth than any other section of the population, almost 40 per cent (Tjønneland, 1996). Indications are that this trend has continued and accelerated. The extent of racial pay discrimination, i.e. differential pay to equally qualified people doing equivalent jobs, has been substantially reduced. The main causes of income inequality is increasingly the structure of the labour market (rewards to occupations, access to employment etc.) and educational differences. The extremely unequal investment in human capital between the racial groups is therefore of particular importance. Decades of 'bantu education', providing inferior education to Africans, is necessarily reflected in labour skills. Even with major efforts from the government, the effects of educational differences will persist for a very long time.

To claim that inequality and poverty — and the close link between distribution and racial divisions — is the cause of violence in South Africa is too simple. To claim that it is without importance to social and political stability is wishful thinking. Distributive concerns will for a very long time have to be a vital factor in politics and policy determination in South Africa. Demands for redistribution are strong and have overwhelming moral force. In the discussion of the constitutional models in the following chapters, the potential for facilitating redistribution and alleviation of poverty will be an important aspect of the analysis.

## Restating the Argument

The political violence plaguing South Africa prior to the 1994 elections was in part a result of regime manipulation. There are, however, also other, more fundamental, sources of conflict manifesting themselves in violence, conflicts that continue to pose serious threats to political stability and democratic consolidation. One interpretation of the underlying pattern of conflict is that what we see is a manifestation of tribal identities and ethnic division. Another interpretation is that the main causes of conflict are structural — the highly unequal and unjust social and economic conditions. The conclusion from this chapter is that there seems to be a complex interplay between cultural/racial/ethnic factors and social conditions, and that the relative strength of the different factors is difficult to determine with respect to both violence, and political mobilisation and voting patterns.

That the malaise is difficult to diagnose has implications for the quest for an effective cure. To the extent that the main cause of instability and violence is political power-play and 'third-force' activities, a political settlement between the conflicting parties, along with the re-establishment of the police as a trustworthy institution is the logical path. Where conflicts are rooted in fundamental structures of society such efforts will not be sufficient to facilitate lasting stability.

A strategy to improve prospects for long-term democratic stability is to tailor the constitution so that the most intractable problems are lifted out of the political domain. Widely different constitutional designs have been proposed as 'solutions' for South Africa, reflecting different interpretations of the 'problem'. The tension between constitutional strategies has made its mark on the new constitution. A useful route to an understanding of its potential and limitations as a normative framework and political instrument, is to examine the approaches towards constitutionalism that influenced the debate, and ultimately the constitution itself. In the following chapters the two major constitutional strategies are presented and analysed. But first there will be a general discussion of constitutionalism and why constitutions matter.

## Notes

1. Source: ANC Department of Information and Publicity, 17 April 1996 (ANC Newswire Root, 17 April 1996, article 37). The 1995 murder figure of 18 933 people excludes the former 'independent' homelands.
2. The murder rate for the US hovers around 9 per 100 000 inhabitants, the equivalent rate for the Soviet Union is 16, for Kenya 6 and for Britain 1 murder per 100 000 inhabitants (ANC Newswire Root, 17 April 1996, Article 37).
3. 66 786 rapes were reported during 1994 and 1995. The figure was given by Safety and Security Minister Sydney Mufamadi in reply to a question in the Senate on 29 March 1996 (ANC Newswire Root, 30 March 1996, Article 6).
4. Source: ANC Department of Information and Publicity (ANC Newswire Root, 29 March 1996, Article 64; and 6 May 1996, Article 61).
5. See Tjønneland (1992: 15–16).
6. There have been rumours and allegations claiming that the violence is (in part) driven by reactionary elements of the former KwaZulu-police and the IFP, who are in control of the provincial government of KwaZulu-Natal.
7. State violence may take different forms. There is the open use of force and direct violence conducted by agents of the state (army and police forces), on the government's behalf, towards opposition groups and communities. Various forms of indirect and covert state violence, planned and executed by state agents with or without the consent of the top political authorities, range from cooptation of and cooperation with conservative black groupings to various undercover activities planned and executed by secret units of the security police; informal repression, death squads, use of black provocateurs etc. In addition to activities in which the state plays a direct role, there are the vigilante groups; violent, organised conservative groupings operating in black communities which receive no official recognition, but are politically directed in the sense that they act to neutralise people opposed to the (apartheid) state and its institutions (Cock, 1990: 89). Due to lack of state action to stop the vigilantes, their activities have been regarded as a form of indirect state violence.
8. M.C. Hudson, cited Horowitz (1985: 54).

9.　The terms originate from No Sizwe (pseudonym for Neville Alexander) and Heribert Adam, both cited in Degenaar (1991: 2).

10.　Buthelezi has a double audience. While appealing to ethnic loyalties and traditional values, he, at the same time, takes care to maintain his adherence to ideas that are central to the conservative establishment inside, as well as outside South Africa; the market economy, private property and protection of minority interests.

11.　However, in the south of Natal the violence also involved conflicts between Zulus, Xhosa and Indians.

12.　Although the hostels officially are single-sex temporary dwellings, entire families have a hostel bed as their permanent home. See Ramaphele (1993).

13.　Many of the migrant workers in Gauteng are Zulus from rural areas of KwaZulu-Natal, but there are also people from other parts of the country as well as large numbers of foreign migrant workers, mainly from Lesotho and Botswana, Mozambique, Malawi and Swaziland (Whiteside, 1991).

14.　The following paragraphs are based on Mattes (1995).

15.　The broad magnitudes of the income inequalities in South Africa are illustrated by the Gini coefficient. In 1975 the Gini coefficient for South Africa was 0.68 contrasted with Ginis of 0.5–0.6 for most semi-industrialised economies (McGrath, 1990: 94).

# PART II
# THE QUEST FOR SOLUTIONS

# 3 Constitutions and Constitutionalism

Against the problem structure of South African society outlined above, this chapter introduces constitutional design as a strategy for addressing social conflict.

The starting point is a set of arguments for 'why constitutions matter'. This serves two purposes. It presents the logic underlying strategies for addressing social conflict by way of constitutional design. It also explicates the understanding of the relationship between the basic norms reflected in the constitution, and the outcome of politics, upon which the analysis in this book ultimately rests.

The second task embarked upon in this chapter is a discussion of constitutionalism and of the relationship between constitutions and democracy. The aim is to show how various traditions feed into the notion of constitutionalism, and how constitutions may serve different purposes. The models presented in this book all propose constitutionalism but are within different traditions, and the underlying concepts of constitutionalism differ.

Thirdly, a conceptual framework is constructed, clarifying the dimensions according to which constitutions vary. This is a tool to be used in the subsequent presentation and analysis of the models. A main concern is to bring out the normative choices that are made — implicitly or explicitly — when constitutions are constructed.

## Do Constitutions Matter?

The significance of formal structures is contested. The focal point of post-World War II political science has been the actual working of the political system, not the formal structures as defined in the constitution.[1] Over the last decade, however, there has been a renewed interest in the study of formal institutions in general, and constitutions in particular. This has been enhanced by the break-down of authoritarian regimes throughout the world, and the focus on the creation of new, comprehensive constitutions. Times of fundamental change — and processes of replacing despised and illegitimate systems — seem to give rise to a profound concern for the norms upon which the state is founded.

## Constitution — a Conceptual Clarification[2]

The constitution is the highest norm of the state system. In order to analyse what kind of institution a constitution is, it is useful to distinguish among the constitution in *formal* sense, the constitution in *material* sense, and the *actual* constitution.

The constitution in the formal sense includes, first of all, the written constitution where such exists. Furthermore, it includes interpretations and clarifications of the constitution, and — where there is a constitutional court with the powers of judicial review — court decisions with constitutional force. In addition, common law principles may have constitutional status.[3] Countries with no written constitution, such as Great Britain, still have a constitution in formal sense as long as there are principles recognised to be the highest norms regulating the life of the state. A formulation of the fundamental constitutional principle in Great Britain could be, 'the parliament is sovereign'.

The constitution in the material sense includes, in addition to the formal constitution, common law principles, ordinary laws and institutionalisation of rules facilitating civilised political competition. The constitution in this sense is the primary subject of this study and the terms 'constitution' and 'constitutional structure' refer to this unless otherwise noted.

The actual constitution is the actual functioning of the country's constitutional life: the behaviour of different state agencies and actors, the bureaucracy, political parties and organisations. When studying constitutions it is important to be aware of the tension between actual public/governmental behaviour and written constitutional paragraphs. The extent to which constitutions reflect the realities of political power varies. 'No one constitution is an entirely realistic description of what actually happens (and) precious few are 100 per cent unrealistic fictions bearing no relationship whatsoever to what goes on' (Finer, 1979: 16). The actual constitution is normally the subject matter of political science.

The actual working of constitutions is only indirectly addressed in this book, in relation to the feasibility of the various constitutional models. Here the primary concern is the formal structures of the state, that is, constitutions in the formal and material sense.

*Constitutional structure* is a key concept. It corresponds to the constitution in material sense, as defined above. The concept designates the basic legal structure of society, including the design of central political institutions (parliamentary/presidential systems of government), principles for the distribution of power (between branches of government and/or between the centre and local levels), the electoral system (design of constituencies, voter rolls, electoral formulae), principles regulating the legal system and its position in relation to the political system (judicial review, bill of rights), and basic principles regulating the economic system (taxation, ownership, the police, health service, educational system etc.). It is the framework regulating the political system and the relationship between the individual and the state — the rules facilitating orderly struggle for political power. The constitutional structure is, in other words, 'the basic rules of the game' of a society, as legally defined.

## Why Formal Structures Matter

The general assumption underlying this book is that the formal set-up of institutions is important for political output. Furthermore, it is assumed that the normative acceptability of the constitution is important for its ability to function as a regulative mechanism.

Figure 3.1 gives a schematic presentation of the ways in which the constitution (the formal basic structure of society as legally defined) is presumed to influence political output. The relationships are complex, and the discussion below does not consider all aspects in depth. Focus is set on the relationships that are most significant for the later analysis and on aspects that may be controversial. A major argument in this respect is that which runs from the normative acceptability of the constitution via regime legitimacy to political output or performance. Crucial to this argument, and to the importance of constitutions in general, is the issue of compliance or constitutionalism in a narrow sense.

## Figure 3.1 Why formal structures matter

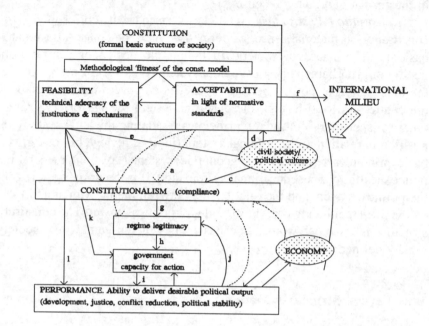

*Is Acceptability Relevant to Stability? the Significance of Legitimacy*

The relationship between the legitimacy of the regime and political performance/stability has been the subject of considerable scholarly interest.

Legitimacy may be understood in Weberian terms, as justification of power or the consent of the population for central political institutions and rules. In modern bureaucratic regimes legitimacy is the ability of the rulers to impose their policies on the ruled, based on a shared belief in the regime's constitutional right to implement its policies. A regime's legitimacy may also be seen in terms of its ability to impose policies upon its subjects which in the short run will have a negative effect, requiring that the ruled have faith in the long term good prescribed, and the commitment of the regime to reach these goals.

What sets democratic systems of government apart from other regime forms is that their stability depends more directly on the consent of a majority of the governed (Diamond *et al.,* 1988: 9). Democratic governments are accountable through periodic elections, and thus are vulnerable to voter dissatisfaction. Legitimacy is closely tied to performance — that is, the ability to provide economic development, political order, freedom, justice and regulation of conflict. At the same time a regime's ability to respond to these demands is in part a function of its legitimacy. (This feed-back mechanism is indicated by the (h), (i) and (j) arrows in Figure 3.1.) As noted by Lipset (1981: 64–70), regimes that lack legitimacy depend more precariously on current performance and are vulnerable to collapse in periods of economic and social distress. The interaction between low legitimacy and low effectiveness is often held to be the primary reason for the instability of Third World regimes (Diamond *et al.*, 1988: 10).

The importance of the link between legitimacy and political performance is generally acknowledged, and it is seen to work both ways as legitimacy is often explained primarily in terms of a feed-back mechanism from political performance. While acknowledging that this is important, I also assume that the character of the constitutional structure itself has an impact on the legitimacy of a regime. This is in part a function of the technical adequacy of the institutions (indicated by the (b), (e), (l) and (k) arrows in Figure 3.1). In addition the normative acceptability of the constitution is assumed to have an independent effect on regime legitimacy. This in turn influences the ability of the government to get its policies enacted, and, eventually, political output or performance. (These relationships are indicated by the (a)/(d)–(c), (g), (h) and (i) arrows on Figure 3.1.) I hold the effect of the normative acceptability of the constitution to be positive and significant where there exists a political culture sharing the ideals reflected in it, and an active civil society.

The normative acceptability of the constitutional principles is not only a matter of the normative qualities of the constitution as a product. For new constitutions in particular, this also depends on its genesis, the character of the constitution-making process.

The impact of the constitution is to a large extent a function of compliance. Formal political structures have little impact unless they are obeyed.[4] Several factors influence governments' constitutionalism, or compliance with formal structures; qualities of the constitution itself as well as exogenous variables.

The acceptability of the basic norms may have a direct effect: (indicated by the (a) arrow in Figure 3.1). If the governing elites find the constitutional principles unacceptable on normative grounds they are less likely to comply with them. The constitution may also further compliance through technical provisions such as judicial review (b).

The indirect influence of the constitution's normative qualities on government compliance is considered even more important. A critical factor determining compliance or constitutionalism seems to be the strength of civil society and the prevailing political culture in society (c).

The impact of civil society is in itself conditioned by technical features of the constitution, such as protection of rights and freedom, and the scope allowed for civil society activity and participation in decision-making (e).

The constitution's normative acceptability also affects the regime's standing in the international milieu which may in turn influence government compliance (f).

The constitutional set-up also influences the power-base of various political actors. The choice of electoral system, the powers of the executive, the presidential/parliamentary form of government, the mode of decision-making, minority vetoes, etc. — are all factors that influence governments' capacity for action (k). By channelling decisions out of the domain of the central government (through constitutional provisions for federalism, segmental autonomy, proportionality clauses, constitutional provisions for affirmative action, etc.) the constitution has a profound influence on political output independent of government action (l).

## Constitutional Stability

An interesting feature of constitutions is their relative permanence. Constitutions tend to be remarkably stable, even in societies undergoing profound changes.[5] What are the causes of constitutional stability?

There are practical reasons why constitutions tend to persist. Rational actors will in most cases regard an existing constitutional structure as a constant to which they adapt. Fundamental constitutional change — starting over — entails considerable transitional costs. It thus functions as an equilibrium point.

There are also psychological reasons why constitutions, once established, tend to have a relative permanence. Most countries have a certain legalistic tradition, and there are barriers against breaking what is recognised as the basic norm of society. This is strengthened by the fact that the constitution often is regarded as resting on a 'higher', or perhaps rather 'deeper', normative foundation.

This belief in the constitution's normative foundation or legitimacy is important for stability. In order to have a factual legitimacy and permanence, the constitution must be perceived as a permanent element of social life. It must be regarded as the stable rules of the game, which is more likely when it is believed to be resting on 'eternal' moral principles. The validity of the normative principles underlying the constitution is not important for day to day politics. But a general belief that the constitution has a legitimacy beyond the fact that historically it was enacted, is an important element of the authority of the constitution, which is in turn, crucial for constitutional stability.

The normative legitimacy of constitutional principles is brought into focus in times of crisis. When the legitimacy of the constitution is questioned and rejected by substantial parts of the politically active population — as was the case with the 1983 constitution in South Africa — the dynamic of constitutional stability works in reverse, unwinding its function as equilibrium point. Even sections of the population not questioning the existing dispensation on normative grounds, cease to regard it as a stable framework which it is rational to adopt to. Its factual legitimacy thus dwindles along with its stability.

The feedback mechanism outlined above, comes a long way in explaining constitutional stability once it is established. This explanation of constitutional stability may be regarded as somewhat circular, but does nevertheless possess considerable explanatory value. The initial establishment of constitutional authority and the constitutional structure as a point of equilibrium, does, however, need additional explanation.

*The Authority of the Constitution*

Montesquieu described the powers of the judiciary as *en quelque façon nulle*, but at the same time the highest authority of a constitutional regime. This paradox opens the path to an understanding of the special qualities of constitutional authority.

Authority, according to Hannah Arendt (1969a) is an alternative, not only to forced obedience, but also to a process of rational argument and conviction. Her view, like that of Plato, is that 'the masses' lack the ability to be convinced by the self-evidence of truth. In order to lead the masses to act in accordance with the truth, it must be transformed into a set of rules. These rules must be tied to the founding of the social order itself, in order to legitimise the existing authorities' demand for obedience.

The most explicit expression of authority in this sense is found in the powers of judicial review.[6] This implies that a court (often a special constitutional court) is given the power to nullify decisions taken through democratic procedures by the legislative and executive branches of government, decisions which derive their legitimacy from being 'the will of the people'. In other words, the bodies that 'the people' authorised to rule and hold accountable through elections, are literally overruled by appointed and non-accountable judges. How can this be justified? The powers of the constitutional court rest first and foremost on its role as 'guardian of the constitution' — the very symbol of the founding of the existing social order.[7] And in constitutional democracies the existing order ultimately weighs more heavily than the current 'will of the people'.

What maintains authority in a society is, according to Arendt, the strength in the trinity of religion-authority-tradition:

> The binding force of an authoritative beginning to which 'religious' bonds tied men back through tradition. (Arendt, 1969a: 125)

'Religious bonds' need not be religious in a strict sense, it includes all forms of *beliefs* in a true and eternal foundation underlying the social order (symbolised by the constitution). This may be the will of God, natural law, or philosophical principles guaranteeing the truth/justice of the social order. The nature of the first principles are secondary and will generally not even be addressed — what is important is the belief that 'something' with unquestionable authority guarantees the truth of the constitution and the social order.

According to Arendt, modernity and secularisation (a break with tradition and loss of religious belief in a sacred beginning of the social order — even loss of belief in truth itself) has eroded the foundation of authority. With the loss of authority one of the mechanisms which has helped regulate society disappears. This confronts us

> without the religious trust in a sacred beginning and without the protection of traditional and therefore self evident standards of behaviour, [with] the elementary problems of human living-together. (Arendt, 1969a: 141)

In times of constitutional crisis the normative foundation of the social order is explicitly questioned. When this happens authority no longer exists. If the rules are still obeyed, rational conviction or force has taken over. Arendt does not believe that it is possible to restore constitutional authority in modern societies. Attempts to restore authority will result in a 'pseudo-authority' where force is what compels obedience.

If her diagnosis holds — what are the prospects for addressing fundamental social problems by way of constitutional design? With the power of the constitution resting ultimately on an unquestioned 'religious' belief in its authority, and the foundation for this authority gone, constitutionalism seem to be unattainable.

But, while acknowledging the relevance of this argument, the conclusion need not be this negative. Even if the constitution is no more than a *modus vivendi* reflecting the powers of different self-interested groups in society, obeyed for strategic reasons or because it is backed by force, it may still provide a relatively stable framework, and thus be of value.

Arendt may be right in that it is impossible to establish new constitutions in modern societies by referring to them being 'the will of God' or reflecting 'the truth' or 'natural law' or even 'justice', but it is not thereby ascertained that there is no alternative foundation upon which constitutional authority can be built.[8]

Initially, and in times of crisis, the norms underlying the constitution are questioned and constitutional legitimacy becomes a matter of rational conviction. If the constitution is based upon principles which the citizens of modern societies, with different moral outlooks, would agree to if they reflected on them, it could gain initial legitimacy.[9] If the principles are reflected in the constitutional structure in such a manner that it generates its own support once established, it becomes an equilibrium to which rational actors adapt, increasingly without questioning its legitimacy. The feed-back mechanism of constitutional stability is set in motion and justification of the principles underlying the constitution is no longer necessary as a driving force. In times of 'routine politics' the constitutional legitimacy is not up for debate — constitutional authority has taken over and is what compels obedience.

The alternative to 'a religious trust in a sacred beginning' is in this argument a consensus on a political conception of justice upon which the constitution is based. This creates a legitimacy which, if properly reflected in the constitution, may develop into authority.

This conclusion has implications for the analysis of the constitutional process in South Africa, the constitution itself, as well as the constitutional models that have been dominating the debate. During apartheid, and particularly in its last period, there was a growing awareness in wide sections of the population of the lack of acceptability of the basic norms underlying the state. In this context the normative acceptability of the post-apartheid dispensation becomes particularly important.

The stability of the new constitutional framework depends in part on its ability to develop authority. This again is a function of the extent to which the constitution is able to generate its own support. Given the lack of 'a religious trust in a sacred beginning' authority will have to be based on an initial rational acceptance of its fundamental principles — a form of 'constitutional patriotism'.[10]

According to this hypothesis — and the general argument for the importance of constitution (see Figure 3.1) — an important aspect of the evaluation of a constitutional framework is to evaluate its normative acceptability in the South African context. Arend Lijphart's and Albie Sachs' models illustrate the complexity of this issue and the range of the debate. Against this background the strengths and limitations of the 'final' South African constitution can be more fully appreciated.

The normative analysis consists of three layers: the presentation of the models brings out central normative choices which are implicit in each of them. Secondly, it is shown how each model can be justified on philosophical grounds. Finally, the models' normative acceptability is considered in relation to the standards set by democracy and human rights norms.

## Constitutionalism

In order to prepare the ground for the discussion of constitutional strategies I will show how different traditions feed into the conception of constitutionalism. The models to be presented in the following chapters take up different elements of constitutionalism, and this in turn accounts for important differences in their constitutional set-up. I will also show how constitutions may preform different functions, and work through a variety of institutional mechanisms.

Modern constitutions require a balance to be struck between *democracy* and constitutionalism in a narrow sense. The embracing of constitutional democracy is striking when we look at the constitutional process in South Africa, and figures prominently in both models presented in this book. The revival of constitutionalism is, however, not particular to South Africa, it has been central trait of democratic transitions throughout the world in the past decade, not least in Eastern Europe (Kumado and Busia, 1991: 3–5).

## Constitutionalism and Democracy

Democracy — the sovereignty of the people, the right of the majority to utilise the powers of the state according to its will — is the foundation of legitimate state power in the modern world. Constitutionalism limits the powers of the state. The competence of the state is restricted in order to protect the citizens' rights and liberties. The two elements, both fundamental elements in the modern notion of liberal democracy, are in many ways antithetical — each restricting the functioning of the other. The tension, or 'the liberal dilemma', may be expressed through the twin concepts of negative and positive liberty.[11] The liberal — negative — rights of non-interference and respect for the private sphere of the individual, limit the domain of the political, and thus the democratic — positive — right of the individual to influence decisions. Constitutionalism implies that there are cases and domains in which the majority cannot legitimately decide — e.g. if it infringes on the basic rights of citizens, or when the constitutional rules themselves are to be altered.[12]

Constitutionalism and democracy are often portrayed as conflicting ideals, but constitutionalism is also increasingly regarded as central to democracy. The private autonomy protected by constitutionalism and the public autonomy expressed through democracy are seen as complementary and internally related (Habermas, 1996: 450-455). Diverging views can in part be ascribed to different traditions of constitutionalism, and different ideals and definitions of democracy.

An exhaustive discussion of democracy is not required at this stage. (Democracy is more carefully defined in Chapter 6, when assessing the democratic qualities of the constitutional schemes.) It suffices to outline two ideal types of democracy, before proceeding to a more thorough discussion of the various concepts of constitutionalism.

## Democracy

'Democracy' designates regimes where the legislative and executive organs are elected at regular intervals, through free elections with universal suffrage and genuine competition between two or more parties. This definition approximates the authoritative definition of *polyarchy* given by Robert Dahl (1971). 'Democracy' also refers to ideals and prescriptive models advocating such forms of government. The twofold use of the concept is important, in Giovanni Sartori's words;

> democracy is uniquely open to, and hinged on, a *fact-value* tension. It can thus be said that only democracy owes its very existence to its ideals ... democracy results from, and is shaped by, the interactions between its ideals and its reality, the pull of an *ought* and the resistance of an *is*. (Sartori, 1987: 8)

For the following discussion it is useful to distinguish between two ideal types; *majoritarian democracy* and *consensus democracy*.

The basic principle of *majoritarian democracy* is 'the sovereignty of the majority' — government by the numeric majority of the people. The electoral system most consistent with this model is the single-member district majority system.[13] This system generally produces a political situation with two parties, one in government, the other in opposition.[14] A basic idea is that the parties will alternate in power as voter preferences change. Majoritarian democracy in ideal form produces clear choices for the voters, and governments that can be held responsible for particular decisions as well as general policies. The governing party is distinct from the regime, preventing dissatisfaction with governmental decisions from turning into hostility towards the regime as such. Majoritarian democracy is often referred to as the *'Westminster model'* after its most influential empirical approximation.

The other ideal type, *consensus democracy*, is based on the principle that no significant sub-group in society should be left without a say in government; democracy as 'government of all the people'. This model emphasises protection of minority rights and diffusion of power between different groups in society. Consensus democracy relies heavily on the elite as political actors, and critics have characterised it as government by elite cartel. Governments are less clearly accountable and the distinction between government and regime more diffuse than in majoritarian democracies. On the other hand it is generally more representative; votes are converted into parliamentary seats and governmental influence with more fidelity through proportional representation, the electoral system integral to consensus democracy.

It is important to keep in mind the distinction between the two ideal types. Disagreement among political theorists on appropriate strategies for establishment and preservation of democratic regimes is largely due to their adherence to one or other form of democracy. Choice of democratic ideal accounts for important differences between the approaches adopted by

Lijphart and Sachs towards the design of a constitutional structure for South Africa.

## *Constitutionalism — Rechtsstaat and the Rule of Law*[15]

The need to distinguish among various concepts of constitutionalism is particularly acute as far as South Africa is concerned. Its legal system and culture is influenced mainly by the British common law tradition but also to some extent by Dutch Roman law. Even more important, impulses from both traditions are reflected in the constitutional proposals to be discussed in following chapters..

The concepts of constitutionalism and *rule of law* — both of which serve as protection against the excesses of majority rule — are often combined into one category. Hereafter I will distinguish between rule of law — the 'British' doctrine of legislation as the basis for political action, irrespective of a written constitution — and constitutionalism, in the sense of a rigid written formal constitution lifting certain vital concerns/rights out of reach of the political process. The most typical form of constitutionalism in this sense is associated with the German concept of *Rechtsstaat*, and for the purpose of this discussion I will use the two terms interchangeably.

While rule of law depends on democracy defined as the sovereignty of Parliament, a *Rechtsstaat* is in principle independent of political form, and will ultimately be in conflict with the sovereignty of Parliament.

The two ideas have important characteristics in common — notably the concept of law as a general principle, equality before the law and certain substantive common-law liberties. But the rule of law is only concerned with one aspect of substantive justice — the legal protection of individual liberty. The *Rechtsstaat* contains a broader spectrum of rights, and the source of rights is common law and natural law rather than political authority. A *Rechtsstaat* presupposes a Bill of Rights which guarantees individual rights *vis-à-vis* the coercive powers of state authority, these rights are legal norms binding on all three organs of state authority (implying a positive duty to concertise them in practical terms) and these rights may never be abolished or their essential core encroached upon (Blaau, 1990: 96).

The difference between rule of law and *Rechtsstaat* is most clearly seen against the circumstances under which the ideas evolved. And the most decisive factor seems to be the prevailing conception of the state. Is the state an opponent of society or is it an institution performing certain functions on its behalf?

The *Rechtsstaat* evolved in 19th century Germany as a way to check the powers of an absolutist regime. It was a situation where civil society (the people) was in opposition to political society (the absolute monarch).

In England, Parliament was seen as the representative of the people, protecting the rights of those who placed its members in office 'civil and political society were not opposed to each other but were two sides of the same coin' (Blaau, 1990: 89).[16] Founding the state on laws given by the representatives of the people implied a merger of individual freedom and political freedom. Where 'the people' checked the executive power through Parliament, the need for a *Rechtsstaat*, separating protection of liberties from political form and defending civil society against political society, did not emerge. The protection of rights and liberties is determined by the quality of the political process and the capacities of Parliament. There is no external standard checking the content of positive laws.

While rule of law is closely linked to the notion of a sovereign parliament, and is concerned with the genesis of the law — the *Rechtsstaat* idea is in principle independent of political form, and how laws come about is regarded as irrelevant when judging their legitimacy. The crucial question is whether they correspond with the constitution.[17]

There are thus important differences between the democratic constitutional tradition, based on the concept of rule of law, holding that the genesis of laws determines their acceptability (i.e. they are acceptable if they are the outcome of a just procedure), and the liberal constitutional tradition, developed from the *Rechtsstaat* idea, operating with an external standard for judging the content of laws. In the legal tradition characterised by rule of law, individual freedom is seen to be best secured through legal recourse offered by private law. The *Rechtsstaat* idea is to protect the rights of individuals *vis-à-vis* state authority through the systematisation of public law to which executive organs are made subject. Only the liberal constitutional tradition is thus constitutional, in the sense that a rigid, written constitution, and not parliamentary sovereignty, is the highest directing normative principle. These differences are also reflected in the respective traditions of judicial review. In the *Rechtsstaat* tradition the power of judicial review is normally vested in a separate constitutional court, ruling only on constitutional and related matters, often with the competence to consider laws on their own initiative. In the *rule of law* tradition the function of determining the constitutionality of legislation is either not preformed at all, or it is allocated to the normal courts of law, and then only when such cases are put before them. The constitutional courts of the *Rechtsstaat* tradition will thus normally have a greater potential for independent action, with the consequent dangers of politisation of the courts and 'legalisation of politics' (Corder, 1992).

The *Rechtsstaat* may be either formal or material. The formal *Rechtsstaat* is associated with: separation of powers between branches of government; the principle of legality: state actions based upon a formal statute; predictability (no retroactive legislation); proportionality (state action should be in proportion to the object pursued, necessary and suitable); and an independent judiciary to protect fundamental rights.

The material or substantive *Rechtsstaat* seeks to merge *lex* and *ius* — in addition to the requirements of the formal *Rechtsstaat*, the law must also reflect proper ethical norms. State authority is not only bound by legality, but also by a set of higher judicial norms, reflected in the constitution.

> The realisation of these norms create a situation which may be described in legal terms as materially just. The constitution therefore, not only binds state authority to uphold procedural safeguards but also obligates the legislature to act in accordance with the requirements of substantive justice when exercising its function of lawmaking. (Blaau, 1990: 85)

The material *Rechtsstaat* is based upon supra-legal norms, that is on a conception of 'natural rights' in some form or other. What is counted as natural rights varies. Civil liberties are always central, so usually are political rights. Cultural, social and economic rights may also be interpreted as natural rights which statutory law is required to respect. A material *Rechtsstaat* is not necessarily a social welfare state, although in some cases it might be.

This discussion shows why constitutionalism may be seen as a useful strategy to achieve widely different objectives.

## *Precommitment or Foreclosure of Issues?*

Constitutions may also serve diverse purposes in other respects. An important distinction runs between constitutionalism as a form of precommitment — necessary for the sake of predictability, as well as for promoting rational long-term preferences — and constitutionalism as a strategy for voluntary foreclosure of issues.

Precommitment through constitutional constraints is needed because ordinary, or first-order, preferences expressed in day-to-day politics may be in conflict with (rational, long term) second-order preferences. The second category of 'preferences about preferences' expressed in the political institutions. These are articulated only in

> the rare moments in a nation's history when deep, principled discussion transcends the log-rolling and horse-trading of everyday majority politics, the object of these debates being the principles which are to constrain future majority decisions. (Elster, 1988: 6)

Constitutional constraints should thus be seen as mechanisms of self-binding, protection against impulsive action/passion, ensuring that the day-to-day political process does not frustrate rational long term goals.

Precommitment is also necessary in order to allow the political process to proceed against a backdrop of set institutional arrangements, without constantly revisiting the basic questions. It is a way to increase the expected stability and duration of political institutions, thus providing a more stable framework for long term planning. Without such constraints democracy itself becomes weaker. Constitutional constraints are stabilising devices limiting the self-destructive forces inherent in unconstrained democracy.

The dark side of precommitment is that basic institutional arrangements are also confining. And precommitment across generations remains a serious problem for democratic theory (Sunstein, 1988: 341). Why should any generation be bound by the decisions of its predecessors?

Constitutionalism may also be motivated by the need to remove certain unresolvable problems from the political arena in order to reduce the risk of system-breakdown and/or generate resources for soluble issues (Holmes, 1988).

The removal of issues from politics is justified by the argument that some matters do not belong in the hands of (potentially oppressive) majorities because they are fundamental rights. And that some matters are likely to undermine the political system itself and thus should be privatised.

There are also problems with constitutionalism as voluntary foreclosure of issues: immunising certain issues from public inspection and debate and maintaining the status quo, usually implies resolving the matter favourably for one or other side. And allowing democratic processes to operate only when the stakes are low, resolving the large issues behind the scenes, is problematic from the point of view of democracy. While foreclosure of issues in some cases decrease factional struggle, the opposite may also occur. If resolution through the political process is unavailable it may give rise to a loss of faith in the system and resort to extra-legal means (Sunstein, 1988: 340).

Technically, constitutional constraints can operate in different ways. They may be set in force by declaring certain changes unconstitutional, or they may be 'automatised' by making the process of change very complicated and demanding, or by irreversibly delegating certain tasks to independent institutions or lower levels of government (Elster, 1988: 4).

The objective of this discussion has been to prepare the grounds for the presentation and analysis of constitutional strategies. Different concepts of constitutionalism, different ideals of democracy, and different demarcations between the constitutional domain and the domain of the political, account for important differences between constitutional models.

In the remaining section of this chapter I will gather these, and other dimensions on which constitutions differ, in a conceptual framework according to which the discussion of the constitutional models can be structured.

## Conceptual Framework for Analysis of Constitutional Strategies

The idea underlying all constitutional strategies is to frame the basic 'rules of the game' in such a manner that society's most fundamental problems and conflicts are accommodated and can be solved peacefully within the system.

The strategies differ on a number of dimensions. They are guided by different ideals, structured towards different objectives, and there is disagreement regarding which mechanisms are the most efficient in achieving the desired result. The framework presented in this chapter is devised as a tool to structure the presentation of the constitutional strategies and bring out their most important characteristics.

The technical set-up necessarily occupies a central position in any presentation of a constitutional structure. In order to assess its potential for functioning as intended under the given circumstances, it is crucial to have an understanding of the mechanisms through which it is seen to work. In addition, it aims at bringing out normative differences between constitutional structures.

The most important dimensions on which constitutions vary are outlined in Table 3.1 below.

**Table 3.1 Conceptual framework for analysis of constitutional models**

| Dimension | Range of variation | |
| --- | --- | --- |
| **(i)  Institutional set-up** | | |
| institutional focus | legal system | political system |
| electoral system | majoritarian | proportional |
| legislature-executive relations | presidentialism | parliamentarism |
| compos. of legislature | uni-cameral | bi-cameral |
| compos. of executive | one party | coalition |
| | single executive | collective executive body |
| decentralisation | unitary state | federal state |
| | highly centralised | highly de-centralised |
| decision-making mode | adversarial | consensual |
| | majoritarian | minority vetoes |
| **(ii)  Interpretation of reality** | | |
| methodological focus | individual | collective |
| problem focus | structural | cultural |
| | inequality, poverty | ethnicity |
| **(iii)  Central value** | justice | stability, cultural autonomy |
| | positive liberty | negative liberty |
| **(iv)  Objective** | transformation | regulation |
| **(v)  Response to pluralism** (the nation-building dimension) | assimilation | separation |
| **(vi)  State-society relationship** | participation | representation |
| **(vii)  The constitutional domain** | democracy | constitutionalism |
| | rule of law | *Rechtsstaat* |
| | precommitment | foreclosure of issues |
| **(viii)  Normative foundation/ justification** | liberalism | communitarian philosophy |
| | contractarian philosophy | |

## (i) Institutional Set-up

A major difference between constitutional models is the importance given to the legal system relative to the political system. The central issue is the existence and strength of a constitutional court with the powers of judicial review.

Within the set-up of the political system there are also crucial differences. The most important are:

- the electoral system, and in particular the choice of electoral formula (the principal difference run between majoritarian and proportional electoral systems);
- the relationship between the executive and the legislature (parliamentary or presidential systems of government);
- the composition of central political bodies (uni/bi-cameral parliament, collective executive body);
- the requirements on decision making (decisions by consensus, minority vetoes);
- degree and form of decentralisation/federalism.

## (ii) Interpretation of Reality

A crucial determinant of differences among constitutional models are their interpretation of reality. This, again, depends on two analytically separate, although related, factors.

One is the methodological focus — whether individuals or groups are seen to be the constitutive element in political society. The second is the problem focus. In the case of South Africa the crucial question is whether inequality or ethic diversity is the most intractable and explosive source of conflicts.

## (iii) Central Value/Concern

Constitutional models may have a normative or a functional emphasis. Constitutions may be regarded primarily as norms reflecting and reforming the basic values of society, or they may be seen as a 'power map' concerned with 'the creation, distribution, legitimative effects and reproduction of power' (Okoth-Ogendo, 1991: 5).

Constitutional models may be guided by a normative focus such as justice, or directed at a functional objective, to achieve stability. This does not imply that the two aspects are not related — few would claim that a constitution perceived as unjust is likely to achieve stability. But the extent to which justice is regarded as a precondition for stability, differs, as do views concerning whether justice is a legitimate concern of the state.

## (iv) Objective/Goal

Constitutional strategies may aim at transformation or regulation. Should the constitution aim at treating the symptoms or cure the disease? Is it possible to transform the social structure of a society and thus solve/reconcile fundamental conflicts? Or should fundamental conflicts be taken as given, and the energy devoted to devising mechanisms capable of regulating them into less explosive patterns?

Differences among the models on this dimension is partly a function of their problem focus, but even when the same problem is addressed, recommendations vary. This is clearly seen in the various responses to societal pluralism.

## (v) Response to Pluralism

Nation-building is important in all constitutional schemes, but the ambitions on this dimension vary. This is illustrated in Table 3.2 below.

In its classical and most ambitious form, the aim of nation building is assimilation: to create one nation (with a homogenous culture and common loyalties) comprising all the citizens of a legally defined state.

Liberal constitutional schemes do not aim at nation-building in the traditional sense, but, based on acceptance of plurality, they seek to encompass all citizens on equal terms within a common political arena, regardless of cultural differences.

Consociational constitutional models build more explicitly onto societal plurality. The aim is peaceful co-existence between largely autonomous (ethnic) groups through mediation and power-sharing. The guiding ideal is that each (ethnic) group has its own political sphere, reducing the common arena to a minimum.

**Table 3.2 Response to pluralism: nation-building ambitions**

| Classical strategy | Liberal strategy | Consociational strategy | Separatist strategy |
| --- | --- | --- | --- |
| **assimilation** nationalist ideology | **toleration** and promotion of inclusive nationalism | **non-interference** power-sharing and co-existence between different ethnic groups | **secession/partition** nationalist ideology |
| 'one state, one nation' | 'together but different' (a common political sphere) | 'separate but equal' (different political spheres) | 'each nation a state' |

Separatist schemes go even further, and argue that no such common arena should exist. Each ethnic group — or nation — should have its own state. In a sense they share the ideology of the assimilationists: one state, one nation — 'each nation a state' is just the other side of the coin.

Underlying the disparate aims on the nation-building dimension are differing views on societal plurality. Some regard it as a problem which can be solved, others regard it as a phenomena which cannot, and should not be attempted (at least not in the short or medium term).

*(vi) Civil Society and the State*

The relationship between the individual, the state and the intermediary organisational network, often referred to as civil society, is conceived differently by different scholars. Some conceive this mainly as a matter of representation of (group/ethnic/segmental/functional) interests, while other scholars stress the importance of individual participation.

Political participation is not necessarily only a matter of voting in elections, but may also include participation in legislative processes, policy-formulation, etc., through intermediate level organisations. Participation may be valued for its function, in the sense of influencing the outcome of politics and ensuring accountability. It may, however, also be viewed as an intrinsic value (Arendt, 1958). In this perspective, participation (mass political activity) may be a goal in itself (Pateman, 1970).

If the relationship between state and civil society is conceived as mainly a matter of interest-representation, individual participation is to a certain extent superfluous. It may even be a problem. Accommodation of, and compromise between, conflicting interests may be easier to achieve if the political leaders representing the groups/interests have a certain autonomy *vis-à-vis* their electorate, which again is easier to attain in a depoliticised situation. Decreasing political participation is not necessarily a negative development in this perspective.

### (vii) The Constitutional Domain and the Domain of the Political

The discussion of constitutionalism in Section 3.2 shows that views differ with regard to what should be contained in the domain of the constitutional and what to leave to the domain of politics.

The size of the constitutional domain, and the balance that is struck between constitutionalism and democracy, varies between constitutional models. What should be safeguarded by 'lifting it up' above politics, and what is legitimately a matter for the arena of parliamentary politics? These differences are related to the concepts of constitutionalism. Constitutionalism may be conceived either as rule of law or as a (formal or material) *Rechtsstaat.*

And constitutionalism may either take the form of precommitment — a way to ensure that day-to-day politics do not frustrate long term goals. Or it may be seen as a foreclosure of issues — an agreement not to address certain issues which are insoluble, or where the potential for damaging conflicts is too acute.

### (viii) Normative Foundation/Justification

The presentation of constitutional models aims at explicating how each of the strategy models may be seen as an answer to the problems of South Africa — as coherent answers according to a particular interpretation of reality. And it is also shown how different traditions in modern political philosophy provide each of them with a normative justification — and question the relevance of the alternative approaches.

A table will be presented in relation to each constitutional model, to show how it is placed within the different dimensions. The framework will also serve as the general structure of the following two chapters, but will not be applied rigidly. It is designed as a tool, not as a requirement, and it is deviated from whenever the presentation of the models seems to benefit from a different ordering.

## Restating the Argument

The main assumptions, presented and argued for throughout this chapter, are that constitutions are potent political instruments, and that constitutional strategies are relevant in relation to the conflicts in South African society discussed in the previous chapter. To place the new constitution in relief it is interesting to look into the suitability of the main constitutional models contesting the ground in the South African constitution-making process, and to consider them both in terms of technical solutions and normative qualities.

The conceptual framework constructed above delineates various dimensions on which constitutional models vary. My argument is that their capacities vary accordingly. The set-up of the formal constitution influence, its potential for being complied with, for enduring, for inducing governments with legitimacy and capacity for action, and consequently its potential for having an impact on political output.

All constitutional strategies share the common presumption that formal structures matter, and that the most difficult conflicts in society should be reflected in the design of the 'basic rules' of interaction regulating the public sphere and the political arena. Still, strategies vary considerably.

What is seen to be the most important problem differs, and this necessarily influences the design of 'solutions'. And ambitions vary. Some strategies aim at eliminating the causes of conflict, transforming the social structure itself, by directing the state activity towards certain constitutionally entrenched goals. Others regard this as an illegitimate or impossible task. Their objective is 'social engineering'; to regulate the societal forces into less conflictual patterns through the introduction of certain constitutional mechanisms. For strategies attempting transformation, 'justice' is the main concern guiding constitutional construction, for those aiming for engineering, it is 'stability'. While focus in the first instance is set on the normative aspects, the second concentrates on technical aspects of the constitution. What are considered to be the 'agents' doing the work, also differ considerably. The electoral system is a fine-tuned instrument favoured by those technically manipulating the constitution for instant effect, while the legal system may be a regarded a better instrument for long-term transformation of the social structure.

Differences between constitutional strategies are addressed in the following chapters according to the conceptual framework presented above.

# Notes

1.  Or rather, this is the case with Anglo-American political science.
2.  In this discussion I draw on Hylland (1991).
3.  An example of a common law principle with constitutional status is found in Norway, namely the principle of parliamentary rule. This principle runs counter to the written text of the constitution where it is stated that the king appoints the cabinet as his councillors. In this case a common law principle, in direct conflict with what is stated in the constitutional text, must be regarded as part of the formal constitution of the country.
4.  A constitution may, however, provide some legitimacy even to a regime not acting in accordance with it. This effect, indicated by the (m) arrow on Figure 3.1 is significant in relation to the function of constitutions in Africa, discussed in Chapter 8.
5.  Constitutional conservatism is, however, relative even in the more established democracies. Thus, the US and Norway are cases of constitutional conservatism (constitutions dating from 1781 and 1814 respectively) whereas France and Denmark are less conservative, their latest constitutions dating from 1959 and 1952 respectively.
6.  Only a minority of established democracies have *judicial* review, with the constitutional court as the guardian of the constitution. The most well known examples of judicial review are the US and Germany (incidentally Arendt's two countries). However, in most democratic regimes there are possibilities of halting the enactment process. In Britain these powers lie with the House of Lords, while in Continental Europe we find the French tradition of *senatorial* rather than judicial constitutional review. In the northern part of Europe (e.g. Norway) the powers to check the legislature were traditionally bestowed in the monarch.
7.  In the USA the 'founding fathers' are still frequently referred to and quoted. In American society and polity the constitution and the constitutional court have a particularly strong position. All questions may, in the last instance, be considered constitutional, and the authority of the constitution thus provides the decisions with legitimacy.
8.  In addition the role of comparative legitimacy should be noted. This includes two elements which, very crudely, may be termed 'the will of the US' and 'the example of the US'. In the current uni-polar world, the hegemony of constitutional democracy is considerable, and may be of great importance for the initial establishment of the constitution. (There are, historically, several examples of durable constitutions established more or less by external dictate, most notably that of Japan.) The other element is that of constitutional democracy as the model which seems to work. Once the constitution is established, the crucial question for its duration is (regardless of how it originally came about), 'does it work'.

9.   To establish a foundation for basic norms, while acknowledging the secular character of modern societies, as well as their fundamental pluralism, is the project of modern contractarian political philosophers such as John Rawls. This tradition is also referred to as modern natural rights theories, because, although their 'natural rights' are less absolutist, the structure of the justificatory argument is very similar. For a discussion of *the natural rights paradigm* see Gilje (1989), otherwise see Rawls (1971, 1985, 1987 and 1989).

10.  The concept of *constitutional patriotism* is developed by Jürgen Habermas (Habermas 1996).

11.  The distinction was first made by Benjamin Constant (1820). 'The liberty of the moderns', the right to non-interference and personal independence, is contrasted with 'the liberty of the ancients' i.e., the liberty to influence public life. The distinction was rephrased by Isaiah Berlin in his famous essay 'Two Concepts of Liberty' (Berlin, 1969) where he distinguishes *positive liberty* — 'who governs me?' — from *negative liberty* — 'to what extent does the government interfere with my life?'.

12.  Restrictions on decision-making usually consists of a requirement of some form of qualified majority (higher quorum, heightened majority, concurrent majorities in various decision-making bodies). Sometimes special procedures are also specified, for example with regard to the time period from the initiation of legislation until it can be passed.

13.  *First-past-the-post* refers to plurality election in single-member constituencies. This system over-represents the largest party and may produce a majority from a mere plurality of votes. (And if the constituencies are 'gerrymandered' or the votes of certain parties very concentrated in a few constituencies, it may even produce a majority of seats from a minority of votes.)

14.  The relationship between the electoral system of 'first-past-the-post' and the two party system, and, opposingly, between proportional representation (PR) systems and multi-partyism, was described by Maurice Duverger as approximating 'a true sociological law'. This is explained both by the *mechanical* effect (since only the winner in each constituency is rewarded, the counting of votes favour the largest competitors) and by the *psychological* effect (since the voters are aware of the fact that the 'third'-party candidate has no chance of being elected, many will hesitate to 'waste' their vote, and thus decide to vote for their second — and more realistic — preference). The psychological effect reinforces the mechanical, working as an incentive towards strategic voting. Sincere voting is less costly in PR systems, which favours party proliferation (Duverger, 1964). In recent political science the validity of Duverger's argument has been debated. FPTP seems only to correspond with two-party systems in societies characterised by homogeneous populations. For the purpose of this book it is important to note that ethnically divided societies seem to represent an exemption to Duverger's 'law' (see Kuhnle, 1987).

15.  Throughout this section I draw on Blaau, 1990.

16.  From the seventeenth century on, Rule of Law — legality and parliamentary sovereignty — acted as a defence against attempts by the king to install an absolutist regime.

17.  Traditionally a systematisation and interpretation of customary law and natural law to secure maximum liberty against a more or less absolute state.

# 4  The Justice Model: Human Rights and Distributive Justice

This chapter is a presentation of what I will refer to as *the justice model,* a strategy for constitutional reform in South Africa.[1] The model can, with some qualifications, be seen as representative of the ANC position throughout the constitutional negotiations.[2] The characteristics of the model are clarified according to the framework for analysis outlined in the previous chapter. The technical set-up is outlined, emphasising the mechanisms through which it is thought to function, and the normative choices implicit in the model are brought out.

A central objective of this chapter is to show how the justice model, as set forth by Albie Sachs, may be seen to apply the ideas of liberal contractarian philosophy to South African conditions. In particular there is a close fit between this model and John Rawls' theory of justice. If there is coherence between the two, Rawls' theory may be seen as a normative justification for Sachs' constitutional model. The discussion centres around two questions. One concerns the construction of rights, and the foundation of their legitimacy. The other is the question of distributive justice and affirmative action.

## Albie Sachs and the Justice Model

> The struggle for self-determination takes the form of a struggle within the frontiers of South Africa to create a new constitutional order. The battle over the Constitution therefore has become as vital for South Africa as the battle for independence was for the people of Mozambique and other colonised territories. (Sachs, 1986: 205)

The constitutional strategy presented in this chapter advocates a procedure for transforming South African society into a more just scheme of cooperation. According to this view, social stability depends on a democratic social structure respecting individual human rights and distributing opportunities and social goods reasonably fairly among citizens. Constitutional construction along these lines has been advocated by Albie Sachs who at the time he wrote this was a member of the ANC Constitutional Committee. After the 1994 transition Sachs was appointed a judge of the newly established Constitutional Court.

In the presentation of what I have termed 'the justice model' I rely primarily on two of Sachs' works, *Protecting Human Rights in a New South Africa (1990a)* and *Advancing Human Rights in South Africa* (1992a).

Sachs does not present a fully-fledged constitutional model. Focus is on the creation of a Bill of Rights as the centrepiece of a new constitution. Much attention is devoted to aspects of the legal system, while other central features of the constitutional framework, elaborated in detail by other scholars, are barely touched upon. On issues such as the design of the electoral system and decision-making bodies, only very general guidelines are given.

By drawing upon other works by Sachs as well as interview material, a more coherent constitutional model is outlined.[3] Even so, his model retains a preliminary character with respect to certain aspects of its content.

This proposal is as much a method or strategy for arriving at the best possible constitutional structure, as a fully-fledged constitutional blueprint or model. The approach is profoundly *procedural*. According to Sachs the best constitution and the best Bill of Rights is constructed through an actual consultation process, involving the widest possible strata of the population. 'The solution' or outcome of this process cannot be defined *a priori*. The procedural character — while making the presentation of the model more difficult — renders the approach particularly interesting. It also invites a comparison between the justice model's specifications for a fair procedure and the actual constitution-making process, which will be undertaken in Chapter 9.

Neither of the models presented here — and probably no model — is complete in the sense that it fully covers all potential aspects of the constitutional structure. Sachs handles numerous constitutional issues in his works, and the legal system and constitutional protection of rights in particular are treated with unusual creativity. The fact that this model is not congruent with the models of the following chapter, and lays emphasis on different institutions and mechanisms, reflects the relative importance given to various sections of the constitutional structure by different scholars. Scholars devoting most attention to the 'specifics' of the electoral system and the set-up of the executive, while ignoring the legal system and the judicial branch of government, do not necessarily consider the latter unimportant, but see it as a constant, while the electoral system is considered the crucial instrument of constitutional engineering.

In the following section the constitutional framework of Sachs' justice model is laid out. The interpretation of the South African situation (on which the model is based) is discussed, along with characteristic features of the institutional set-up. The objectives of the model are explicated, and particular attention is devoted to expose the mechanisms which, according to Sachs, can further these goals.

## The Conceptual Framework

In the previous chapter various dimensions were outlined on which constitutional models differ. Following this analytical framework, the objectives of Sachs' justice model are now to be examined.

### South African Reality According to the Justice Model

Sachs' constitutional model is based on an understanding of South African society in which devastating poverty and inequality is seen to be the major source of conflict and unrest. This is the legacy of apartheid, and thus particularly unjust, and meaningful change requires that these problems are actively and ably addressed by the state. It is therefore necessary to construct a constitution that ensures a potent government with maximum ability for political action, a legal framework that secures the direction of change, while safeguarding basic rights of the individual against the state.

The multi-ethnic character of South African society is recognised, but ethnicity is rejected as a politically significant force in a democratic South Africa. Ethnicity presently appears to be of importance, but this is a function of policies pursued by the apartheid regime. Race and ethnicity are 'artificial' political cleavages. If not emphasised and encouraged by the political system, the importance of ethnicity will dwindle. The question of race must be addressed, due to the overwhelming economic importance of racially defined boundaries, but as far as possible the state should be 'colour blind'. Ethnic identity and ethnic tension between black groups has been actively encouraged by the apartheid state, and granting these divisions political significance is regarded as a way to uphold the old system.

**Table 4.1    The justice model according to the conceptual framework for analysis**

| Dimension | The justice model's position within the range of variation | |
| --- | --- | --- |
| (i)   **Institutional set-up** | | |
| institutional focus | **legal system** | political system |
| electoral system | majoritarian | **proportional** |
| legislature-executive relations | **presidentialism** | parliamentarism |
| compos. of legislature | uni-cameral | **bi-cameral** |
| compos. of executive | **one party govern.** | coalition government |
| | **single executive** | collective executive body |
| decentralisation | **unitary state** | federal state |
| | highly centralised | **decentralised** |
| decision-making mode | **adversarial** | consensual |
| | **majoritarian** | minority vetoes |
| (ii)  **Interpretation of reality** | | |
| methodological focus | **individual** | collective |
| problem focus | **structural** | cultural |
| | **inequality, poverty** | ethnicity |
| (iii) **Central value** | **justice** | stability, cultural autonomy |
| | **positive liberty** | negative liberty |
| (iv)  **Objective** | **transformation** | regulation |
| (v)   **Response to plurality** ( nation-building ) | assimilation / **toleration** / separation | |
| (vi)  **State-society relationship** | **participation** | representation |
| (vii) **Constitutional domain** | democracy | **constitutionalism** |
| | rule of law | *Rechtsstaat* |
| | **precommitment** | foreclosure of issues |
| (viii) **Normative foundation/ justification** | **liberalism** | communitarian |
| | **contractarian philos. John Rawls** | philosophy |

*The Constitutional Set-up*

The constitutional set-up advocated by Sachs is guided by the twin concerns of making the state a powerful instrument of social change, and of safeguarding citizens' rights and liberties from illegitimate state intervention.

In order to strengthen the state's potential as an agent of change, Sachs' constitutional set-up provides for a unitary, relatively centralised state; decision-making procedures based on majority rule; and a delimitation of the political domain which — while respecting and protecting the private sphere — facilitates extensive state regulation of the economy. Federalism is rejected:

> it is a way of depriving majority rule in South Africa of any meaning, by drawing boundaries around race and ethnicity. This would prevent the emergence of a national government, keep the black population divided, prevent any economic restructuring of the country and free the economically prosperous areas of the country of any responsibility for helping develop the vast poverty-stricken areas. The issues are really ones of self-interest dressed up as principle. (Sachs, 1990a: 152)

Although the need for local government and decision-making bodies at different political levels is emphasised, this is a matter of creating opportunities for participation and increasing implementation capacity, not for limiting the powers of the central government. The dangers of excessive concentration of power in a single authority are recognised, but the need for checks and balances are seen to be met by other constitutional arrangements (such as separation of powers and a Bill of Rights). Furthermore, he argues, strong forms of local government can be developed without dividing the country into 'a myriad of group political areas' (Sachs, 1990a: 153). Local government should be encouraged, not as competing centres of political power, but in a manner harmonising its workings with national political goals.

The principle of *majority rule* is central to Sachs' model. This does not, however, imply a majoritarian electoral system, akin to the British system of 'first-past-the-post'. A form of proportional representation (PR) is held to be the most favourable electoral system for South Africa, provided that it is firmly within the frames of universal suffrage and a common voter roll.[4] Rather than applying to the electoral system, 'majority rule' refers to governmental decision-making procedures. Sachs is firmly against institutionalisation of coalition governments or constitutional guarantees for minority vetoes. The right of the majority to make decisions is, according to this view, not only the crux of the idea of democracy, but absolutely essential if South Africa is to become a more just society.

Sachs argues that the constitution should open for, and encourage, state regulation of the economy in order to promote social equality and distributive justice. The right to private ownership should be respected, but in ways that do not prohibit restructuring and, most notably, land reform. The market and private enterprise should be allowed to operate, but not without restrictions. What is envisioned is thus a mixed economy, or a regulated market economy (Sachs, 1990a: 165–68).

These features of the constitutional set-up, are intended to secure a potent government. But Sachs recognises the need to limit the powers of government, even when democratically elected. While majority rule is necessary and valuable, it may interfere unduly with the rights of citizens. The individual should be protected from illegitimate state intervention by a Bill of Rights, entrenched in the constitution and justiciable, that is, persons alleging infringements of their rights are to be given opportunity to seek a remedy by recourse to the courts (Sachs, 1990a: 191). The Bill of Rights should not only protect individual civil and political liberties, but also social, economic and cultural rights.

A system for separation of powers is suggested. According to the principle advocated by Montesquieu, and institutionalised, e.g., in the political system of the USA, power should be divided between a democratically elected legislative assembly, the executive (preferably a directly elected president), and a constitutional court with powers of judicial review (Sachs, 1990a: 191).

In Sachs' constitutional proposal the powers of the state will also be checked by institutions facilitating civil society participation in the decision-making process. And also through the establishment of institutions such as the Ombud and a Human-Rights Commission to oversee the implementation process (Sachs, 1992b: 24[5]).

*Central Concerns: Normative versus Functional*

The focus of this model is on the normative qualities of the constitutional set-up. It is based on the conception that important social problems and conflicts cannot be solved merely by 'technical regulations', but come down to normative questions of choosing between values. A stable, smoothly functioning system is not necessarily a goal in itself, only if the system is reasonably just. Normative qualities, the fairness of the political system, are in this sense primary to functional aspects.

Justice is primary in another respect as well. The legitimacy of the state is seen to depend, first and foremost, on the perceived fairness of the system. The stability of a democratic political system in South Africa depends on it being considered legitimate by the majority of the population. Unless the basic rules of society are perceived to be just, they are unlikely to generate the support necessary for stability. Given the history of South Africa and the bizarre social structure it has produced, the government's dedication to distributive justice is particularly crucial for long-term legitimacy.

While functional aspects are not centre stage in this model, they are not ignored. In order to provide fair 'rules of the game' for South African society, the political system must be designed so that it is likely to generate a stable and workable political and economic situation. 'Once the principle of democracy and majority rule is accepted, the question of preserving the material wealth of the country takes on special importance' (Sachs, 1986a: 209). Questions such as economic feasibility are crucial, but all solutions will have to be found within the limits set by justice.

### Objective: Transformation versus Regulation

Sachs criticises consociational models (presented in Chapter 5) for being problem evasive. And he maintains that the problems of South Africa call for a problem confronting strategy. Rather than attempting to 'engineer' South African society, in the sense of balancing its differences and divisions to achieve political stability, Sachs wants a constitution which, through providing for a fair and democratic political process, works to transform the social structure itself. Gradual transformation of South Africa into a more just society, providing genuinely equal opportunities to all citizens, is the objective of this model. South Africa's social conflicts should be addressed in a manner aiming at their solution, not merely 'regulated' to prevent open conflict.

*Civil Society and the State: Participation versus Representation*

The relationship between citizens, civil society organisations and the state is conceived mainly in terms of participation, rather than as representation of interests. Participation should be encouraged at all levels: in the electoral process, in legislation and implementation, and in the construction of the constitution itself.

An uncomplicated electoral system, facilitating meaningful participation by all adult South Africans, regardless of education, is a key concern. Furthermore, participation should be stimulated through institutionalising consultation processes whereby civil society organisations are drawn into decision-making. This also serves to increase government accountability.

The idea of involving the largest sections of society possible in the drafting process, is rooted in ANC tradition. It is developed by Sachs in relation to the creation of a Bill of Rights for South Africa, and referred to as *participatory formulation of rights*. He envisages a strategy utilising the relatively developed South African civil society: existing organisations and associations (labour unions, women's groups, associations for disabled people, commercial organisations, farmers' organisations etc.). A central component of this strategy is also to stimulate the formation of new organisations. Organisations may be asked to make formulations of rights that they find to be of special importance for their particular situation, or they may be asked to comment upon or reformulate drafts (Sachs, 1990a: 16). The idea is to ensure that the Bill of Rights is in accordance with South African culture and needs. And, at the same time, to educate and deepen the consciousness of those involved, and increase the support and legitimacy of the resulting document. Participation in the creation of the constitution works to kindle an obligation towards it. Participation in decision-making is advocated as a general element of politics, also beyond the constitutional process, and is seen as a method to increase the legitimacy of the political system. Participation in the legislative process, formulating what are to count as general rules, furthers an understanding of the legitimate claims of 'the others' and thus contribute to reconciliation and nation-building.

Participatory formulation of rights, reflects the idea that the fairness of the process through which the constitution comes about is a criterion for its acceptability. The significance of these ideas stands out more clearly when viewed in the light of Rawls' philosophical method.

## The Constitutional Domain

What should be enshrined in the constitutional domain and what is to be left for politics? The size of the constitutional domain is an important aspect of any constitutional set-up. Sachs advocates a comprehensive Bill of Rights as part of the constitutional framework. It is to guarantee important civil, political, cultural, social, economic and environmental rights. Within the last three categories the rights should guarantee an *expanding minimum floor*. The goals of government activity in the areas of social policy, economic policy and environmental policy, as well as the direction of change, should be laid down in the constitution itself.

Left-wing theorists have traditionally held constitutions to be the prize the property-owning classes require in order to accept democracy. It has been viewed as a conservative institution — a guarantee against confiscation by the propertyless majority. Those who have still favoured it have done it out of the conviction that it is in the interest of the propertyless majority to give such guarantees in order to gain indispensable minority support.

In this perspective the justice model is very interesting. In light of the focus on distributive justice and redistribution, the emphasis on constitutionalism seems paradoxical. The argument is two-fold. Constitutionalism promotes reconciliation and answers to the fears of different parts of the population by securing their rights and providing an orderly framework for politics. His second and primary argument in favour of constitutionalism is that it is the most effective and suitable device for orderly change. Constitutionalism in his view is a tool of transformation and justice, not of conservation and inequality.

In the justice model, constitutionalism is seen as pre-commitment — necessary both for the sake of predictability, and to promote rational long-term preferences, first and foremost distributive justice.

The fundamental charge against constitutionalism as pre-commitment — that it is an institution whereby the dead are ruling the living — also pertains to the justice model. A central question in this respect is how difficult it should be to change or amend the constitutional structure. This issue is not explicitly addressed but some form of entrenchment is clearly envisioned.

The justice model is a material *Rechtsstaat*. Sachs specifies a wide spectre of norms that the actual legislation should be in accordance with in order to be just. These should be reflected in a constitutionally entrenched Bill of Rights, binding on the legislature as well as the executive. Sachs explicitly recognises the need to subjugate all three branches of government to a Bill of Rights and a rigid written Constitution. He proposes a judiciary exercising its powers in terms of the material *Rechtsstaat* principle, endowed not only with procedural testing powers (which the South African judiciary had even under the *apartheid* regime), but also with substantial testing powers — checking the content of legislation against 'natural rights' principles as they are enshrined in the constitution.

But the justice model draws on the rule of law tradition as well. Although the ultimate criterion is compatibility with the constitution, the constitution itself is justified by being the outcome of a just procedure, a procedure reflecting the moral sentiments prevailing in society. Emphasis is placed on the importance of a correct political procedure to ensure, as far as possible, the justice of the outcome.

With such an all-encompassing constitution, little space seems to be left for the domain of politics. Sachs acknowledges that this may be objectionable and underscores that the constitution only should specify a range, or set limits, on the various issues. Specific policies are not to be included in the constitution. The means through which the constitutionally defined ends are to be pursued, are matters to be decided on in the political domain. Still, the constitutional domain is very extensive in this model.

## Societal Plurality and Nation Building

'Different, but equal and together' characterises the views of the justice model on social plurality and nation-building (see Table 3.2).

Sachs explicitly states that cultural pluralism, religious and linguistic diversity must be tolerated, even encouraged. The cultural, religious and linguistic rights of all citizens should be given constitutional protection. But the differences in culture (or ethnic identities) should not be reflected in the political system. All should participate on equal terms in the same political arena.

There is, however, a certain ambivalence regarding the the nation-building dimension. On the one hand, cultural diversity is characterised as an asset. 'Each cultural tributary contributes towards and increases the majesty of the river of South African-ness' (Sachs, 1990a: 179). On the other hand, considerable emphasis is placed on the creation of over-arching loyalties. It is explicitly stated that organisations are not to be allowed to 'function as a cover for political mobilisation on a divisive, racist or ethnic basis' (Sachs, 1990a: 26). An inclusive South African nationalism is to be encouraged.

Nation-building in the classical sense seems to be an implicit long term goal, even though assimilation is explicitly rejected.

*Institutional Measures: What are the Mechanisms Doing the Work?*

How is the objective of transforming South Africa into a more just society to be advanced in this model? Two strategies are specified. Firstly, Sachs focuses on ensuring a potent government, capable of reaching the necessary decisions, and with sufficient powers to ensure implementation of laws and policies. A unitary, relatively centralised state, with decision-making procedures according to the principle of majority rule, a strong executive (preferably democratically elected to increase legitimacy), and a constitutional foundation for affirmative action policies and regulation of the economy, enable the state to function as an agent of change.

Secondly, transformation is to be advanced through the legal system. The direction of change is to be laid down in the constitution (through social and economic rights guaranteeing an 'expanding minimum floor'). These goals, along with the civil, political and cultural rights of individuals, are to be enshrined in a constitutionally entrenched Bill of Rights, and protected by a constitutional court with the powers of judicial review. These mechanisms, along with facilities for civil society participation in decision-making and control on implementation, are to increase government accountability and guard against abuse of state power.

This constitutional model relies overwhelmingly on the legal system, both as a guardian against state abuse, and as an agent of change. A crucial question in the assessment of this model is whether South Africa's legal system would be capable of carrying the burden placed onto it by this constitutional model. Another important issue, given the politically important role of the courts, and in particular the Constitutional Court, is the possible danger of politisation. The potential of excessive legal activism increases where the powers of judicial review are as wide as envisaged in this case (O'Malley, 1996). A related matter bearing on the perceived impartiality of the court is the procedure of appointment. Who appoints the judges? This is an important aspect of the separation of powers between the judiciary and the other branches of government. We will return to the problems of overload of the legal system, and its independence and neutrality in later chapters.

## Where Do These Ideas Come From?

This constitutional proposal seems to draw its roots from a number of sources. Many of the elements in the constitutional set-up he outlines are found in the political systems of established democracies.

Much of Sachs' constitutional framework is property common to the liberal democratic tradition. Several central features resemble the political systems of the United States and Germany: the central position of a Bill of Rights, the emphasis on the constitution and a constitutional court with the powers of judicial review, as well as the separation of powers between the branches of government.

For other aspects of the model Sachs has looked elsewhere. The concept of affirmative action originates from the USA, and has been used in, for example, India and Sri Lanka. The ways in which the state is required/allowed to regulate the economy, has much in common with the functioning of the political process in Scandinavian countries. Social and economic rights are included, to a lesser extent, in the constitutional structures of these countries (although not necessarily in the written constitution), as is the Ombud, and some of the procedures envisioned for civil society participation in legislation processes.

Despite Sachs' emphasis on 'majority rule', the justice model is more in line with the German or Scandinavian political systems than the British form of government usually associated with the concept of majority rule. The emphasis on constitutionalism and a constitutional court as protection against abuse of power from a democratically elected government, separates it from the 'Westminster model' of more or less unchecked majority rule. This trait is strengthened by the fact that Albie Sachs favours a PR electoral system to the British single member district majoritarian system. Nevertheless, Sachs' justice model seems to be guided by the ideal of majoritarian democracy rather than consensus democracy.

Sachs' concern for social justice and strong emphasis on participation reflect ANC ideology and tradition. Extensive participation and consultation in decision-making processes figure prominently in ANC history.[6] There also an influence from ideologies of 'participatory democracy' and 'African democracy' that also should be seen in the context of Sachs' years in exile — many of which were spent in Mozambique.

So far, Sachs' constitutional proposals may seem like a random collection of elements — as eclecticism without a guiding idea. The rationale underlying the model is easier to see when we look to modern political philosophy.

Sachs' emphasis on *justice* as the primary virtue of social institutions, is parallel to perhaps the most influential tradition in contemporary political philosophy, often referred to as 'the new contractarians' or liberal theories of justice.

The American philosopher John Rawls is the most important figure within this tradition, and one of the most influential political philosophers of our times. His book *A Theory of Justice* (1971) spurred a whole new 'industry' of normative political philosophy. His way of addressing the fundamental questions — 'what is a just society' and 'how can social institutions (and in particular constitutions) be normatively justified in modern, fundamentally plural, societies' — evoked interest far beyond the ranks of philosophers, especially among economists, political scientists and lawyers. In later years Rawls revised and elaborated on themes from *A Theory of Justice*. Some of the ideas that, for our purposes, are the most interesting and fruitful, are found in two of his later articles, 'The Idea of an Overlapping Consensus' (1987) and 'The Domain of the Political and Overlapping Consensus' (1989).

## Sachs' Model — an Application of John Rawls' Theory of Justice

For someone familiar with the writings of John Rawls, reading *Protecting Human Rights in a New South Africa* is an intriguing experience. The parallels between central ideas in this book and the Rawlsian ideas are striking. There are parallels in the general theoretical framework, in the structure of the arguments as well as in terminology. I will argue that *Protecting Human Rights in a New South Africa*, and Sachs' constitutional recommendations in general, can be read as a creative and innovative application of Rawlsian ideas to the South African context.

Sachs does not refer to Rawls, nor to any of the theorists elaborating on his ideas. When asked, acknowledged having read some of Rawls' writings and been exited by them: 'I found nothing in them that was not compatible with my ideas'.[7] What, if anything, in Sachs' justice model that originates from his reading of Rawls, is of minor interest. What is important is that by 'co-reading' the two writers, new light is shed on the works of both. The justice model is given greater depth and coherence, underlying assumptions are brought out, and, if the model can be shown to be in accordance with the principles of justice, Rawls' theory may serve as a normative justification for Sachs' constitutional proposal. John Rawls' theory, on the other hand, is given a very interesting interpretation.[8]

Sachs' constitutional proposal for South Africa is guided by the twin concerns of distributive justice and protection of individual rights and freedoms. Rawls started out from the same point of departure when constructing his famous theory of justice — 'Justice as Fairness' — as an alternative to the utilitarian ideas dominating political thinking.

## Rawls' Philosophical Method and Sachs' Idea of Participatory Formulation of Rights

Rawls argues that we share two deeply held intuitions or convictions about how society ought to be organised: it should secure its members a high level of welfare, and it should respect and protect the fundamental rights of all citizens. Furthermore, he holds that the latter principle — that all human beings have certain rights that the welfare of the society as a whole cannot legitimately override — is normally given a certain priority. Utilitarianism only takes the first principle into consideration and defines the right way to organise society as the organisation that maximises 'the good'. ('The good' is defined by utilitarians as total or average utility or rational wants-satisfaction.)

According to Rawls, utilitarianism, by equating 'the right' with maximising 'the good', and concentrating solely on utility or welfare, violates our deeply held conviction that all members of society have the right to a certain rights protection. He sets out to construct principles of justice that respect, and give a certain priority to this intuition, while at the same time pay due regard to economic considerations in order to facilitate a high level of welfare.

The method Rawls uses to generate and justify his principles is a variety of the theory of 'the social contract', developed and employed by philosophers such as Hobbes, Rousseau, Locke and Kant (see Gilje, 1989). In sophisticated forms of social contract theory, such as in the works of Kant, 'the social contract' is not conceived as an actual, historical, contract binding on those who enter it. The idea is, rather, that if the norms regulating society were such that it would be rational for all members of society to prefer this state of social cooperation to an anarchic state of nature, the state would be regarded as just and as a social contract binding on all.

The same idea of *rational consent* underlies Rawls' theory; a just state is a state regulated by principles with which it would be rational for all persons to agree. As a device to bring out the principles that would be agreed upon by free and equal rational persons, Rawls constructs a fair hypothetical ('mental') choice-situation. The manner in which this *original position* is constructed, guarantees that principles chosen under these 'mental conditions' are just.


## Procedural Justice

Rawls' theory of justice is *procedural*. The principles are just because they are the outcome of a fair procedure — it is the fairness of the procedure itself which justifies the resulting principles. Similarly, to Sachs, an important criterion for the acceptability of a certain constitutional framework, is the process of its construction and adoption.

Why is Rawls' *original position* a fair choice-situation? Rawls bases the claim primarily on two features characterising the *original position*. First of all, the parties have the properties that we see as relevant for taking moral decisions, and only these. Secondly, they are placed behind a *veil of ignorance* covering all information about their own social position, resources and preferences, only letting through enough general knowledge about society to permit the parties to choose adequate principles (Rawls, 1971: 17–19).

In the 'original positions' of actual politics — when new constitutions are to be created and agreed upon — there is, unfortunately, no possibility for pulling down a veil of ignorance. Unfortunately, because it is reasonable to presume that if it were possible to hide from the delegates to the South African Constitutional Assembly all information about the colour of their skin, their gender and age, their ethnic, linguistic, religious and cultural background, their social position, their economic resources and their political convictions, party affiliation and constituencies, only letting through general information about the social, economic and political conditions of South African society — if this were possible, then the resulting document would be reasonably fair. It would be fair because, in order to protect their own interests, all delegates would have to think him/herself in all social positions, and ensure that — whoever (s)he turned out to be, the situation would be as favourable as possible.

But is there any way in which the same result can be achieved in practical politics? Is there a substitute for 'the veil of ignorance'?

Yes and no. Sachs proposes a procedure for constructing a just constitution. Unlike Rawls' procedure, which by definition produces a just result, Sachs' method is one of imperfect procedural justice. In practical politics justice cannot be guaranteed, but some methods are more likely to generate just results.

The veil of ignorance ensures impartiality — the parties cannot but give all points of view equal consideration and weight. Sachs' strategy for constitutional construction — 'participatory formulation of rights' — strive towards the same result: impartially through due consideration of all interests. This procedure is fair, because (and to the extent that) it takes into consideration the points of view of the widest possible strata of the population — collected through an extensive consultation-process involving various forms of civil society organisations. In addition, fairness demands that the resulting constitutional proposal is adopted in a democratic manner. Both Sachs and Rawls hold democratic procedures of decision-making, although not capable of guaranteeing a fair outcome, to be the best opportunity available. Democratic processes are also fair in the sense that all parties are — at least in principle — given equal influence.

## *Justice According to External Criteria and the Idea of Reflective Equilibrium*

In addition to setting *procedural* criteria (that is, criteria that the process of constitutional construction will have to meet) Sachs also points to *external* criteria with which the constitutional framework will have to be in accordance in order to be acceptable. These are to a large extent derived from what he describes as the 'international human rights culture', containing certain 'universally recognised fundamental principles'. These include the equal dignity and worth of all persons, the inviolability of the person, freedom of movement, the right to vote, freedom of expression, conscience and religion, freedom from torture and cruel, inhumane and degrading treatment, prohibition of servitude, slavery and forced labour and the requirements of due process of law (Sachs, 1990a: 40–41).

Rawls, too, prescribes a form of coherence with external criteria. Although his principles are the outcome of a choice situation characterised by pure procedural justice, and thus are justified by definition, Rawls argues that they should be checked against our considered judgements. If the principles are not in coherence with our most deeply held intuitions and convictions, the set-up of the original position should be evaluated and possibly adjusted. Alternatively, in course of the reflective process, we come to change our deeply held convictions, until an equilibrium is reached (Rawls, 1971: 20–22).

## The Idea of an Overlapping Consensus

But, how do we know that these external criteria are just? In a modern world, characterised by value-pluralism, whose 'deeply held intuitions and convictions' are authoritative? Rawls argues that the premise on which a theory of justice should be based should be 'thin' and of such a quality that it could be supported by people with differing moral and religious outlooks. It should be based on a conception of the person, and an understanding of rationality on which there is a general *overlapping consensus*.[9]

Sachs' strategy for *participatory formulation of rights* seeks to generate an overlapping consensus on constitutional principles. Formulations submitted by groups and associations with widely different needs and interests, are to be united into a single document, taking all perspectives into consideration. In this manner a common set of rules, acceptable to people with different conceptions of 'the good' and different moral/religious outlooks, are thought to take form. Although the result might not be acceptable to all the various ideologies in South African society, the method could contribute to the development of an overlapping consensus.[10]

So far we have concentrated on Rawls' *method* and concluded that Sachs' 'participatory formulation of rights' approach may be interpreted as a just procedure for constitutional construction, in certain respects parallel to the Rawlsian ideas of overlapping consensus and reflective equilibrium. *The veil of ignorance* is to some extent substituted by this method of taking different perspectives into consideration. The complete impartiality characterising the original position, is, however, not attained.

The aim of the following section is to show how Rawls' principles of justice are reflected in Sachs' constitutional model. A high level of coherence is necessary if Rawls' theory is to be regarded as a normative justification for the justice model.

## Figure 4.1 The idea of an overlapping consensus

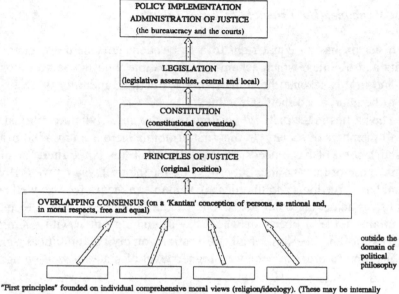

"First principles" founded on individual comprehensive moral views (religion/ideology). (These may be internally incompatible, but each must support, or be compatible with the 'Kantian' conception of the person.)

## Rawls' Principles of Justice and Affirmative Action

First of all, what are the principles of justice emerging from Rawls' just procedure?

The parties in *the original position* (who have the ability to reason rationally, but who do not know anything about their own preferences, resources or relative position in society) are forced to consider the interests of all social positions when choosing principles to regulate society. These 'rules of the game', are so crucial in determining the prospects different citizens have for realising their personal plans of life, that the parties in the *original position* would choose a conservative strategy, making sure that no social position comes out worse off than necessary (Rawls, 1971: 95–99).[11] Rawls argues that the following principles would be chosen in the *original position* (the principles are cited from Rawls, 1993: 5).

## First Principle: The Principle of Equal Liberty

Each person has an equal right to a fully adequate scheme of equal basic rights and liberties, which scheme is compatible with the same scheme for all; and in this scheme the equal political liberties, and only those liberties, are to be guaranteed their fair value.[12]

The parties in the *original position* would secure civil and political rights for all members of society. In this first principle there is an implicit principle of satisfaction of basic needs, to the extent that this is required for citizens to make use of their political liberties in a meaningful way (Rawls, 1993: 7). Equal basic freedoms and liberties are valuable in themselves, as well as vital means for achieving other goals. They should only be restricted to increase the total scheme of liberty or when they are incompatible with a similar set of freedoms and liberties for all. Restrictions on civil and political rights are not justified in order to achieve a higher level of material well-being.[13]

## Second Principle

Social and economic inequalities are to satisfy two conditions: first they are to be attached to positions and offices open to all under conditions of fair equality of opportunity; and second, they are to be to the greatest benefit to the least advantaged members of society.

The second principle, to which I will refer as 'the difference principle' takes economic efficiency into consideration. If unequal distribution creates a surplus, and this surplus is divided so that all members of society get a share of it (for instance through progressive taxation), it would not be rational for anyone to object to the unequal distribution. Social and economic inequalities are justified if they result in a situation where the worst-off member of society is better off than he or she would be under a system where all resources are equally distributed.

In order to be just, social and economic inequality must, however, be linked to positions open to all under conditions of reasonable equality of opportunity.[14]

Rawls' theory only identifies abstract principles of justice and general guidelines for their application. It does not make specific recommendations regarding electoral systems, composition of legislatures, division of powers, local government, entrenchment clauses or special majority requirements. Neither does this theory specify how the economy is to be regulated or which social and economic policies ought to be enacted in order for the difference principle to be satisfied. The theory defines a range rather than a specific result.

Does the constitutional structure proposed by Sachs fall within the Rawlsian range? The first principle of justice is reflected in Sachs' constitutional proposal, including the recognition of the material conditions required for political liberty. The process for *participatory formulation of rights* is designed to ensure that the Bill of Rights will satisfy the principle of equal liberty.

It is not as straightforward to see what Rawls' second principle requires. Satisfaction of the difference principle and the restrictions represented by the just savings principle and the principle of equal opportunity depends fundamentally on the actual workings of the system. Coherence cannot be determined *a priori*. However, looking at the constitutional structure outlined by Sachs, I would argue that the concerns expressed in an abstract manner in Rawls' second principle, could be 'translated' into more concrete provisions and policies through Sachs' conception of *affirmative action*. Concerns for affirmative action permeate the entire constitutional proposal.

There is no authorised definition of *affirmative action*.

[W]e are unaware to this day of the term ever having been defined in legislation or international covenants. Modern conventions, however, frequently have articles which make it plain that any special treatment to favour language, cultural, religious and educational rights of formerly oppressed groups, and any moves to overcome the disadvantages imposed by past gender and race discrimination, shall not be regarded as violating human rights principles. (Sachs, 1992b: 11)

The term originates from the United States where it has been used to designate provisions and programmes giving preferential treatment to members of certain groups considered to be in a disadvantaged position — such as ethnic or racial minorities, women (or in a few instances, men), or people from certain geographical areas.

*Affirmative action* usually refers to quotas and special admission requirements for disadvantaged groups.[15] These may differ in content as well as in scope. Some merely require that individuals from the disadvantaged group(s) are admitted or employed if he or she is otherwise as qualified as alternative applicants. Stronger provisions require accepting qualified members of the disadvantaged group(s) despite better qualified applicants. Special quotas may be defined for the disadvantaged group(s) in schools, universities and in the civil service. And private institutions may be required to admit or employ a minimum quota of the group(s) in question. Affirmative action schemes are most commonly used for admittance to higher education and as part of employment policies, but they are also applicable to areas such as housing, or land-reform programmes.

Sachs operates with two different concepts of affirmative action. 'Affirmative action in the narrow sense', is affirmative action as defined above. For Sachs, this is only one (and not the most important) element of 'affirmative action in the wide sense'. Affirmative action in the wide sense embraces a full set of strategies and principles associated with a social-democratic welfare state. Before examining Sachs' programme for affirmative action in more detail, his justification for making affirmative action a central part of the constitutional structure, is summarised.

## Justifying Affirmative Action in South Africa

> We ... need, the substantive rightness of a broad constitutional principle that requires that active steps be taken to secure equal chances in life for all. We also ... want a sense of procedural security. Thus we need clearly defined pointers both as to what the principle embraces and as to how it is to be applied. The actual working out we will have to leave to future practice. (Sachs, 1992b: 12)

Sachs'. central concern is that a democratic South African constitution needs to confront and respond to the injustices which are tearing the country apart — the injustices which produced demands for a new constitution (Sachs, 1992b: 44). A 'post-apartheid constitution', is not only a matter of chronology. It requires that everything apartheid produced is taken into account.

According to Sachs, grand scale affirmative action is particularly suitable in South Africa where case by case proof of past exclusion is superfluous. The evidence of discrimination is in apartheid law, separate institutions of government, unequal budgets etc. 'The whole of apartheid law amounted to no less than a systematised and unjust form of affirmative action in favour of the whites' (Sachs, 1992a: 98). In order to deal with this legacy the realities of race have to be taken into account. 'To ignore the realities of racial inequalities should be an example not of being colour-blind, but of being totally blind' (Sachs, 1992a: 99). In the light of the alternative — i.e. permitting continuing racial disadvantage — racial quotas are regarded as a necessary evil.

Life chances are grossly unequal in South Africa: 'colour rather than need or ability is still the greatest factor in deciding who will wear shoes or who will go barefoot' (Sachs, 1992a: 98). To believe that the injustices and inequalities produced by past race discrimination will go away simply because the laws which enforced the discrimination are repealed, is wishful thinking. These inequalities replicate themselves from generation to generation. 'Illiteracy, ill-health and poverty get handed down as a bitter bequest' (Sachs, 1992a: 99). Without active steps to prevent it, inequality continues as before, only this time regarded as natural, or as the fault of the disadvantaged. 'What a painful paradox it would be if, after decades of struggle and sacrifice, we succeeded in doing what apartheid could never do, namely, in legitimising inequality' (Sachs, 1992b: 6). Affirmative action is Sachs' strategy for preventing constitutional principles such as equal rights and freedom of association, from resulting in a privatisation of misery and a fatalising of inequality.

## Affirmative Action in the Wide Sense

Affirmative action is a strategy designed to deal with the differences in life-chances created by apartheid in a firm, orderly and principled manner. In the widest sense, affirmative action covers 'all purposive activity designed to eliminate the effects of apartheid and to create a society where everyone has the same chance to get on in life' (Sachs, 1992b: 14). According to Sachs, the main means of guaranteeing that people will at last get their rights, is not special programmes, but a political system applying the principles of good government (Sachs, 1992b: 43). 'Affirmative action' in this sense, includes far more than is normally associated with the term.[16]

The strategies and principles which make up *affirmative action in the wide sense* is outlined in the following paragraphs.

*Equal Protection*

Even though affirmative action may entail differential treatment, it rests fundamentally on a principle of *equal rights* and *anti-discrimination*. Constitutional clauses guaranteeing equal protection under the law serve to end discrimination against blacks, while at the same time protecting whites against retaliatory domination or abuse.

'Equal protection' means that public funds should be spent on citizens equally as citizens (Sachs, 1992b: 18). This implies a re-direction of government spending away from the white minority. Sachs recommends that this principle should be institutionally supported by a Human Rights Commission and the courts. Manifestly active and fair means for dealing with racism are necessary for the sake of stability as well as for justice, otherwise people may begin to take the law into their own hands (Sachs, 1992: 19). Since court proceedings tend to be lengthy, expensive and conflictual, regionally based, semi-autonomous government agencies should attempt to solve disputes by conciliation. In this way conflicts can be resolved in a speedy and inexpensive manner, emphasising mediation. '[T]he culture of rights is strengthened, as law, culture and behaviour interact' (Sachs, 1992b: 20).

Constitutional guarantees for freedom of association and constitutionally guaranteed space for social organisations, are crucial in ensuring equal protection. The organs of civil society are the principal guarantors that good government will exist. They may 'see to it that government tries neither to overstep nor to understep the mark' (Sachs, 1992b: 22) and help people secure their rights against the state. Sachs underscores that neither laws nor institutions can guarantee the viability and effectiveness of the new anti-apartheid legal arrangement. The promotion of a democratic political culture and an active civil society is thus a central concern of his approach.

Another means to guarantee equal protection is the Ombud whose function is to 'deal with the officious official'. The Ombud is a constitutional paradox: the state appoints an official paid out of state funds to control the actions of the state. Although the office is far to weak to handle the whole question of dealing with racist structures and patterns of behaviour it is needed to deal with problems of abuse and maladministration that cannot be handled elsewhere in the constitution (Sachs, 1992b: 25).

*Regional Equalisation*

According to Sachs' constitutional proposal an important concern of affirmative action in the wide sense, will be to promote *regional equalisation*. There are huge inequalities between the regions of South Africa. Transfer of resources from rich to poor regions will therefore be an important element in reducing poverty and promoting a more equal economic and social development. According to Sachs, governments should be constitutionally committed to further regional equalisation and necessary institutions should be provided for. These may include fiscal arrangements ensuring a flow of revenue from rich to poor regions. These resources, invested in infrastructural development, may progressively overcome inequalities between poor and rich regions.[17]

*An Expanding Floor of Rights*

The principle of an expanding floor of minimum social, educational and welfare rights, is the central idea of Sachs' conception of affirmative action.

> The basic idea is to impose a duty on Parliament to adopt legislation which, taking account of the resources of the country, grants progressively increasing rights to every citizen. It focuses on certain core or fundamental areas of human existence, establishing the notion of an expanding list of entitlements to nutrition, health, education, shelter, employment and welfare. In a sense, this is a pro-active extension of the principle of equal protection. It re-enforces the notion of equal opportunity by demanding at least equal starting-off points for everyone. (Sachs, 1992b: 28)

Affirmative action in the wide sense emphasises social, educational and welfare rights. And the idea of an *expanding floor of rights* is an attempt to go beyond simply setting out these rights as something to be aimed for. The justice model seeks to provide constitutional protection for social rights and establish criteria and mechanisms for making them enforceable.[18]

Institutionally, the principle should be backed by the courts and a Social Rights Commission which would supervise the implementation of social rights programmes, assist the courts on social rights questions, and be a source of information for legislative authorities as well as for the public (Sachs, 1992b: 34).

*Affirmative Action in the Narrow Sense*

The principal aim of the constitutional programme for affirmative action is to open up opportunities for all. This requires giving special attention to those most injured or excluded by previous discrimination through making available provisions of affirmative action in the narrow definition of the term. Quotas may be necessary to deal with special blockages or impediments, but Sachs underscores that affirmative action in the narrow sense cannot carry the burden of transforming South Africa into a more just society, and that it can never be a substitute for good government and progressive social programmes (Sachs, 1992b: 15). Well-targeted quotas may play an important role in the short term. The medium and long-term answer is to build up a system of general education and personal mobility.

Affirmative action programmes, narrowly defined, may take a variety of forms and involve a wide variety of agencies. Precise methods should be adapted to the concrete realities and practices of each specific area. General principles and supervising organs should be enshrined in the constitution while the actual design of programmes and institutions should be done in cooperation with expertise in each particular field.

The essence of affirmative action programmes is to enable people who have been denied of qualifications to acquire them. Opening up the civil service, etc., does not mean appointing unqualified persons on the basis of colour or gender. Representativity, cultural diversity, etc., should be taken into account, but only when at least basic requirements for the position are satisfied. Race and gender preferences are required to overcome structured, self-perpetuating inequalities, but only for a determinate period. And no-one should be excluded from consideration on grounds of race or gender, nor should quotas be used as ceilings.

Furthermore, Sachs underscores that all forms of affirmative action must proceed according to the rule of law. The circumstances when quotas, timetables and monitoring should be used, procedures be followed, and agencies responsible for investigation and supervision, should be determined by legislation, as should the role of the courts.

*Theoretical Foundations of Affirmative Action*

Sachs' programme of affirmative action rests on two different theories of justice. According to *the level playing field theory,* affirmative action is permissible/required to create conditions of equal opportunity. *The theory of compensatory justice*, holds that affirmative action is obligatory to compensate victims of past discrimination.

*The level playing field theory* corresponds to Rawls' theory of justice. It expresses the idea that the basic rules regulating society should be such that all citizens are given equal opportunity when competing for positions and, more generally, in pursuing what they regard as 'the good' in life.

Some would undoubtedly object that there is a fundamental difference, in that Rawls' theory only require equal opportunity in a formal sense, while Sachs' focus is on substantive justice, and that Rawls' (formal) equal opportunity principle thus runs against Sachs' conception of affirmative action in the narrow sense. This is, in my view, a misinterpretation of both. Rawls — like Sachs — underscores that the justice of the basic institutions is related to the actual functioning of the system over time, that is, to how it actually distributes resources and opportunities in society. Institutions characterised by formal equality, but producing grossly unfair results, are not just. Substantive justice is clearly taken into consideration in Rawls' theory. And, likewise, formal equality of opportunity — equal rights and non-discrimination — are basic principles underlying Sachs' approach.

The level playing field theory is 'forward-looking' in the sense that it considers how the working of the basic structure of society will influence current and future distribution of resources and opportunities. The theory of compensatory justice, on the other hand, is backward looking. The historical past has created a grossly unequal distribution — e.g. of land — in South Africa, and action should be taken to rectify past injustices. The theory of compensatory justice corresponds to views presented by the libertarian philosopher Robert Nozick in his book *Anarchy, State and Utopia* (1974). It is a critique of, and an alternative to, Rawls' theory, and the two theories seem irreconcilable.

What may seem as an anomaly in Sachs' approach is explained by the fact that his project differs from Rawls' in one important respect: Rawls' concern is with *ideal theory*. Due to the pervasive influence of the present, unjust, structure of South African society, differential treatment is called for — at least for a limited period of time. Such concerns are not relevant to Rawls, who is working within the domain of ideal theory, and thus confines himself to questions concerning what a just society should look like, not addressing the question of how to get from an unjust to a just situation. When asking 'what is a fair society', history is irrelevant, but when addressing the question of 'how may South Africa become a (more) just society', history clearly cannot be ignored. The theory of compensatory justice, while irrelevant in a just society, is of vital importance in a transition phase.


### Does Rawls' Theory Justify Sachs' Model?

From the above section we know that the overall idea of affirmative action corresponds closely with Rawls' theory of justice. Previously we have seen that Sachs and Rawls depart from the same premise: individuals have certain rights that the state should protect, and which the welfare of society as a whole cannot legitimately override. Both regard justice to be the primary virtue of social institutions, but hold that within the limits set by justice, economic efficiency should be encouraged. The two scholars devise similar procedures for producing just results, and Rawls' two principles of justice are reflected in the constitutional structure of the justice model. Likewise, the scope of their projects is the same: Sachs' constitutional proposal and Rawls' theory of justice are both formulated for *the basic structure of society*.[19] The principles are to be used to assess the justice of society's political, economic and political institutions taken as a whole, on the basis of their effect on fundamental rights and distribution of resources over time. They constitute a standard for evaluating whether the basic 'rules of the game' are fair.

There is, however, a difference in concern: Rawls occupies himself with ideal theory, while Sachs in his writings is striving to find solutions for his troubled country. To him the question of *what is a just society* is highly relevant — but insufficient. What matters even more is *how to get there*. Nevertheless, although ideal theory is not Sachs' concern his constitutional approach is clearly guided by the ideal of a just society — a just society in the Rawlsian conception. The difference in concern is thus no obstacle to seeing Rawls' theory as normative justification for the constitutional structure presented by Sachs.

Are there any reasons not to conclude that Rawls' theory of justice provides a normative foundation for Sachs' constitutional model? At least one important objection can be raised. It concerns the size of the constitutional domain in Sachs' theory.

## *The Size of the Constitutional Domain versus the Domain of the Political*

Rawls illustrates how, theoretically, his principles of justice may be brought to bear on politics through a four stage sequence (Rawls, 1971: 195–201).

After the principles are chosen in the *original position*, the *veil of ignorance* is partially lifted. The parties are now to see themselves as delegates to a constitutional convention, choosing adequate constitutional principles for their society. They still do not know their position in society, but have all relevant facts about the long-term circumstances of their society. And they are to choose constitutional provisions in accordance with the two principles of justice. A just constitution, according to Rawls, must protect the fundamental freedoms and liberties of all citizens, and make provisions for some form of democratic political system.

At the legislative stage, the parties are to see themselves as ideal legislators, enacting laws and policies following the rules set out in the constitution. At this stage the requirements of *the difference principle* should be taken into consideration. At the fourth stage the parties are to see themselves as ideal bureaucrats and judges implementing the laws and policies enacted by the legislature, through procedures specified in the constitution and legislation. At this stage the *veil of ignorance* is completely lifted; all information is to be considered, but the parties are still ideal in the sense that they are presumed to be committed by the principles of justice.

The justice model is in line with Rawls' theory in that the constitutional domain should protect fundamental freedoms and liberties for all citizens, and provide for a democratic system. The conception of an expanding floor of basic rights also seems to be a reasonable interpretation of the obligation imposed by the difference principle. The different institutions, such as the Human Rights Commission, the Social Rights Commission and the Ombud, included in Sachs programme for affirmative action, are a way to ensure that the implementation of laws and policies acts according to procedures specified by the constitution and the legislature.

The important difference is that Sachs wants to address distributive questions, along with important institutional questions, within the constitutional domain. His recommendation is to address distributive concerns in the constitution in the form of social rights imposing a duty on future governments to extend basic social rights to all. The constitution should provide a general scheme for this extension, and provisions for bodies accountable for the process.

(T)he Constitution lays down a general scheme for ensuring that resources are devoted in a systematic and law, governed way to the progressive extension of basic social rights to all. It also sees to it that appropriate bodies are made responsible and accountable for the process. (Sachs, 1992b: 41)

Legislation is to specify the ways and means for progressive extension of social rights and make the rights enforceable. This is the outcome of the political process, but must conform with the principles of the constitution. Parliamentary, regional and local government committees and the Social Rights Commission are to ensure that the matter in question is given constant attention. The courts, ultimately the Constitutional Court, are responsible for ensuring that constitutional principles are applied and to ensure that proper procedures are followed and the correct criteria adopted (Sachs, 1992b: 42). The scope of judicial review is considerable, creating a wide scope for legal activism (see Corder, 1992; O'Malley, 1996).

Rawls argues that distributive concerns should be left to politics. Delimitation of the constitutional domain — so that it contains all the 'constitutional essentials', and only those matters which properly belong within this domain — is a major concern of Rawls. The disagreement on these matters is important for the overall verdict on whether the constitutional structure of the justice model is justified by Rawls' theory.

According to Rawls, distributive concerns (the difference principle) is of such a nature that it is open to *rational disagreement* concerning what is required in terms of institutions and regulations.[20] The 'constitutional essentials' should constitute a limited, but sufficient, social unity to facilitate orderly and peaceful political competition — a process for solving distributive questions. If equal basic liberties and equal opportunity are safeguarded in the constitutional domain through the establishment of a democratic political system, concerns for a fair distribution are best left to the political process itself.

There is no procedure that — even in principle — can *guarantee* that specific constitutional provisions are just, and even less so for laws and policies.[21] The only possibility is to rely on a combination of an imperfect procedure and appeals to coherence with external criteria (the principles of justice themselves reflected in the constitution). A democratic political system is, although not perfect, the most adequate political procedure. Unless the outcome of the democratic process is manifestly unjust (according to the principles of justice) democratic decisions (reached through 'majority-rule' decision-making procedures) should be regarded as authoritative. In a democratic system, respecting fundamental rights and freedoms, there is always a possibility to influence decisions, and thus distribution. If, however, the laws and policies enacted do not over time result in a distribution of resources that is reasonably just, the constitution should be altered. Particularly in cases where the scope for rational disagreement is large it is dangerous to substitute appointed judges for elected representatives.

Sachs is not unaware of the fact that it is controversial to address social rights in the constitutional domain rather than to leave concerns for distributive justice to politics (Sachs, 1992b: 28). But he sees this mainly as a problem of social rights undermining basic civil and political rights.[22] This does not answer the objection voiced by Rawls against including social rights and other distributive concerns in the constitutional domain. Rawls' argument is that the constitutional domain should include those, and only those elements on which there is likely to be an overlapping consensus among citizens (committed to justice). Only provisions required by the principle of equal liberty, and the principle of equal opportunity, belong to these 'constitutional essentials'. On the difference principle there is too much room for rational disagreement.

Is the justice model's approach to distributive issues 'unrawlsian'? Although social rights clauses guaranteeing an expanding floor of basic rights are enshrined in the constitutional domain, and general objectives and institutions responsible for implementing them are identified in the constitution, the actual programmes and policies are to be the result of the political process. And social rights are made contingent on resources and social conditions.

The duties placed on governments by constitutional social rights are only duties to devote their efforts in a certain direction. And this is in a sense also presupposed in Rawls' theory. Even though the difference principle is not included in the 'constitutional essentials', a constitutional structure which over time does not produce a reasonably fair distribution, is not consistent with justice, and should be altered.

Lastly, although the justice model prescribes constitutional protection of social rights, it is not rigid as to whether this will necessarily have to be included in the actual written constitution. '[W]hether the floor of rights idea is in the constitution or not, it should be high on the agenda of any new government' (Sachs, 1992b: 29).

A question mark remains as to whether Rawls could have accepted the comprehensive constitutional domain outlined in Sachs' constitutional model. The inclusion of social and economic rights as part of the constitution places the justice model close to the welfare state pole of the material *Rechtsstaat*. Rawls, on the other hand, while deriving the same set of 'natural rights', includes mainly civil and political liberties (included in the first principle of justice) in the constitution. While clearly advocating a material *Rechtsstaat*, he argues that in matters concerning distribution of resources the Parliament should be regarded as sovereign. In spite of this, Sachs' constitutional structure should, in my judgement, be regarded as a legitimate application of Rawls' theory to South African conditions.

We may thus conclude that Sachs' justice model is provided with a philosophical justification through its coherence with Rawls' principles. This is no guarantee of 'truth' or even 'justice'. There are normative premises underlying Rawls' theory on which there may be rational disagreement. And, as will be shown in the next chapter, alternative models may have alternative philosophical justifications. Still, Rawls' philosophical justification provides the justice model with a solid normative foundation.

## Restating the Argument

This chapter has presented the justice model as a constitutional strategy for South Africa. The model, derived from the writings of Albie Sachs, generally coincide with the constitutional position of the ANC. The model focuses on mechanisms for transformation of the social structure of South Africa into a more just scheme of cooperation, which is seen to be a precondition for long-term democratic stability. Poverty, and social and economic inequality — the legacy of apartheid — is regarded to be the main problems, and the model includes a comprehensive programme of affirmative action to combat them. Central to this programme is the idea of a constitutionally guaranteed expanding minimum floor of basic social rights. The model holds that distributive justice should be a constitutional pre-commitment, binding on future governments, and that the constitution also should provide some basic means to advance this goal.

The justice model stresses the principle of majority rule. The set-up of political institutions is aimed at producing a potent government as an engine of change. The direction of change is to be laid down in the constitution through clauses guaranteeing an expanding floor of social rights, thus placing duties on future governments to engage in affirmative action in the wide sense. Balancing this strong state, the Bill of Rights is designed to protect citizens from illegitimate state intervention.

The justice model, in most important respects, parallels Rawls' theory of justice and coheres with his principles. Rawls' theory thus provides Sachs' constitutional model with a philosophical foundation.

Some criticism of the justice model has been voiced in the course of the discussion. The extensive constitutional domain — the inclusion of elements on which there is room for rational disagreement and the limited space for politics — poses problems from the point of view of democracy, as well as on practical accounts. These, and other problems will be elaborated on in later chapters. A major objection raised against the justice model is the fact that it pays little attention to the multi-ethnic character of South African society — a matter which is the primary concern of the constitutional model to be presented in the following chapter.

## Notes

1. Sachs himself does not use the term *justice model* to designate his constitutional proposal, nor does he present it as a constitutional *model*.
2. On many issues it is difficult to talk of a unified ANC constitutional position, particularly in the period before 1994. The ANC is an alliance that includes the Congress of South African Trade Unions (COSATU) and the South African Communist Party (SACP). The broad and diverse base of the organisation is reflected in the organisation's elite, and various groups and sections of the organisation represent different ideological orientations. Until the early 1990s the dominating stance was skepticism and rejection of constitutionalism. On issues such as the right to private property, and aspects of the right to life (abortion, the death penalty) there are widely differing views. When I say that the justice model is representative of the ANC position, this refers to the core leadership, and the party's experts on constitutional issues.
3. Personal discussions with Albie Sachs, Bergen, March 1991. It is important to note Sachs' double role, as an academic (Professor of Law) and a political activist. When asked about constitutional issues not covered in his writings, his reply would often be in terms of 'we', signalling that, as a member of the ANC National Executive Committee, and serving on the party's Constitutional Committee, he would generally be in line with the ANC position. Although he writes in his personal capacity, his views to a large extent reflect the ANC position in the constitutional negotiations.
4. The electoral system does not receive much attention in Sachs' work. Purely on the basis of what is written it might seem that a majoritarian electoral model would be most in line with his thoughts. However, when asked (personal interview, Bergen, March 1991) about his views on the issue, he stated that his preferences was for a PR-electoral system. This was around the time when the ANC position on this issue started to swing towards proportional representation.
5. The page numbers refer to a somewhat more inclusive draft version of the article included in Hugo (1992), and also in Sachs (1992a).
6. The clearest example is perhaps the process leading up to the formulation and adoption of the Freedom Charter in 1955 (Mandela, 1994/95).
7. Personal interview, Bergen, March 1991.

8.  Difficulties are also exposed through the comparison, both in Rawls' theory and in Sachs' constitutional proposal.

9.  The idea of an 'overlapping consensus' is central to Rawls' work. In order for principles of justice to be relevant to modern societies, characterised by fundamental value-pluralism, they cannot be justified by reference to universally and eternally true principles. Rather, it should be based on an *overlapping consensus* in society. Political philosophy should limit itself to formulate principles for the political domain, and as far as possible avoid relying on general and comprehensive moral conceptions (Rawls, 1987, 1989). The idea is illustrated in Figure 4.1.

10. This is partly seen to be a result of the pedagogic effects of the process of rights-formulation on those who participate. When a civil society organisation primarily concerned with the interests and needs of its members is to suggest a formulation which is to count as a general rule and thus must be acceptable to all — an understanding of the legitimate interests of 'the others' is prone to emerge.

11. Rawls argues that when choices of fundamental importance are conducted under uncertainty, it is rational to adopt a position of risk-aversion, that is, choose according to a *maximin strategy*. Rational choice theorists have criticised this point in his theory. It is argued that maximin is not the only rational strategy under conditions of uncertainty (when no risk calculation is possible). The maximin strategy is consistent with rationality, but it is not the only rational strategy (Elster, 1986: 6). However, in the case in question, a conservative strategy is the more plausible choice, in light of the fundamental implications of the worst possible result.

12. This formulation diverges markedly from previous formulations of the principles in the sense that it is underscored that the principle of equal liberty does not simply mean that all are entitled to equal political liberties in a formal sense.

13. Rawls qualifies this point by stating that this does not necessarily hold in societies in which the level of economic development is under a certain (not identified) level. This may be a potential objection to applying (this part of) Rawls' theory to South Africa.

14. Those presently inhabiting society are not permitted to exploit available resources to the extent that later generations are left with less (just savings principles). This element is stated more explicitly in the earlier formulations of the principles of justice (see Rawls, 1971: 302).

15. This is also how the term 'affirmative action' is used by Lijphart, see Chapter 5.

16. When key concepts, with a certain set of connotations, are stretched to cover more than the conventional content, confusion is prone to arise (which often seems to be why the manoeuvre is conducted). In this case there may be tactical considerations for using the term 'affirmative action' rather than talking about social reforms and adoption of a social-democratic welfare state (which the recommendations for 'affirmative action in the wide sense' resembles). The fact that Sachs strives to make the proposals for affirmative action acceptable to people with different political views is reflected when he repeatedly underscores that the strategy of affirmative action is 'ideologically open' (Sachs, 1992b: 12), 'the even-handed alternative' and 'still an open concept ... Yet it contains the full possibility of establishing relatively painless lines of advance for the benefit of all' (Sachs, 1992b: 49).

17. The need for regional autonomy as a means to maintain the cultural identity of South Africa's ethnic groups are often raised as an objection against centralism. Sachs' reply is that '[C]ultural distinctness can be retained without perversely and offensively regarding isolation, poverty, lack of clothing and hunger as a cultural right' (Sachs, 1992b: 26).

18. The expanding floor of rights argument and Rawls' second principle are guided by the same logic: a just distribution of primary social goods should be ensured, both because these goods are important in themselves, and because they are crucial all-purpose means for achieving other goals. Distributive justice is necessary to ensure fair equality of opportunity to all citizens.

19. The question of scope is important. The principles of justice do not necessarily apply to the separate elements of the social structure, or to sub-systems seen in isolation, nor to questions of private justice (e.g. between members of a family) or questions of international justice. Rawls does not exclude the possibility that his principles may be of relevance in these areas, but this is not what they are devised for, and his theory does not provide justification for such use.

20. Rational disagreement will exist, even between rational people with an obligation towards justice. For example, due to different experience, different world-views and moral doctrines, and uncertain knowledge about economic and social effects of different measures.

21. In contrast to the principles of justice which are justified by being the result of a fair procedure.

22. This critique is partly refuted by arguing that social rights are not to be weighed in a competitive scale against the rights to freedom. A firm constitutional commitment towards the preservation of fundamental freedoms is required quite independently of whether social rights are realised. Both sets of fundamental rights should be protected in an appropriate manner, and wherever possible, so that the different sets of rights reinforce each other. And when circumstances require that one cluster of rights must give way to another, it is important to safeguard the most fundamental rights within each category. Thus, 'torture can never be constitutionally justified, even in times of famine to find out where food is being hoarded. By the same token, property rights can never be invoked to justify destruction of food in order to keep prices high' (Sachs, 1992b: 30).

# 5 Consociational Models: Power-Sharing for Stability

The theme of this chapter is *consociational models,* also called power-sharing. For decades variants of consociationalism have been proposed as suitable for South Africa.

The consociational model's position on various dimensions is outlined in Table 5.1 and each element of the conceptual framework is elaborated on in the first part of this chapter.

The ANC position, of which Albie Sachs is representative, has been to discount consociational solutions for South Africa as 'self-interest dressed up as principle'. There is some truth in the oft-repeated argument that the strongest proponents of consociationalism are found among those who benefited from apartheid, and that they discovered power-sharing only when they realised their power was set to go. Political groups naturally tend to look to their own interests when favouring one option over another. Although there may be reason to question the motives of certain political players it should not be inferred that consociationalism as such is unacceptable on moral grounds. The ontology and the normative judgements implicit in the consociational approach stand out when seen in light of communitarian political philosophy. There is a discussion of central themes in communitarian philosophy in the last part of this chapter, which seeks to bring out the logic underlying the consociational model. The consociational model is laid out as a coherent answer to a particular interpretation of the problems of South Africa.

## Arend Lijphart and Consociational Democracy

How to avoid severe conflict between (ethnic) groups in a divided society is the central concern of consociational theorists.[1] Favoured 'regulative mechanisms' vary between scholars, but common to all recommendations for consensus-orientated solutions for South Africa, is that they have seen ethnic conflict as the country's most fundamental and explosive problem, and sought ways to depoliticise them by drawing up a constitutional structure characterised by power-sharing between groups.

Arend Lijphart is a Dutch, American-based political scientist who for years has advocated the consociational model as a remedy for divided societies. This presentation is based mainly on his proposal for 'Power-Sharing in South Africa' (1985), and his theoretical works on consociational democracy, but is supplemented with contributions from other scholars within this school of thought.

The model of consociational democracy with its focus on minority rights, decisions by consensus and autonomy for each group in its own affairs, has for decades evoked interest in South Africa, particularly in the white academic and political establishment. References to Lijphart's theories were made during the work on the 1983 revision of the South African Constitution (Davenport, 1987: 465) and has continued to be a point of reference for the National Party (NP). The constitutional principles set forth by the NP in September 1991, were almost completely in accordance with the consociational model.[2] Generally the model can be seen to reflect the core concerns of the NP and their negotiating position throughout the constitution-making process.

Parties to the right of the NP, the Freedom Front (FF) and the Conservative Party (CP), have also supported varieties of consociationalism, stressing the cultural autonomy element. The representatives of the Democratic Party (DP) have been strong proponents of federalism and decentralisation of power, core elements of most consociational recommendations for South Africa.

Interest in and support for consociationalism is not limited to the white establishment. The Inkatha Freedom Party (IFP) and its leader Chief Mangosuto Buthelezi are among the fiercest proponents of consociation and federalism in South Africa. This is not a newfound interest. Already in 1982 Lijphart served as a member of the Buthelezi commission, drawing up a proposal for constitutional reform in KwaZulu and Natal.[3] So while Sachs' justice model reflects the ANC position in the constitutional negotiations, most other parties favour some form of consociationalism.

Lijphart's constitutional model for South Africa is an application of his general theory of consociational democracy on which he has elaborated since the 1960s. His first book on the subject was published in 1968; *The Politics of Accommodation: Pluralism and Democracy in the Netherlands*. In 1977 came *Democracy in Plural Societies: a Comparative Exploration*, a widely read book, in which he analyses the political systems and experiences of a number of severely divided societies throughout the world.

The basic question throughout is why do some deeply divided countries function as stable democracies over extended periods of time, while others are torn apart by violence and civil strife? From his 'comparative exploration', Lijphart extracts a number of features which are regarded as conducive to democratic stability in plural societies, and a set of institutional arrangements that make up the *consociational* model of democracy.

He concludes that plural societies adopting majoritarian political systems rarely manage to function as stable democracies over time. Plural societies lack the most basic premise for the functioning of the majoritarian system: shifting majorities. A central assumption in the theory of majoritarian democracy is that the parties will alternate in power as voter preferences change. In plural societies voting patterns are more or less determined by group membership, and groups tend to be extremely stable. Majoritarian democracy under such circumstances implies permanent minorities — without any say in government, and without any hope of being in majority in the foreseeable future. An adversary 'winner take all' system, under such circumstances, tends to result in lack of legitimacy for the regime within the minority group. Conflicts are prone to be channelled into extra-parliamentary, and often violent forms. Consociational democracies, according to Lijphart, include mechanisms countering these tendencies.

The basic principle of consociational democracy is representation: no significant sub-group in society should be left without a say in government. Institutionally the principle is backed by a proportional electoral system, constitutional clauses ensuring minority representation in the executive body, and minority protection through mutual vetoes and substantial segmental autonomy in internal matters. The key elements of Lijphart's consociational model as applied to South Africa are outlined in the following paragraphs.[4] The interpretation of South African reality underlying consociational solutions is discussed and the constitutional set-up is laid out, along with the objectives of the model on different dimensions. Focus throughout the presentation concentrates, as it does in the consociational model itself — on the logic and structure of ethnic conflict and on measures to abate it. Through which mechanisms do the consociational model further conflict regulation? Particular attention is devoted to the design of the electoral system — the centrepiece of consociationalism, and an issue where influential scholars within this tradition diverge.

## Table 5.1 The consociational model

| Dimension | The consociational model's position within the range of variation | |
|---|---|---|

| Dimension | | |
|---|---|---|
| (i) **Institutional set-up** | | |
| institutional focus | legal system | **political system** |
| electoral system | majoritarian | **proportional** |
| legislature-executive relations | presidentialism | **parliamentarism** |
| composition of legislature | uni-cameral | **bi-cameral** |
| composition of executive | one party | **coalition** |
| | single executive | **collective executive body** |
| decentralisation | unitary state | **federal state** |
| | highly centralised | **highly decentralised** |
| decision-making mode | adversarial | **consensual** |
| | majoritarian | **minority vetoes** |
| (ii) **Interpretation of reality** | | |
| methodological focus | individual | **collective** |
| problem focus | structural | **cultural** |
| | inequality, poverty | **ethnicity** |
| (iii) **Central value** | justice | **stability, cultural autonomy** |
| | positive liberty | **negative liberty** |
| (iv) **Objective** | transformation | **regulation** |
| (v) **Response to pluralism** (the nation-building dimension) | assimilation/**non-interference**/separation | |
| (vi) **State-society relationship** | participation | **representation** |
| (vii) **The constitutional domain** | democracy | **constitutionalism** |
| | rule of law | ***Rechtsstaat*** |
| | precommitment | **foreclosure of issues** |
| (viii) **Normative foundation/ justification** | liberalism | **communitarian** |
| | contractarian philosophy | **philosophy (catholic communitarian and protestant organological thought)** |

## The Conceptual Framework

The positions of the consociational model on the various dimensions of the conceptual framework developed in Chapter 3, are presented in Table 5.1 above. In order to make explicit the differences in objectives between the consociational approach and the justice model, and between various consociational theorists, the subsequent presentation and discussion is more comparative than the equivalent sections of the previous chapter, and thereby more critical. However, at this stage the primary aim is to explicate different aspects of the model, rather than to evaluate them. An assessment of the models is taken on in Part III.

### South African Reality According to the Consociational Model

From Lijphart's perspective, South Africa is fundamentally and indisputably *a plural society*. Plural societies are characterised by sharp divisions along ethnic, linguistic, cultural, racial, religious or ideological lines. They are heterogeneous not only in the identification of different religious, cultural, or ideological groups, but in the division into more or less separate subsocieties. Different sections of the community live side by side, but separately, within the same political unit. In the words of J.S. Furnivall, 'They mix but do not combine' (1948: 304). In deeply divided societies these segmental divisions form the basis of conflict groups. Plural societies differ with regard to the kinds of segmental cleavages as well as the *degrees* of plurality, hostility and violence (Lijphart, 1977a: 17–18).

Methodological questions are crucial in order to understand the difference between Sachs and Lijphart with regard to how they conceive South Africa's problems. What constitutes the most fundamental elements of society? What are the building blocks that the political system should utilise and build onto? Sachs holds that the constitutional structure should basically regulate relationships between *individuals* — the basic elements of society — and between the individuals that make up the state, and the state itself. Lijphart, on the other hand, assumes that in deeply divided societies, such as in South Africa, individuals have strong, constant, more or less ascriptive loyalties to their (ethnic) group. These bonds are seen to be so fundamental to personal identity that (ethnic) *groups*, rather than individuals, should be regarded as the main political building blocks. Inequality between the groups is of more fundamental importance (to individuals also) than inequality between individuals.

> Conflict groups in deeply divided societies do not generally conceive of equal and interchangeable individuals as the foundation stone of democratic decision-making. To them the basic political unit is the segment or the conflict group. At least one conflict group — usually the smaller one — bases its claims and demands upon the equality on each segment rather than of the number of individuals comprising them. (Nordlinger, 1972: 35–36)

Lijphart regards ethnic divisions (between various African groups, Indians, 'coloureds', Afrikaans- and English-speaking whites) as the main cleavages in South Africa. His prediction is that unless adequate constitutional precautions are taken, ethnic conflict will become more and more manifest and explosive in a post-apartheid situation. This assumption is based partially on his interpretation of conflict-patterns in South African society, but even more on the experience of other countries with a diverse ethnic make-up; political parties in severely divided societies tend to split along ethnic lines.

> The comparative empirical evidence on the strength and persistence of ethnicity is overwhelming. In South Africa it is therefore highly probable — nay, virtually certain — that the ethnic factor will reassert itself under conditions of free association and open electoral competition. (Lijphart, 1985: 122)

Ethnic identity is (at least partly) an ascriptive matter, changing very slowly. Under these circumstances party strength becomes a matter of demography, the resulting political situation is one where the same party/parties rule permanently, while others face perpetual minority status. The state becomes the property of the ruling ethnic group, with little or no loyalty among members of other groups. In spite of formal institutions facilitating orderly political competition, conflicts tend to take extra-parliamentary routes of expression, resulting in regime break-down and political instability.

A reason for ethnic affiliations to be conducive to severe conflict is, according to this interpretation, that ethnicity is integral to identity. Once politics is conceived in terms of ethnic differences, losing out in the struggle is threatening in a fundamental sense. And, although ethnic conflict usually involves competition for material resources, the central issues tend to be non-negotiables: religious, linguistic and cultural questions with no easy way to 'share the cake'. And symbolic demands are generally less compromisable than claims that can be quantified.

Interpreting the South African reality is a controversial task and the main criticism of Lijphart's constitutional proposal for South Africa has been that his diagnosis is wrong. Yes, South Africa is culturally heterogeneous, there may even be ethnically related conflicts, but South Africa is not plural in the sense presupposed by Lijphart's theory. With the exception of some minor groups of Afrikaner nationalists, it is not a society of distinct segments, eager to safeguard their cultural purity. On the contrary there is a common feeling of being, and wishing to be, South African. Lijphart's solution for South Africa is founded on invalid premises and would not work, critics argue.

We will return to the question of whether the conditions in South Africa are such that the consociational theory applies, in later chapters.

## Constitutional Set-up and Institutional Measures

The basic units, or building blocks, of this model are the different segments that constitute South African society: the various ethnic groups. Identification of segments poses special problems in the South African context. Racial classification under apartheid made South Africans sensitive to the categorisation of people, and a political system building onto predefined groups would have difficulties gaining legitimacy. Lijphart, being aware of this problem, proposes institutions which allow segments to emerge spontaneously.[5] This way the controversial and vexatious issue of whether the segments should be defined in terms of race, ethnicity, culture, or some other criteria, is avoided.

Complete freedom of association, individual freedom of affiliation and free competition between groups and parties, are preconditions for the spontaneous emergence of segments. The most important 'device' for making segments emerge, is a proportional electoral system allowing fair representation of smaller groups. Once segments emerge, measures of *corporate federalism*, channelling resources and political autonomy over essential 'internal affairs' to each group, strengthen the process of group formation.

Although Lijphart opts for a system where the different segments of South African society emerge spontaneously, he does make certain predictions concerning the number of segments, their relative size, and which cleavages will become most decisive. This is necessary in order to argue for the suitability of the consociational model for South Africa. His 'comparative exploration' of plural societies resulted in a list of factors conducive or unfavourable to the success of this model. Several of these factors concern the number, size and composition of segments. Lijphart's central assumptions are that divisions will be predominantly ethnic (rather than racial, socioeconomic or based on rural/urban differences), it is assumed that several groups will form, and that none of them will be dominant, or at least not comprise a majority of the population. All of these are factors regarded to be conducive to the success of the consociational model.

The favourable conditions, and the extent to which they exist in South Africa, are more thoroughly discussed below. At this point it is sufficient to note the criticism raised against the consociational model on account of insufficient concern for the socioeconomic conditions of South Africa. Critics argue that the magnitude of inequalities between the segments in South Africa, are such that consociational democracy under these circumstances would counter, rather than produce, stability. Lijphart admits that ethnic and socioeconomic cleavages are likely to reinforce each other in South Africa and that inequalities between the segments will be considerable. This, according to findings from other countries, is an important disadvantage to successful consociation. Lijphart denies, however, that inequality represents an unsurmountable difficulty to the success of consociational democracy in South Africa. He argues that this unfavourable condition is sufficiently outweighed by other, positive, factors, and that redistribution will also be possible within a consociational political system. We will return to this line of criticism when discussing the feasibility of this model for South Africa.

Consociational theory, as an empirical explanation of political stability in divided societies, points to rapid introduction of universal suffrage as an unfavourable factor. Dramatic extension of the suffrage tends to stimulate the fears of the privileged minority of being politically overwhelmed and dominated, resulting in opposition towards majoritarian institutions and a resort to violence or governmental repression to win a struggle that cannot be won at the ballot box. This is a fairly accurate description of the fears of the white minority in apartheid-South Africa, but in this case Lijphart did not recommend a prolonged process of gradually extended suffrage. Realising that electoral reforms were long overdue in South Africa, and that no less than universal suffrage would be acceptable to the majority, he argued that this should be granted even though it puts additional strains on the institutions for conflict management.

## The Electoral System

The electoral system is regarded by consociational theorists as the most powerful lever of constitutional engineering. According to Lijphart the most favourable electoral system for South Africa is *party-list proportional representation* ensuring all groups a representation equivalent to the number of votes they receive (Lijphart, 1987 and 1990). This electoral system requires no pre-definition of groups, and allows even relatively small groups to be represented in the legislative bodies. Consociational theory proposes this as an alternative to 'first-past-the post', the electoral system characteristic of majoritarian democracy, permanently under-representing, or shutting out, minorities.

Party-list PR should, according to Lijphart, be used for legislative elections at all levels, federal, state and local; it produces the best proportionality and promotes coalition-building by stimulating proliferation of parties. A plurality of parties, dividing the black electorate, will be necessary for PR to produce a coalition government in South Africa, PR can obviously not prevent an electoral majority from gaining a majority of the seats.

The justice model and the consociational model agree on the main features of the electoral system, and a party list proportional system was agreed upon for the 1994 general elections. Still, this does not reflect a general consensus on this issue. The debate over the electoral system continued throughout the constitution-making process. There is a tradition of majoritarian elections in South Africa and the loss of a clear link between representatives and voters in party-list PR is pointed out as a disadvantage by those favouring a constituency-based system (Faure, 1996).

There are also other lines of criticism. Donald L. Horowitz is among the most influential critics from within the ranks of consociational theory.[6] He shares most of Lijphart's basic premises, but in *A Democratic South Africa?* (1991) he expressed doubts about the prospects of sufficient party proliferation to prevent a black majority government in South Africa with a Party-list PR electoral system. He also argues that even if sufficient party-proliferation is achieved, Lijphart's strategy would fail to result in democratic stability; it would only produce 'coalitions of convenience', not 'coalitions of consensus'. While he shares Lijphart's belief that coalitions are crucial accommodative arrangements, any coalition will not do. Incentives are needed to make politicians compromise. 'Coalitions of convenience', merely aggregating the number of seats necessary to form a government, are insufficient to produce inter-ethnic compromise in a severely divided society. Unless there are incentives for politicians to seek votes across the ethnic divide, coalition governments will not provide accommodation.[7]

Because there are no incentives for pooling of popular votes, Lijphart's electoral system, according to Horowitz, lacks the very engine of compromise. Horowitz himself proposes *the alternative vote*, as the best electoral system for South Africa, with the single transferable vote, as the second-best option. Although the alternative vote is a majoritarian system, and the single transferable vote is a proportional system, they resemble each other in that they are both 'preferential systems'.[8] When applied to *heterogeneous constituencies*[9], they permit inter-ethnic vote pooling, and reward moderation. Moderate candidates are likely to receive a larger share of second and third preference votes. Conflict reduction is furthered, not by external constraints, but by *internal incentives*, affecting the selfish calculations of politicians. They will promote conflict reduction because it is in their self-interest. No change of hearts and minds is needed. Preferential electoral systems motivate politicians to seek second-preference votes 'across the border' and thus support compromises at the top of the coalition by electoral incentives at the bottom. Party-list PR lack such incentives, and this is the crux of Horowitz' critique of Lijphart's approach.[10]

Lijphart rejects this critique and Horowitz' alternative.[11] He argues that the moderating effect of coalition-building *per se* is underestimated, and that the (sparse) historical evidence from alternative vote systems shows little proof of it providing incentives towards moderation, being more proportional, or better for minorities than majoritarian systems. The alternative vote can only work well if there is a multi-party system without a majority party — if a party can win on first preferences second preferences are irrelevant. The alternative vote is less conducive to party proliferation than PR-systems, and a multi-party system is essential to coalition-building which in turn is necessary for accommodation.

Horowitz' subsidiary proposal, the single transferable vote (being a proportional system) is more agreeable to Lijphart, but he holds that it has serious disadvantages for plural societies; because voters are asked to rank candidates, it is best suited for five or six mandate districts. The risk of *gerrymandering* is high when district magnitude is low, and this is highly undesirable in plural societies. In addition, intra-party choice reduces party cohesion, which in turn negatively affects inter-party negotiations (Katz, 1980).

The most important argument against Horowitz' alternative is, however, that preferential systems are much more complicated for the voters than party-list PR. This poses considerable problems in a country such as South Africa, with a large number of illiterate or semi-literate voters. This is a weighty argument, and politically Horowitz' critique has been incapable of displacing Party-list PR as an alternative for South Africa among those favouring a consociational solution.

## The Executive: Grand Coalition and Mutual Veto

There are several interesting aspects to consider with regard to the set-up and role of the executive branch of government. Two crucial matters for constitutional engineers are (a) the relationship between the legislature and the executive, and (b) the composition of the executive.

With regard to type of executive the main alternatives are presidential government and parliamentary government. Lijphart strongly favours the latter. Presidential systems entail concentration of power in the hands of one person, it is inimical to the formation of coalitions, and the president, being one person, inevitably represents only one segment.[12] Again, Horowitz is in disagreement with Lijphart, arguing that presidentialism may be a useful conflict-regulating practice given that the president is properly elected.[13]

The executive is an important institution in several respects. In order for legislation and policy decisions to be regarded as legitimate within the different segments, representation of all groups is essential. Proportional representation in the legislature is crucial, but it is not enough. If executive decisions are reached according to the principle of majority rule, with one (or a few) parties monopolising the executive, little is gained. To prevent this, the consociational model prescribes constitutional provisions to ensure decisions by consensus and guarantee minorities a share in political power.

A stable governing coalition between political parties, always involving the major conflict organisations, is regarded as an effective conflict-regulating practice. Coalitions may be formed by political agreements prior to the elections with the avowed aim of conflict regulation, or be more *ad hoc* if no party is able to govern independently. Government by *grand coalition*, collegial executive bodies where all or most major segments are represented, may also be institutionalised through constitutional provisions. For South Africa, Lijphart recommends that the executive at the federal level should be chosen by the legislature on a proportional basis and that there should be a rotating chairmanship. Executives at all levels of government should be proportionally constituted — elected or appointed — collegial bodies.

Grand coalition government is thought to be a logical extension of proportional representation in legislative bodies. It ensures all segments a voice in government, and increases the likelihood of wide support for government policies. It facilitates decisions by consensus and stimulates cooperative attitudes among the leaders. Elite cooperation transcending segmental cleavages is considered to be of vital importance for the political stability of consociational democracies; because the habits, sentiments and loyalties of followers are difficult to alter in the short run, efforts to contain conflict must begin at the top.

Lijphart recommends that even relatively small groups be granted veto power: an absolute veto on the most fundamental issues, such as cultural autonomy, and a suspensive veto on non-fundamental questions. The mutual veto provides that decisions cannot be reached unless they are acceptable to all major groups. The mutual veto may apply to the legislative and other political bodies in addition to the executive body.[14]

According to Horowitz, Lijphart once again commits the fault of relying on *external constraints*, such as formal constitutional guarantees for segmental interests (Horowitz, 1991). Coalitions, in order to work, must be a result of politicians' self-interest. Rules from outside, that the politicians are to obey even when it is not in their interest, are seldom effective. They are usually resented by the group(s) on which they are imposed and are seldom durable — unless they are part of a larger bargain in which there are rewards, outweighing the resentment.

## Segmental Autonomy

In 'classical' democratic theory it is assumed that mutually reinforcing divisions (i.e. close correspondence between party support and basic social divisions) creates conflicts too intense and clear-cut to allow compromise, thus endangering democracy (Lipset, 1959: 31, 88–89). Lijphart's argument is the opposite: regulatory outcomes have in some cases occurred *precisely because* of mutually reinforcing divisions. Distinct lines of cleavage between sub-cultures, and minimisation of inter-segmental contacts, reduce the probability for antagonisms to be acted out in a violent fashion.[15]

A basic assumption of the consociational model is that 'high fences make good neighbours'. From this assumption flows the importance of granting each segment autonomy to decide its own internal affairs. Depending on the nature of the conflict, the groups may run their own schools, churches, cultural councils, etc. Where the segments are geographically concentrated, territorial federalism is advocated, otherwise this will have to take the form of corporate federalism.

In South Africa segments are likely to be relatively interspersed, but with some strongholds, and Lijphart recommends that group autonomy be introduced by combining territorial and corporate federalism. The country should be divided territorially, drawing the state boundaries in such a way as to yield economically and administratively effective states with as homogeneous populations as possible. Because complete homogeneity cannot be attained, the states should also have consociational constitutions. Decentralisation is good for stability because it multiplies the political arenas and thus lowers the political stakes in each contest. The local political bodies will be more homogeneous than those at federal level. This will increase intra-group competition relative to inter-group competition at the local level.

There would also be a need for non-territorial units to cater for the 'own affairs' of the segments without a territorial base in the federation. Cultural and educational autonomy could be organised through private associations, publicly funded on a proportional basis, or through publicly organised *cultural councils*.

Lijphart views a properly constructed federal solution as useful for plural societies, including South Africa. Other theorists oppose this view, regarding federalism as more harmful than helpful:

> In the modern world ... segregation (i.e. territorial isolation) has meant more than just cultural and social autonomy; it has meant also unequal access to education, to the economy, and to political power. It is by maintaining and promoting such inequalities that segregation has promoted communal conflict. (Melson and Wolpe, 1970: 1127)

Some consociational theorists hold that isolating segments increases the probability of civil war. Although federalism may facilitate conflict regulation by providing territorially-based segments with a greater measure of political security, it is as likely to contribute to exacerbation of conflict as to conflict regulation and should not be generally recommended. Granting territorially distinctive segments partial autonomy may also lead to demands for greater autonomy, and secession and civil war may follow. Besides, the states of a federation will inevitably include individuals belonging to segments whose territorial base is elsewhere, and their demands and needs may be ignored by the dominant segment (Nordlinger, 1972).

The issue of federalism is particularly interesting in this context because it has been one of the most widely debated issues of the constitutional negotiations in South Africa.

## Central Concerns: Normative Versus Functional

Lijphart is indisputably normative in the sense that he explicitly promotes consociational democracy as a constitutional model for South Africa.

With regard to the model itself, the focus is on functional aspects of the constitutional set-up. The aim is to achieve social stability through various technical mechanisms for conflict regulation and 'social engineering'. While this may seem a purely technical matter, a particular idea of the good for society is also implicit in this constitutional model. While for Albie Sachs justice is the primary virtue of social institutions, the basic values for Lijphart are *stability* and *cultural autonomy*. These are the primary goals that should be pursued when a constitutional structure is designed. This difference in the conception of the good for society is reflected throughout their proposals, and it is closely related to their identification of problems.

## Objective: Regulation Versus Transformation

Consociational models are based on the assumption that the basic conflicts of severely divided society cannot be 'solved'. Ethnic loyalties are extremely stable, and should be regarded as constants. To aim for the perfect under these circumstances is the worst enemy of a workable solution; attempts to create social unity will just exacerbate conflicts. Efforts to abolish ethnic affiliations are likely to be — at best — fruitless. It is, however, not at all fruitless to attempt to limit their impact, and this is precisely what consociation is about. Rather than attempting to transform society through assimilation, consociational 'engineers' occupy themselves with technical mechanisms, attempting to channel existing conflicts into less centrifugal and violent forms.

Attempting to transform society necessarily implies, according to consociational thinking, that some groups' conception of the good is affirmed while others are rejected. The state should limit itself to pursue the 'neutral' goal of maintaining stability through constitutional mechanisms regulating the conflicts into less explosive forms.[16]

## Civil Society and the State: Representation Versus Participation

Representation and depolitisation are the two key-words expressing the relationship between state and civil society as envisioned in the consociational model. As opposed to the justice model, in which participation is seen to be crucial, consociational models conceive the relationship between the state, the individual and the intermediate organisational network mainly in terms of representation of group interests. An appropriate understanding of the role of the state versus the individual, and the perceived character of the intermediate organisations and their leaders, is essential to understand the workings of the consociational model.

### The Role of the State

According to consociational theory the primary function of the central government in plural societies should be to mediate between the segments of society. The individual citizen is not irrelevant, but the mediating layer between the individual citizens and the state is of more fundamental political importance. Lijphart conceives the intermediate level organisations of the future South Africa to be divided along ethnic lines, with political parties and civil society organisations corresponding to form clearly distinguishable ethnic segments.

This conception of the state and the role of the central government is fundamentally opposed to the justice model, in which the most fundamental function of the state is to serve as a guarantor of the rights of individual citizens.[17] In consociational theory, rights protection is seen as a means rather than as a goal in itself. It is a way to advance the primary objective of the state, to regulate the relationship between adverse groups in society, and hinder destructive conflict. Because of the perceived importance of group identity in plural societies, groups, rather than individuals, should be the primary subject of rights. The state should guarantee certain fundamental rights to all individuals, but on other dimensions individual rights should be protected according to the culture and resources of each segment or group.

## The Role of the Elite in Consociational Theory

The role of the political elite is crucial in consociational theory: only the leaders of the conflict groups are seen to be capable of making a direct and positive contribution to the development and implementation of necessary conflict-regulating practices. The conflict group members are too numerous, too scattered, too fragmented, too weak, and too unskilled (Nordlinger, 1972: 40). The model relies heavily on the elite as political actors, and the preferred relationship between the group leaders and their constituency is one in which the leaders enjoy considerable autonomy. The segments should ideally be represented by one set of leaders, automatically empowered to enter into deals and compromises. Contact between segments other than at top-level, should be minimised in order to reduce tension.

Lijphart places much emphasis on the freedom of leaders to enter into consociational arrangements, but devotes little attention to the constraints, and the structure of incentives within which leaders work. He merely assumes that political elites enjoy a high degree of freedom of choice, and may resort to consociational politics in a deliberate effort to counteract the centrifugal tendencies inherent in plural societies. Other consociational theorists have, however, analysed the factors influencing elite behaviour.

According to Nordlinger (1972), elites are motivated to engage in conflict-regulating behaviour by a desire to ward off pressure from external states, to maintain or increase the level of economic well-being, to acquire or retain governmental offices and power, and/or to avoid bloodshed among the leaders' own segments. Elites will be most motivated if no conflict group forms a majority or expects to do so in the foreseeable future, and when the elites believe in the very real possibility of civil strife.[18]

Nordlinger also argues that politically secure conflict group leaders are more prone to promote regulatory efforts. Structured elite-dominance within their own conflict groups is a necessary condition for conflict-regulating outcomes. Leaders must enjoy extensive independent authority to take action and make commitments without being accused of ignoring, dominating, or coercing their followers. Non-elites must either be apolitical, have acquiescent attitudes toward authority, be organised in patron-client relations, or be mass parties with extensive organisational capabilities (Nordlinger, 1972: 86–87).

The emphasis in consociational theory on the role of the elite has given rise to widespread criticism, and the democratic qualities of the model has been questioned. This critique will form part of the analysis of the model in Chapter 8 below.

## The Constitutional Domain and the Domain of the Political

Consociational models limit the domain of the political, perhaps even more so than the justice model, but in a somewhat different manner.

In the consociational model the scope of political decisions is limited and the political domain fragmented through functional and geographical federalism. Decisions by consensus and minority vetoes hamper the process of decision-making and sometimes result in non-decisions, which also limit the role of politics.

Furthermore, important issues are taken out of the political domain through constitutional clauses guaranteeing proportional representation and proportional allocation of positions and resources.

Constitutional constraints are primarily set in force by making the process of change very complicated and demanding and by irreversibly delegating certain tasks to independent institutions — procedures which may be carried out mechanically once established. In contrast, the justice model relies on constitutional constraints to operate through judicial review, declaring certain changes unconstitutional — a method which inevitably comes down to a matter of judgement.

In the consociational model, constitutionalism is motivated by the need to remove certain unresolvable problems from the political arena in order to reduce the risk of system-breakdown as well as generating resources for soluble issues. *Voluntary foreclosure of issues* is seen to promote democracy by creating an institutional foundation that is beyond debate, on the basis of which other issues can be solved (Holmes, 1988a).

## Proportionality as Voluntary Foreclosure of Issues

Proportionality is a conflict-regulating practice which can be applied in several ways to reduce the degree and scope of competition. The principle of proportionality, that all groups influence a decision in proportion to their numerical strength, is the standard of political representation in Lijphart's consociational model, distributing elective government positions according to relative electoral strength, in the legislature as well as the executive body.

The principle may also be applied to the allocation of appointive government positions and scarce resources to the segments in accordance with their population size or relative strength. Lijphart holds that proportionality should be the normative target for appointments to the civil service, including the police, the armed forces and the judiciary. The civil service represents major career opportunities, and to distribute these proportionally is a way to allocate resources to the different groups. It is also a method to ensure that members of the different segments are treated equally by government agencies.

Proportionality takes some potentially difficult decisions out of the political arena. When each segment is ensured a share of parliamentary seats, civil service appointments or educational funds, roughly proportional to their share of the electorate or population, these issues are only open to intra-group competition, limiting the scope for inter-group competition.

There are, however, also problems with the constitutional foreclosure of issues: immunising certain issues from public inspection and debate and maintaining status quo, often imply resolving the matters favourably for one or the other side. Allowing democratic processes to operate only when the stakes are low, resolving the large issues behind the scenes, is problematic from the point of view of democracy. While this kind of privatisation through politics may decrease factional struggle, the opposite may also occur. If resolution through the political process is unavailable this may cause a loss of faith in the system and resort to extra-legal means (Sunstein, 1988: 340).[19]

## The Consociational Rechtsstaat

The consociational model is within the *Rectsstaat* tradition. There is little influence from the British legal tradition where the *rule of law* is ultimately based upon Parliamentary sovereignty.

Furthermore, is it a formal *Rechtsstaat*, protecting the rights and liberties of citizens through a systematisation of public law, to which the state is made subject. A rigid framework of public law regulates the functioning of the legislative and executive organs, thus protecting the interests of citizens and groups in society. Unlike the material *Rechtsstaat* of the justice model — where statutory law and government actions are required to be in accordance not only with the principles of legality, but also with some principle of justice — consociationalism is not concerned with material justice. The constitutional framework of the consociational model will not — even if complied with — necessarily produce a just society.

We have seen that neither the justice model nor the consociational model hold rule of law to be sufficient to curb the powers of state authority. More stringent controls and safeguards are needed to protect rights and liberties against Parliament as well as the executive. Where legislatures are sovereign the government may legally abuse power.[20] We thus have two cases of constitutional democracy. In both models democratic institutions figure prominently. But in neither is democracy, in the sense of parliamentary sovereignty, the ultimate norm of the state system.

## Societal Plurality and Nation-Building

Traditional theories of nation-building prescribe assimilation, or at least measures furthering the growth of inter-ethnic nationalism (see Table 3.2 above). Nation-building is conceived as process whereby new, national sentiments and loyalties are learned. Sachs' justice model, although recognising the problems with this strategy, and less maximalist in its objectives, is still within this paradigm. Whether — or how — some form of political community can be maintained if such nation-building does not succeed, is largely ignored.

The 'engineers' of consociational democracy are more modest about goals, and assume that it is necessary for ethnically divided states to live with ethnic cleavages rather than attempting assimilation. While Sachs advocates for a society characterised by people who are 'different, but equal and together', all competing on equal terms within the same political arena, Lijphart, and consociational theory in general, opts for a system of 'separate but equal', with ethnic groups competing as far as possible on different political arenas. Since habits, sentiments and loyalties of followers are difficult to alter in the short run, efforts to contain conflict must begin at the top. Agreement among group leaders is more likely and is a necessary and important step towards accommodation.

Consociational theory regards excessive social plurality as a problem, but not a problem to be solved. Rather it is a phenomenon to take into account. Its impact should be limited through institutional mechanisms. Overarching loyalties are regarded as an asset, particularly at the elite level, but a democratic system can function with very little overarching loyalty at non-elite level, if the segments are kept isolated. Again, 'high fences make good neighbours'.

## Conditions Conducive to Consociation

What are the conditions that make the likelihood of a successful outcome better in some plural societies than in others?

According to Lijphart consociation is most likely to succeed where there are (1) no majority segment, (2) equally sized segments, (3) three to five segments, (4) a relatively small total population, (5) a foreign threat perceived as a common danger, (6) overarching loyalties, (7) absence of large socioeconomic inequalities, (8) geographically concentrated segments, and (9) traditions of political accommodation.

He underscores that the relationship between these conditions and successful consociation is probabilistic in nature (Lijphart, 1985: 115). They are favourable conditions, but neither are necessary preconditions for consociationalism to succeed, nor are they sufficient to guarantee a successful outcome. Although criticism raised against the various conditions may weaken their empirical explanatory value, Lijphart maintains that this does not weaken the normative applicability of the model, because, in his own words 'even if most or all of the favourable factors are lacking, it is still possible to have a successful consociation' (1985: 116).

## Where do these Ideas Come From?

Lijphart is one among a host of consociationalists. One of his most important predecessors, and probably the first to state the theory, was interestingly an African economist, Sir Arthur Lewis in his book *Politics in West Africa* (1965). Other important scholars of consociational democracy are Eric Nordlinger, J. Steiner, G. Lembruch, Kenneth D. McRae and Hans Daalder.

The political systems of the Netherlands, Belgium, Switzerland and Austria are central to Lijphart's model, and to consociationalism in general.[21] Lijphart does, however, examine a number of countries in different parts of the world in order to extract and 'test' his model. Severely divided societies, such as Lebanon and Sri Lanka, which demonstrated for a period the potential of consociation to degenerate later into violence and civil war, provide important knowledge of the forces furthering conflict-regulation and those counteracting it.

Lijphart does not explicitly relate to any philosophical school or tradition. His roots, both personally and with regard to his theory of consociationalism, are, however, drawn from the Low Countries, where protestant organological theory and catholic communitarianism are influential traditions.[22] Many of his ideas concerning social cohesion and political organisation reflect such ideas, which, interestingly, also have exercised considerable influence on Afrikaner ideology (see Sparks, 1990).

Lijphart's theory also parallels the communitarian tradition in contemporary political philosophy, and this link will be explored in the following paragraph. To facilitate a structured discussion, the main arguments of communitarian scholars will be discussed as a unified position. A preliminary word of caution is, however, appropriate: the *communitarians* form no unified school of political theory.[23] The views of the different scholars subsumed under this label vary considerably.

## Communitarian Philosophy as a Normative Justification for Consociational Democracy

There is little indication in Lijphart's work of any direct interest in communitarian philosophy. Many of the ideas common to Lijphart and contemporary communitarians may also be traced to other sources such as catholic political thinking and calvinist organological theory.

I do, however, believe that to discuss Lijphart's basic ideas and assumptions in the light of some central communitarian ideas, yields important insights. The significance of consociationalism as an alternative response to the pluralism of modern societies, stands out in this perspective. The consociational model, rather than appearing to be an assemblage of empirical cases, now becomes a fully-fledged philosophically based alternative to the liberalism of Rawls and Sachs. (And, interestingly, communitarian philosophers have taken considerable interest in the works of Lijphart and other theorists of consociational democracy (Kymlica, 1989).)

*Community, Identity, Culture: the Communitarian Critique of Liberalism*

This discussion is structured around the three main criticisms that communitarians raise towards liberal political theory: Rawls (and by implication also Sachs) is addressing the wrong question; the moral ontology (the view of the person and the relationship between individual and community), on which these theories rest, is not valid; and, consequently, their solution is wrong.[24]

*Liberalist Theory Address the Wrong Question*

The communitarian approach challenges the very enterprise of Rawls and Sachs by arguing that they fail to ask the right questions.

> It is all very well to stipulate abstract first premises ... and then deduce conclusions about what practices are legitimate. But practice precedes theory; and it is hard to see why persons in actual societies should take any notice of such abstract principles or their deductive implications. (Kukathas and Pettit, 1990: 92)

Communitarians have an altogether different approach to moral philosophy:

> Our concern is not to stand back from our circumstances to try to judge our moral practices from some independent or impartial point of view. The end of moral reasoning is not judgement but understanding and self-discovery. I ask not 'what should I be, what sort of life should I lead?', but 'who am I?'. To ask this question is to concern oneself first and foremost with the character of the community which constitutes one's identity. It is to concern oneself with politics — the activity of attending to the demands of the community — rather than with such philosophical abstractions as justice. (Kukathas and Pettit, 1990: 106)

While liberal theories hold that 'justice is the first virtue of social institutions' and sets out to find universal norms on which to construct a just society, communitarians depart from a position of cultural relativism and argue that moral principles can be understood only as accounts of the practices which prevail in actual societies.

Not only do they reject the relevance of contractarian arguments — scrutinising society's arrangements from a hypothetical, ideal, standpoint —

they also reject the idea that procedural justice alone can provide an adequate basis for social institutions. Morality, they argue, is rooted in practice — in the particular practices of actual communities. The idea of evaluating or re-designing existing societies in the light of abstract principles of morality, is thus implausible. There are no universal principles of morality or justice. The foundation of morals lie not in philosophy but in politics. Appropriate rules or laws can only be discovered by examining the values of our own community and moral tradition — and then searching for institutional solutions to protect them (Kukathas and Pettit, 1990: 95).

## The Question of Moral Ontology

Communitarians challenge a fundamental contention shared by Rawls and Sachs; namely that a community is an association of independent individuals, and that the justice of community is reliant on the terms of association. On the contrary, communitarians argue, the very existence of individuals capable of agreeing to form associations, or assenting to terms of agreement, *presupposes* the existence of a community.

The liberal idea imply a certain conception of the person: 'person-hood' must be independent of interests and attachments, so that these are open to assessment and revision. This, according to communitarians, is a flawed conception. Interests and loyalties are integral to our identity. In a manner similar to Hegel's critique of Kant, the communitarians criticise liberalism's 'claim for the priority of the right over the good, and the picture of the freely choosing individual it embodies' (Sandel, 1988: 61). Rawls' theory makes no sense, because it presupposes a capacity we do not have: the capacity to choose or construct a morality without self-knowledge or moral experience. His principles, therefore, cannot supply the foundations for evaluating our social institutions or moral practices (Kukathas and Pettit, 1990: 96–97).

Communitarians challenge the moral individualism of liberal theory, where only individuals are seen as 'self-originating sources of valid claims' (Rawls, quoted Semb, 1992: 5). Rather, they hold particular historical communities to be the primary *subjects* of values (Cohen, 1986: 457). A position which they argue gives a 'fuller expression to the claims of citizenship and community than the liberal vision allows' (Sandel, 1988: 61).

Liberal theorists, such as Rawls, rely on a conception of the self as free and independent of particular desires and ends, a self capable of choice, in order to establish a framework of rights that will enable us to realise our capacity as free moral agents, consistent with a similar liberty for others. The communitarian alternative is constructed on the basis of a contrasting conception of the self; a radically situated self, (partly) defined by particular circumstances and the communities from which identity is derived. While liberals may grant that communities — such as the family, the tribe or ethnic group, or nation — have a psychological importance for the individual, the communitarian claim goes further. They hold that communities have moral claims of their own (Sandel, 1988: 62). Since the individual is (at least partly) defined by the community, the good of community is a precondition for, and thus prior to, the rights of the individual.

## What is at Stake for Politics? The Communitarian Alternative

Philosophers like Rawls are looking for the wrong thing: universal principles for an ideal form of political association. This problem, communitarians hold, only exists in the mind of the philosopher. The important problems arise *within* political associations and must be solved through the practices and traditions which are central to the particular association. Instead of looking for universal principles — abstractions created by philosophers — political theory should turn inwards to try to discover the meanings implicit in our discourses and practices (Walzer, 1982 and 1981).

Liberals and communitarians propose different responses to the pluralism that characterises the modern world. Liberalists advocate toleration of different ways of living. Like Kant, Rawls strives to de-link his just principles of society from a particular conception of 'the good', defining 'the right' independently. In liberal theories the good society is perceived as a framework of rights, liberties or duties within which people may pursue their separate ends, individually or in voluntary association.

> The good society is governed by law and, as such, is regulated by right principles or principles of justice. These principles are discoverable and stable. And they are principles which do not themselves presuppose the rightness or betterness of any particular way of life. (Kukathas and Pettit, 1990: 93)

While liberals regard the expansion of individual rights and entitlements as unqualified moral and political progress, communitarians are critical of the tendency of liberal programmes to displace politics from smaller forms of association to more comprehensive ones. They are critical to both libertarian liberals, defending the market economy, and egalitarian liberals (such as Sachs), defending the welfare state. Both entail concentration of power, and erode 'those intermediate forms of community that have at times sustained a more vital public life' (Sandel, 1988: 63).

Communitarians attempt to replace the liberal idea of a pluralist secular society with a more communitarian ideal of an organic, and spiritually unified social order, 'the ideal of a uniform and common culture which integrates and harmonises the interests of the individual and the community' (Kukathas and Pettit, 1990: 94). Rejecting the idea of justice as the first virtue of social institutions, their alternative is a society governed by a concern for the common good, in which the good of community itself is pre-eminent.

A consociational democratic solution, hedging the communities so vital to identity, and their values and practices, is a constitutional solution in line with communitarian thought. Rather than devices to further some universal principle of justice for individual citizens, it is structured towards increasing the good for community; a stable framework within which each culture can develop.

## The Communitarian Critique Considered

The communitarian critique is partly refuted, partly incorporated by Rawls. He explicitly acknowledges that his concern is not to supply a universal standard of justice but to discover those moral principles which might best serve his own society, with all its particular concerns. His starting point is prevailing moral beliefs and intuitions of modern liberal democratic societies. The *original position* is designed only to enable us to see more clearly what is presumed to be already there (Kukathas, 1990: 107). The same respect for the particular circumstances is found in Sachs' constitutional proposal. The idea of *participatory formulation of rights* is set forth as a method for securing coherence between constitutional principles and existing social norms.

It may also be argued that Rawls' conception of the person does not differ radically from that of the communitarians: he does not deny that in actual life, socialisation and culture is integral to identity. What is argued is that we have an idea of the person in which his or her particular ends are not included, and that this idea (of persons as free and equal) is more relevant to our moral judgements. Also for communitarians the self is only partly constituted by its context and its goals or ends. Although the communitarians hold the identity of the self to be the product of (political) experience, they seem, like Rawls, to accept that the *person* is prior to his ends (Kukathas and Pettit, 1990: 108–9).

Although the aspirations of Rawls and Sachs are not universalist in the sense that they regard their theories to be valid for all societies, their perspective is clearly different from the cultural relativism of the communitarians. Although they settle for a political standard supported by an overlapping consensus, rather than eternal and universal norms, they are searching for a common moral standard by which to evaluate social practices within a political community. An enterprise communitarians reject.

The liberal project of which Sachs and Rawls are exponents devotes the political domain towards accomplishment of greater freedom of choice for a greater number, and leaves the deeper structures to the private sphere, or just assumes their existence as given. A problem with the open liberal society is that while it provides openings for choice — opportunities for setting goals in life and freedom to pursue them — these are only possibilities. Possibilities are incomplete, communitarians argue, as long as they only consist of abstract choices. It is first when certain deeper structures or social bonds are added to these possibilities, that they become meaningful. The value of social ties is a mine field for liberals. They are generally of an absolute nature, recognising no shades of grey; people either belong or they do not — and if they do not they have no rights to claim. Religion, while historically a politically destructive force, is also a source of social bonds and meaningful deep structures. When old structures disintegrate, the search for meaning becomes more frenetic, and people become all too willing to be tempted by postulates providing a sense of belonging (Dahrendorf, 1991).

Communitarianisms seem to provide an answer to the question of why the open society is insufficient. Their theory explains the search for the tribal society and the homogeneous nation: without deep structures of social belonging, choices and possibilities do not seem to carry much meaning.

Is the open society with free citizens an impossible project? Is it inevitably in conflict with the need for social bonds, containing ideas of protection, boundaries and definitions? Or can the open society have a real identity. Jürgen Habermas seems to envision a *volounté générale*, manifesting itself through a continuous dialogue upholding the fundamental norms of society (Dahrendorf, 1991). In a sense, this is also what Sachs aspires towards. Communitarians would argue that constitutional patriotism is an abstract, rather than emotional matter, and hardly satisfies a longing to live for, and pass on to future generations, deep structures in society.

**Table 5.2. The justice model and the consociational model according to the conceptual framework for analysis**

| Dimension | | Justice model (Sachs) | Consociational model (Lijphart) |
|---|---|---|---|
| (i) | **Institutional set-up** | | |
| | institutional focus | legal system | political system |
| | electoral system | proportional | proportional |
| | legislature-executive relationship | presidentialism | parliamentarism |
| | compos. of legislature | bi-cameral | bi-cameral |
| | compos. of executive | one party government | (grand) coalition gov. |
| | | single executive | collective executive body |
| | decentralisation | unitary state | federal state |
| | | decentralised | highly decentralised |
| | decision-making mode | adversarial | consensual |
| | | majoritarian | minority vetoes |
| (ii) | **Interpretation of reality** | | |
| | methodological focus | individual | collective |
| | problem focus | structural | cultural |
| | | inequality, poverty | ethnicity |
| (iii) | **Central value** | justice | stability, cultural autonomy |
| | | positive liberty | negative liberty |
| (iv) | **Objective** | transformation | regulation |
| (v) | **Response to pluralism** (nation-building) | toleration | non-interference |
| (vi) | **State-society relationship** | participation | representation |
| (vii) | **The constitutional domain** | | |
| | | constitutionalism | constitutionalism |
| | | *Rechtsstaat* | *Rechtsstaat* |
| | | precommitment | foreclosure of issues |
| (viii) | **Normative foundation/ justification** | liberalism | communitarian philosophy |
| | | contractarian philos.. (John Rawls) | (catholic communitarian and protestant organological thinking) |

**Restating the Argument**

This chapter has presented the consociational model as a constitutional proposal for South Africa. Focus has been set on clarifying the model's position with regard to the institutional set-up as well as the underlying normative values. The presentation is roughly parallel to that of the justice model in the previous chapter, and important differences between the models have been noted in the course of the presentation.

The main institutional differences between the justice model and consociational solutions for South Africa are summarised in Table 5.2 above.

While both Sachs and Lijphart advocate proportional electoral systems as part of their models for South Africa, this is much more integral to, and prominent in Lijphart's approach, where the principle of proportionality permeates the entire constitutional structure. The decision-making procedures should be characterised by consensus rather than majority rule, the executive should be a proportionally constituted coalition with rotating chairmanship, and all groups should have a mutual veto. Sachs' approach, on the other hand, envisions a strong executive. While both models suggest a two-chamber parliament, the senate is, in Lijphart's view, to play a more significant role as the protector of the different segments. Lijphart favours a federal solution rather than a unitary state, and extensive decentralisation of power to local authorities as well as non-geographical political bodies, such as cultural councils. His proposal is designed to ensure that not in any sphere of government could a majority party impose its will or objectives on other parties. The system is so carefully counter-balanced that all legislation would be the result of inter-party agreements and trade-offs. It is a consociational system, but without ethnic groups enjoying constitutional status as such (Schlemmer, 1991: 66).

The role of rights, as well as of the courts, varies considerably between the two models. While Lijphart's model does not preclude a bill of rights, this is not recommended either. The only rights a consociational model is required to safeguard, for the sake of stability, are the collective rights of the different communities that make up society. Allocation/redistribution of resources by the state through affirmative action provisions is suggested in both models, but while this is required by justice in Sachs' model, it is a matter of stability for Lijphart.

Lijphart's consociational model is criticised from different camps. Part of the critique is internal, articulated by scholars who share the same objectives and the same interpretation of the plural nature of South African society, but who disagree on the way problems should most adequately be handled. Due to the prominent role the electoral system is seen to play in consociational models, disagreement on this part of the constitutional set-up is rife and has been given special attention.

External critique of the consociational model is even more abundant. Its methodological qualities are questioned — the fact that the model is so firmly empirically based has lead critics to argue that it is only a random set of constitutional elements, assembled from some (predominantly European) countries which have some superficial traits in common. And it is argued that to apply, or recommend this 'assemblage' to a different political setting is illegitimate. The above presentation of the model rebuts this criticism by explicating how the consociational model — like the justice model — is a coherent constitutional 'solution'. When viewed in the light of communitarian philosophy, the consociational model appears as an independent and complete theoretical construct, based on a particular moral ontology and supported by a philosophical justification. The problems addressed by the two schools of thought differ, however, as do their conceptions of the person and their relation to society. The solutions differ accordingly. Both models may thus be regarded as supported by a philosophical justification — which one is seen to be the more 'valid' is a matter of judgement. The adequacy of the different justification strategies in the South African context is the theme of the following chapter, where various forms of criticism raised against the consociational model will also be discussed.

A main objective has been to present exponents of the two constitutional models that have dominated the South African debate as coherent strategies for addressing what each of them considers to be the most fundamental problems of the society. To assess their solutions is the task of the following chapters. Whether the models are valid generalisations, and on methodological accounts applicable to South Africa, is discussed in Chapter 6. Their normative acceptability is the focus of Chapter 7, while their feasibility in the light of the conflicts and problems of South African society, is considered in Chapter 8. Throughout the analyses one should bear in mind that the ultimate aim of the discussions are to shed light on the questions to be discussed in the last part of the book: the character of the new South African constitution and the prospects for constitutionalism in South Africa.

# Notes

1. Scholars use different terminology. 'Ethnic accommodation', 'conflict regulation', 'conflict management', and 'power-sharing' are terms used in very similar models and here they are used interchangeably with 'consociational democracy'. Lijphart distinguishes between the consociational model as a constitutional framework for plural society and consensus democracy as an ideal type. Although they overlap to a considerable extent, they are analytically distinct.

2. Key elements in the constitutional principles presented by the national party were as follows. a) Executive power should rest with a coalition government consisting of the three largest parties and should be a collective executive body with rotating premiership, required to make decisions by consensus, and backed by a mutual veto. b) Bi-cameral parliament with the first chamber composed according to the principle of proportionality (PR elections). In the second chamber the regions have an equal number of representatives, equally divided between the three largest parties in each region. The second chamber should have extensive powers. c) Federalism and substantial local autonomy. 'One city, one tax base, one administration', is accepted, but combined with special voter requirements for local elections (according to property and tax paying abilities). The constitution should also open for neighbourhood committees for protection of social and welfare interests at community level (National Party, 1991).

   When asked to comment on the NP constitutional principles (personal interview, Bergen, 16 September 1991) Lijphart replied that — except for some 'minor but important flaws' (most importantly the voting-qualifications) which he considered to be bargaining chips and signal to the white electorate — the principles were in coherence with the consociational model, although perhaps not in the form best suited to South African conditions.

3. The final report and recommendations of the commission is found in Buthelezi Commission (1982). See also Lijphart (1985: 78).

4. The following presentation is based on Lijphart's statement concerning optimal consociational guidelines for South Africa (Lijphart, 1985: 80).

5. While Lijphart's primary recommendation for South Africa is to facilitate spontaneous formation of groups, he does not exclude the possibility of predefining segments. A workable solution might be a 'mixed arrangement' permitting one, or a few, groups to officially designate themselves as separate segments; register on separate voter's rolls; have a specified number of representatives in parliament; run their own schools, and so on — while other citizens participate together in free PR elections, forming associations for cultural autonomy when this is needed or wanted. All registration would have to be on a completely voluntary basis. However, as Lijphart himself is well aware, even this 'mixed arrangement' would be offensive to many South Africans.

6. Donald L. Horowitz is one of the world's foremost experts on ethnicity, particularly known for his 1985 book *Ethnic Groups in Conflict*. He agrees with Lijphart and consociational theorists in their interpretation of the problems of South Africa and the significance of ethnic conflict, and is generally within the same paradigm. His solutions — particularly regarding the electoral system, but also in favouring a presidential system — differ, however, so markedly that he cannot comfortably be counted among the 'consociationalists'. The following critique is thus something in between an internal debate within the consociational camp, and an external critique.

7. According to Horowitz, Lijphart is overlooking the distinction between mere seat pooling and vote pooling. *Vote pooling* is an exchange of votes of the respective supporters by

two parties 'a pooling at the grass-root level', while *seat pooling* takes place at the 'top', after the election, in order to gain enough seats to form a government.

8. Voters rank the candidates in their constituency in order of preference, and if their first preference is not 'counted' their second or third preference is.

9. Heterogeneous constituencies are electoral districts composed of significant members of two or more than two ethnic groups.

10. 'Consociationalism comes down to statesmanship, not electoral incentives. If the experience of severely divided societies shows anything at all, it is that statesmanship alone, statesmanship without tangible reasons, statesmanship without rewards, will not reduce conflict' (Horowitz, 1989: 22).

11. The following answer to Horowitz' critique is summarised from Lijphart, 1991a.

12. An additional criticism of presidentialism is its inflexibility, resulting from the fixed term of office, and the fact that it operates according to the rule of 'winner-take-all', thus tending to turn politics into a zero-sum-game (Linz, 1990).

13. Horowitz bases his argument mainly on the experiences of presidentialism in multi-ethnic Nigeria (Horowitz, 1985 and 1991).

14. Horowitz points to the contradiction between the idea of one-person-one-vote and special rights for particular groups, detracting from the effects of universal suffrage. This 'undemocratic' trait of consociationalism endangers long-term minority protection.

15. Not all consociational theorists agree with these views, holding that voluntary inter-segmental contacts do not aggravate the conflict or make its regulation more difficult. On the contrary, unconstrained inter-segmental contacts may actually promote tolerance and understanding between segments (Nordlinger, 1972).

16. But, it may be asked whether in South Africa, where inequalities are enormous and the majority demands change, it is more neutral to go for 'stability' than 'justice', or regulation rather than transformation.

17. Sachs does not deny that individuals have fundamental loyalties to ethnic, linguistic, religious or ideological communities, and that the existence of these communities are of importance for their identity and fulfilment. Cultural rights should be recognised, but as individual rights, not bestowed in some sub-group of society as a collective unit (Sachs, 1990a: 39).

18. In South Africa all of these motivations are found to some extent, varying in intensity between the leaders of different groups. To avoid bloodshed within their own ranks has been a concern of leaders of all groups, particularly in the phase of negotiations leading up to the adoption of the interim constitution.

19. This argument is frequently put forward in relation to South Africa. It is used to oppose consociationalism, as well as to defend it. Proponents of the model argue pure majoritarianism also implies a foreclosure of issues namely those posed by (ethnic) minorities. They will, when in effect permanently excluded from political influence, lose faith in the system and resort to extra-legal means. This is not only a normative problem, but also a practical one — threatening civil peace and political stability. The potential for violent action from right wing Afrikaner nationalists, if not accommodated within the system, is frequently put forward as an argument for power-sharing. On the other hand it is argued that consociationalism's foreclosure of redistributive issues is likely to result in lack of legitimacy for the regime throughout the poor majority, and ultimately in system break-down.

20. In a full democracy based on universal suffrage, with a mature democratic culture and high regard for civil liberties, Sachs would probably hold that 'self imposed restraints' might suffice. But in South Africa, with the previous record of 'abuse through law' a

Rechtsstaat checking power through 'external constraints' is seen to be needed, both by proponents of the justice model and consociationalism.

21. The primary cases of consociational democracy upon which Lijphart bases his theory is Austria from 1945 to 1966, Belgium since the end of World War I, the Netherlands from 1917 to 1967, and Switzerland since 1943. In addition he refers to Lebanon from 1943 to 1975 and Malaysia since 1969 as relatively successful consociation (Lijphart, 1985: 89). For a fuller list of analysis of consociationalism, and applications of the consociational model to different countries, see Lijphart, 1985: 84.

22. Catholic communitarianism and the calvinist organological theory, as formulated by J.R. Thorbecke and Abraham Kuyper are discussed in von der Dunk (1982) and Swensen (1990). Similarities are striking, e.g. Lijphart's principle of segmental autonomy may be seen as a reflection of the *subsidiarity principle* of catholic communitarianism and its calvinist counterpart of *sovereignty in the internal sphere*.

23. Central scholars within this tradition are Michael Sandel, Michael Waltzer, Charles Taylor and Will Kymlica.

24. For more details of the debates between liberals and communitarians see Mulhall and Swift (1996).

# PART III
# ASSESSING THE
# CONTENDERS

# 6  Methodological Critique: Valid Models for South Africa?

We now proceed to the assessment of the rivalling constitutional models. In this chapter methodological aspects are considered: are the models valid generalisations? Each of the models includes institutional mechanisms designed to produce a desired result. Are there reasons to doubt that they would function according to their intention? And are the conditions in South Africa such that the theories apply?

Are the proposals acceptable on normative grounds? This question is raised in Chapter 7, which focuses on the normative qualities of the consociational model and the justice model respectively: are these constitutional models in accordance with central democratic and human rights norms? Normative questions are important in light of the assumption that the legitimacy of the new constitution depends on it being perceived as democratic and in accordance with internationally accepted human rights norms. And, furthermore, that the legitimacy of the constitution — internally as well as in the international milieu — is crucial for the government's ability to implement and sustain policies, and for political stability.

Are there reasons to believe that the models, if they had been implemented in South Africa in their pure form, would 'deliver' the results that they were designed to produce? Their feasibility in South African circumstances is the theme of Chapter 8, where we examine some serious pitfalls to which each model is susceptible to fall victim. The analysis carried out in the following three chapters seeks to clarify the constitutional models' potential to function as frameworks regulating South African politics, and expose their shortcomings. The aim is to develop tools for assessing the framework of the new South African constitution, presented and analysed in the last part of the book.

## Are the Models Valid Generalisations?

There are several aspects to this question. The first regards the causal relationships between institutional mechanisms and desired outcomes. Are these sufficiently substantiated? Second, is it specified under which conditions these mechanisms operate? And third, are conditions in South Africa such that the preconditions for applying the models are satisfied?

The previous presentation of the models shows that they differ in several respects, some of which are highly relevant to this discussion. One difference between the models in particular renders a symmetric analysis difficult. While the consociational model is inductively arrived at, generalising from empirical cases, the justice model is primarily a product of deductive inference from fundamental norms. While both models are normative, in the sense that they have been put forth as ideals for the actual constitutional structure in South Africa, the consociational model is also empirical. It is used to explain the (absence of) democratic stability in plural societies. It thus lends itself to empirical 'testing' in a way that the justice model does not.

The most pressing question regarding generalisation of the justice model concerns the norms upon which it is founded: is this liberal individualism relevant to an African country?

## Is the Justice Model a Valid Generalisation?

The discussion in Chapter 4 concluded that the justice model, as laid out by Albie Sachs, could be regarded as an application of John Rawls' theory of justice to South African conditions. Rawls, when developing his theory, specifies certain conditions which must be present in a society in order for his theory to be valid: citizens must share certain fundamental moral sentiments. Most importantly, there must be an overlapping consensus on a certain conception of the person. Individuals must be regarded as, in moral respects, free and equal and capable of rational reasoning (Rawls, 1987). And the individual must be seen as the morally relevant unit.

In addition, certain *circumstances of justice* must apply to society in order for Rawls' theory — and by implication Sachs model — to be applicable. It is developed as a way to organise societies marked by pluralism, with different comprehensive moral views (religion, ideology) and different conceptions of 'the good'. It presupposes material conditions characterised by *moderate scarcity* and that orderly structuring of society, facilitating cooperation, will create an economic surplus. The fact that cooperation generates a surplus that no one would have any part of unless an orderly community existed must also be generally recognised (Rawls, 1971: 126–30).

Are these conditions satisfied in South Africa? Pluralism is indisputably a characteristic of South African society — racial, religious and cultural differences are ample and highly visible. Likewise, it is generally accepted that an economic surplus arises from societal cooperation.

The two other conditions are less obviously satisfied. Do South African citizens share certain fundamental moral sentiments? More specifically, are there reasons to assume that an overlapping consensus exists, or can be developed, on the 'Kantian' conception of the person, upon which the justice model rests? And is the material condition satisfied? Is South Africa characterised by moderate scarcity?

## Moderate Scarcity as a Precondition

Rawls' theory is developed for a society with *moderate* scarcity. He maintains that economic development must be over a certain (not specified) level, for the priority of the first principle to apply. Below this level equal basic rights may (justly) be restricted to achieve a higher level of economic well-being. Is South Africa above this level? There is widespread poverty in South Africa but there is also considerable wealth. The country is included among the 'developing middle income countries' in international statistics. In order to determine whether it satisfies the condition of moderate scarcity it is necessary to look at Rawls' argument for including the condition.

Unless there is some scarcity, in the sense that there are fewer resources than are wanted by the citizens, Rawls' theory is superfluous — rules regulating the distribution of and competition for resources are not called for. This, however, is hardly a relevant 'problem' in any society — and certainly not in South Africa. On the other hand the scarcity must not, according to Rawls, be too extreme if his theory is to be applicable. The condition rests on the assumption that under conditions of extreme scarcity, rights cannot be effectively established, so that it may be rational to sacrifice some civil and political liberty in order to achieve development (Rawls, 1971: 542).[1]

The condition of moderate scarcity gives rise to two questions. Is the relationship presupposed by Rawls, between civil and political rights, on the one hand, and economic development on the other, in fact accurate? And, if it is, what is the crucial level of economic well-being above which the theory is valid?

Rawls' assumption is that economic development may be promoted by sacrificing liberty. This is a point of considerable scholarly dispute. The assumption of such a trade off was influential within development economics and political science in the 1960s and early 1970s. The 'trade-off' argument has, however, been opposed both on empirical and normative grounds. It seems that if indicators other than economic growth are included in the definition of development, that is, if the general level of welfare, is seen as an aspect of development, there is less empirical evidence supporting the trade-off argument (Dick, 1974; Goodin, 1979; Howard, 1983).

If we support the conclusion that the trade-off argument is invalid — that limiting civil and political rights does not promote economic development at any level of well-being — then there is no lower limit to the range of prosperity for which Rawls' theory is valid. No further inquiry is necessary to conclude that South Africa is within the range.

If we conclude that the trade-off relationship does hold in some cases, there are still reasons why this is unlikely to be the case in South Africa. In complex industrialised economies, such as the South African, the amount of information required for efficient resource allocation is formidable. Civil and political rights provide information and incentive structures facilitating efficient production and enabling redistribution.[2]

We may conclude that the 'circumstances of justice' on which the justice model is based are present in South Africa. One question remains, however. Are there reasons to believe that an overlapping consensus exists among South African citizens, on the conception of the person underlying the justice model?

## South Africa and Liberal Individualism

Is a theory based on liberal individualism relevant to an African country? Rawls is explicitly founding his theory on moral sentiments developed in western liberal societies after the Reformation, and the conception of the person which he assumes enjoys general support in this culture, despite the variety of different comprehensive moral outlooks. Is there a similar overlapping consensus in South Africa? Is there general agreement on the individual as the morally relevant social unit? And is there a widespread conception of all persons as, in moral respects, free and equal?

The discussions in Chapter 5, of consociational theory and the communitarian critique of liberalism, demonstrate that not all observers of the South African situation hold this to be the case.[3] They doubt the importance of the individual in plural societies, generally, and also in the case of South Africa, and hold that other social units, in particular ethnic groups, are politically more relevant. Others point to the importance of *ubuntu* in South African tradition. The concept means broadly that 'each individual's humanity is ideally expressed through his relationship with others and theirs in turn through a recognition of his humanity' (Sparks, 1990: 14).

> There was not much room for individualism in the Western sense, for the emphasis was on the group and the individual was assigned his role within it. Yet the result was not oppressive or even stifling. In fact these traditional African societies placed a high value on human worth, but it was a humanism that found its expression in a communal context ... There is a word for it in the Nguni languages, *ubuntu*, that captures the essence of this particular kind of participatory humanism, which has survived the urbanisation of South Africa's industrial revolution and is visible today in the communal spirit of the ghetto townships ... *'Ubuntu ungamntu ngabanye abantu'* goes the Xhosa proverb — 'people are people though other people'. (Sparks, 1990: 14)

The prevalence of communal sentiments is said to be reflected in the traditional modes of decision-making, emphasising mediation and consensus.

Excessive individualism is not the only criticism which may be voiced against the justice model. It may also be questioned whether all groups in South Africa can be said to support a conception of persons as equal in moral respects and thus entitled to equal liberties and equal standing as citizens. Here, it is not African tradition which is seen to be the main obstacle, but rather the moral sentiments of Afrikaner nationalism.

Notions of 'chosen people' and racial superiority are salient in Afrikaner thought. These ideas — held to originate from the prominence of Calvinism in Afrikaner ideology, and strengthened by the influence of Scholars of German Romanticism, such as Fichte and Herder — are said to have a strong and pervasive grip on the Afrikaner mind (Sparks, 1990). If this is correct, the development of an overlapping consensus on a 'Kantian' conception of the person — where all are seen to be free and equal in moral respects and thus entitled to equal rights — is unlikely.

Other scholars argue, however, that ideas of racial superiority, and Afrikaners as the chosen people, are not integral to Afrikaner ideology in this fundamental sense. Although such traits are present today, they were not particularly strong in Afrikaner political and social ideology prior to the late nineteenth century. Rather than being integral to Afrikaner thinking, the ideas emerged as a product of capitalist development in South Africa. Being contingent upon a particular social situation, they are probably of a transient nature (du Toit 1983). According to this latter interpretation the development of an overlapping consensus is less improbable.

A certain lack of coherence seems to exist between the moral sentiments upon which the justice model is constructed, and (parts of) political tradition and thinking in South Africa. Is this sufficient to dismiss the model as valid for South Africa? I will argue that it is not. Although the ideology of sections of South African society rejects the conception that all people are, in moral respects, equal, it is also a fact — vividly demonstrated in the anti-apartheid struggle and in the recent phase of transition to democracy — that support for equal political rights and equal protection of individual liberties are widespread in South Africa.

Even if they are right, those who argue that a 'communal spirit' exists in South Africa today continuing pre-colonial traditions, this does not in and by itself present problems for liberal theories of justice. While regarding the individual as the morally relevant unit, they do not deny the existence and importance of social ties such as family or cultural communities. What they do hold is that under modern conditions, in societies characterised by pluralism, and where the state possesses powers of repression and control unknown to traditional societies — the individual needs special protection. In practical terms it may, however, be difficult to reconcile the institutionalised manifestations of such beliefs and social bonds, such as traditional leadership and common law, with the structures of the state.

There is no definite answer to this discussion, but in my judgement there is no reason to conclude that the circumstances in South Africa are such that the preconditions underlying the justice model is violated. The model should, on methodological grounds, be regarded as a valid normative model for South Africa.

## Is the Consociational Model Valid for South Africa?

My recommendation of a consociational form of government for South Africa is based on the argument that it is by far the best solution for the problems of this country ... and on two further firm convictions: (1) the theory of consociational democracy is a basically valid empirical theory; and (2) South

Africa satisfies the criteria for its application as a normative theory. (Lijphart, 1985: 83)

Are there reasons to doubt Lijphart's firmly held convictions? Is the consociational model empirically valid? And is it applicable to South Africa?

## The Empirical Validity of the Consociational Model

The general claim of consociational theory is that in plural societies consociationalism will always stand a better chance in securing democratic stability than majoritarian democracy (Lijphart, 1977: 106; 1985: 86). The realistic choice for fragmented societies is, as repeatedly argued by Lijphart, not between consociational and majoritarian democracy, but between consociational democracy and no democracy at all. While homogeneity is a sufficient condition for democratic stability, and a necessary condition for majoritarian democracy, even plural societies can develop into stable democracies if they adopt consociational institutions, facilitating coalescent elite behaviour.

These claims have given rise to ample and diverse criticisms. The proposition that consociational democracy will yield peace and durable democracy, is challenged — as is the inverse proposition that majoritarianism in plural societies will result in violence and democratic collapse. It is also argued that, rather than being a response to the problems of plural societies, consociationalism cause segmented cleavages (Sartori, 1994: 72). And the conditions under which consociationalism is favourable, are subject to considerable controversy. The criticism will be reviewed in the following sections, and the objective is to consider the validity of Lijphart's general claim.

Does consociational democracy increase the probability of democratic stability in plural societies? In order to test Lijphart's claims reliable and valid measurements for the relevant variables must be found. The universe for which the theory is supposed to be valid, that is, plural or fragmented societies, must be isolated, as must the mechanism supposedly causing the desired outcome, that is, the model of consociational democracy. A way to measure democratic stability must also be found in order to determine the success or failure of the model. In addition, the background conditions favourable to the workings of consociational democracy should be explicated in a way that makes it possible to measure them and determine their relative strength.

Much energy has been devoted to defining the variables, but precise measurement has proven difficult. As Lijphart himself notes, strict 'testing' is not possible, any assessment will necessarily be impressionistic (Lijphart, 1985: 88).

## Is there an Orderly Universe of Consociationally Regulated Plural Societies?

The extent to which a society is *plural* or fragmented, is determined according to several criteria: whether the segments can be clearly identified and their size exactly determined; whether boundaries between political, social and economic organisations coincide with segmental cleavages; and the stability of electoral support for segmental parties (Lijphart, 1985: 87).

Lijphart is criticised for failing to distinguish sufficiently between diversity and fragmentation (Steiner, 1986: 212; Sartori, 1994: 71). Diversity is a necessary, but not sufficient condition for fragmentation. The fact that religious, ethnic, racial or linguistic diversity exists does not necessarily imply a plural society. Switzerland should, for example, be regarded as a case of linguistic diversity rather than fragmentation since political cleavages and linguistic lines do not coincide (Steiner, 1986; Barry, 1975b). That a society is multi-linguistic or multi-ethnic is not a sufficient condition for it being plural in the sense presupposed by the consociational model. There must also be conflict between the ethnic or linguistically defined groups. This criticism is often raised against applying the consociational model in South Africa.

Whether the decision-making practices in the countries used as examples of consociationalism, in fact do correspond with the model, is disputed (Barry, 1975a; Steiner, 1974; Steiner and Obler, 1977). Likewise, there is disagreement as to whether the societies in question are in fact plural in the sense presupposed by consociational theory. Halpern (1986) has put this strongly. She holds that every case that can be located within the universe of plural societies successfully regulated by consociationalism may be contested (Stokke, 1991: 7).

Assuming that precise criteria could be found to determine whether a society is plural in the relevant sense, will consociationalism under such conditions yield civil peace and maintain democracy? The various elements of consociational democracy are thoroughly discussed in Chapter 5. Here it suffices to repeat the key characteristics of consociational decision-making: proportionality, grand coalition governments, minority veto and segmental autonomy.

Critique against the likelihood of achieving democratic stability though these measures centres on the following. In grand-coalition governments decision-making is slow, and it is further hampered by minority vetoes, potentially precluding decisions altogether. This 'massacre of political power', and consequent inability to reach decisions, may lead to stagnation and instability. Furthermore it is argued that proportionality plays down the role of individual merit and capability, thus reducing political and administrative efficiency. Consociational democracy is also criticised for being too expensive since segmental autonomy requires multiplication of governmental and administrative units (Sartori, 1994; van den Berghe, 1981; Venter, 1983).

Lijphart responds to this criticism by arguing that quick decisions are not necessarily good decisions. To illustrate this claim he compares economic development in consociational European countries such as Austria and Switzerland, with majoritarian Britain. Furthermore, he argues that the minor efficiency losses inflicted by proportionality and segmental autonomy, is of no significance for democratic stability, and far outweighed by the positive aspects of these measures (Lijphart, 1985: 99–100).

Another common criticism is that consociation creates rather than resolves problems of pluralism (Nagata, 1979: 506). Daalder (1974) argues for example that the 'Great Pacification' in the Netherlands in 1917 was the prelude to the Dutch 'verzuiling' rather than a response to it. Lijphart — acknowledging that consociationalism, at least initially, may strengthen segmentation — denies the relevance of this criticism. The aim of consociationalism is not to 'cure' fragmentation. Instead the segments of society are used as constructive elements of stable democracy (Lijphart, 1977: 42; 1986: 106).

*Democratic stability* is defined by Lijphart as 'the maintenance of civil peace and a democratic system of government' (Lijphart, 1985: 87). And 'democratic system of government' is defined according to Dahl's concept of 'polyarchy', as a political system where governmental positions are open to competition between all individuals and groups, with an inclusive level of political participation and where civil and political rights are guaranteed (Dahl, 1971).

With regard to Lijphart's primary cases there is general agreement about the stability of Austria, the Netherlands, Switzerland, and — at least until recently — Belgium.[4] There is, however, disagreement as to whether these countries are in fact consociational — or democratic. As will be discussed in Chapter 7, doubts are expressed as to whether the consociational model satisfies the conditions of democratic government, or rather should be considered as examples of non-democratic government by elite cartel.

Even scholars considering the countries to be both plural, democratic, and consociational, have questioned the causal relationship between the factors. Stability has been ascribed to other factors: to the prevailing pattern of political strength, forcing the political elites to collaborate (Beyme, 1985, cited in Stokke, 1991: 10); and to the level of post World War II prosperity (Steiner and Obler, 1977; Barry, 1975a). The direction of the causal relationship is challenged (Boynton and Kwon, 1978; Van Schendlen, 1983, 1984; Venter, 1983). Does consociationalism produce democratic stability or is stability rather the cause of, and a precondition for, consociationalism? And, finally, doubts are expressed as to whether power-sharing measures are necessary in plural societies (Barry, 1975b; Sartori, 1994): Cannot even majoritarian systems produce democratic stability if all parties behave with moderation and tolerance? While Lijphart rejects this criticism as naive, Barry's point appears to be supported by Eriksen's analysis of Mauritius. In Mauritius a successful multi-cultural compromise has proved durable, in spite of a political system inspired by the Westminster model, including a 'first-past-the-post' electoral system resulting in the numerically dominant group, the hindus, ruling permanently (Eriksen, 1992: 227).

Other causes of criticism are the cases of Lebanon and Cyprus, where consociational experiments ended in civil war. Lijphart claims that the Lebanese case is one of external conflict projected on internal divisions, rather than the result of an inadequate political system (Lijphart, 1985: 92). Cyprus he admits to be a consociational failure, but argues that this was not due to consociationalism, but in spite of it. While conditions in Cyprus were extremely unfavourable, the general argument holds; if it is ever to achieve democratic stability this will have to be attained through consociation. Lijphart, while maintaining that his theory is the superior choice for plural societies, underscores that consociationalism does not necessarily guarantee peace and democracy (Lijphart, 1985: 89). What he does hold is that it is better suited than majoritarian models.

Despite ample criticism it does not seem possible to write off consociational democracy as an empirical model explaining the stability of plural societies. The applicability of consociationalism as a normative model is, however, a different issue.

Lijphart, when boldly claiming that there is no harm in trying consociation, since no other form of democracy will work anyway, fails to consider the fact that a consociational failure may leave the country considerably worse off than before. Consociationalism, as admitted by Lijphart, is likely to initially deepen societal cleavages and tension. This may not be a problem if consociationalism succeeds in utilising the segments constructively to build democratic stability, but it may be fatal if the attempt fails. Failure to take this sufficiently into consideration limits the utility of the 'solution'. An assessment of the extent to which conditions in South Africa are favourable to consociation is thus of great relevance.

## Is the Consociational Model Applicable to South Africa?

Are South African conditions such that the consociational model, according to its own criteria, is applicable? Lijphart himself gives the following assessment of favourable and unfavourable conditions in South Africa compared with five other consociational countries.

**Table 6.1  Favourable and unfavourable conditions for consociational democracy in South Africa, Belgium, Cyprus, Lebanon, Malaysia and Switzerland**

| Condition | South Africa | Belgium | Cyprus | Lebanon | Malaysia | Switzerl. |
|---|---|---|---|---|---|---|
| 1. No majority segment | ++ | - | -- | ++ | - | - |
| 2. Segments of equal size | + | + | -- | + | - | -- |
| 3. Small number of segments | - | 0 | 0 | - | ++ | ++ |
| 4. Small population size | + | ++ | 0 | ++ | ++ | ++ |
| 5. External threats | 0 | 0 | -- | -- | 0 | 0 |
| 6. Overarching loyalties | + | 0 | - | 0 | 0 | ++ |
| 7. Socioeconomic equality | -- | - | - | - | -- | + |
| 8. Geogr. concentr. of segm. | - | - | + | - | - | ++ |
| 9. Traditions of accommodation | 0 | + | 0 | ++ | + | ++ |
| Total score | +1 | +1 | -7 | +2 | 0 | +8 |

A five point scale is used as follows:
 ++ Very favourable; + Favourable; 0 Neutral; - Unfavourable;  -- Very unfavourable
Source: Lijphart, 1985: 120.

## (1) No Majority Segment

That no segment comprises a majority of the population is, according to Lijphart, the most important condition. He holds this to be a likely development in South Africa, and estimates that the two largest segments each will contain about one fifth of the population — but this presupposes that segments form according to ethnic lines.

From previous chapters it follows that there are considerable disagreement on the importance on ethnicity in South Africa, and also on the likelihood of splits within the African community. In the light of this, Lijphart's confidence is rather surprising. The impact of apartheid on the ethnic question, although not completely neglected, seems under-estimated.

The 1994 elections under Lijphart's recommended electoral system (party list PR) produced an overwhelming 62 per cent majority for the ANC. And the experiences of the local government elections, two years down the line, do not indicate significant loss of voter support, nor are there signs of splits in the party along ethnic lines.

Although it is still too early to determine the long-term political influence of ethnicity, the first two years of democracy (under a dispensation with strong consociational traits) seem to weaken Lijphart's hypotheses regarding segment formation.

## (2) Equally Sized Segments

Lijphart also assumes that the segments will be roughly equal in size, thus facilitating negotiation among segmental leaders. But, again, this depends on the outcome of the process of segment formation, and again, the developments so far seem to have weakened Lijphart's argument.

## (3) Number of Segments

The optimal number of segments is, according to Lijphart, between three and five. Bargaining becomes difficult as the number of segments increases, while a twofold division almost inevitably results in a majority and a minority, and direct confrontation. Lijphart assumes the number of segments in South Africa to be around 14 (Lijphart, 1985: 36).[5] This, although a large number, is not considered unmanageable.

Other scholars have considered a division into three 'cultural heritage groups'; Afrikaner, English and African, a more likely development in South Africa (Adam, 1983). Although this, when viewed in isolation, leaves us with a more manageable number of segments, the first (and more important) condition of 'no majority' is undermined.

This prediction is more in line with the voting patterns so far. The ANC draws support from a majority of voters in all African language groups, and also in the 'coloured' population. The National Party draws support from a majority of voters in all segments of the white population, and among all groups of Afrikaans-speakers, including the coloured population of the Western Cape, while their support in the African population is very limited. The small Democratic Party is supported almost exclusively by white English speakers. The more explicitly ethnically based parties, the Inkatha Freedom Party, the Freedom Front and the Conservative Party, draw support from only a minority within their own segment (Mattes 1995).

## (4) Population Size

While South Africa's 1996 population of an estimated 37.9 million[6] is larger than the optimal size for consociational democracy, Lijphart regarded the country's size as a positive factor. The reasons why small size is seen as favourable is that in smaller countries political leaders are likely to know each other personally, the decision-making process is less complex, and the foreign policy burden is lighter. South Africa's strategic location and important role in the region, adds, however, to the foreign policy burden.

## (5) External Threats

External threats may strenghten internal unity, but only if they are perceived as a common danger by all groups. Under apartheid the international stance towards South Africa was interpreted differently by the regime and the opposition. One party's friend is the other's enemy. This has been regarded as an unfavourable condition to consociation (Adam and Giliomee, 1979; Schlemmer, 1978). Lijphart — not commenting on the effect of this situation for the establishment of consociationalism — argues that the international threat will disappear as soon as a consociational solution is found, and that this is of little significance to the maintenance of the system. Developments since the start of the democratic transition seem to support this assumption.

## (6) Overarching Loyalties

A sense of belonging together furthers consociation. Barry, warning against applying the consociational model as a normative model to divided countries, underscores this point. Consociationalism is particularly unsuitable for countries plagued by ethnic conflict because this involves not only questions concerning how the country is to be run, but whether it should be a country at all (Barry, 1975b: 503).

While this warning seems appropriate to countries in Eastern Europe and the previous Soviet Union, for example, where the upsurge of ethnic sentiments has lead to demands for self-determination, there is little indicating a similar development in South Africa. Although an 'overarching sense of belonging together' hardly exists, there is a strong commitment to the territorial unity and identity of the South African state. Although the IFP's federalist policy proposals come close to demands for self-determination for KwaZulu-Natal, and there are Afrikaner nationalists supporting the idea of a separate white *Volksstaat*, most separatist rhetoric can be seen as a strategy for increased autonomy. True separatists comprise a very small segment of the South African population.

## (7) Socioeconomic Equality

Where there are large socioeconomic differences among the segments, consociation is difficult because the poorer segments are likely to feel discriminated against, and the more prosperous, threatened. Socioeconomic equality is therefore, in Lijphart's own assessment, an important favourable condition. This condition is clearly not favourable in South Africa.

The failure to address class conflict and economic inequality is a major criticism voiced against consociationalism in the South African context (Nolutshungu, 1982; Southall, 1983; Frankel, 1980).

> (It is) not only misleading, from the point of view of social science, but cruel from the point of view of those affected, to propose (consociationalism) as a recipe for conflict management in societies where ethnic tension is founded on injustice. (Zolberg, 1977: 142)

Lijphart's response to this criticism is that consociational countries have not performed any worse than their non-consociational neighbours with regard to socioeconomic reforms or reduction of inequality (Lijphart, 1985: 98).[7] Inequality, even in the magnitude found in South Africa, is not regarded an insuperable obstacle to consociationalism. Contrary to 'most of the other factors, it is not necessarily a static condition, and it can be improved by deliberate political action, including preferential treatment for the disadvantaged segments' (Lijphart, 1985: 125). Redistribution, according to Lijphart, may be accomplished in a consociational system — given sufficient economic growth, a condition which he is confident will be satisfied in South Africa (Lijphart, 1985: 125). His assessment of South Africa as a 'basically wealthy country', which, when its international respectability is regained, will draw sufficient new investments to stimulate the economic growth necessary to facilitate substantial redistribution, appears to be far too optimistic in the light of what is now known about the state of the South African economy and the international economic situation (Deng and Tjønneland, 1996).

## (8) Geographical Concentration of Segments

Geographical concentration of segments is regarded by Lijphart as a favourable factor, primarily because it allows for territorial federalism to be used as an effective consociational measure.[8] While the segments in South Africa have certain areas of relative concentration, the ethnic groups live relatively interspersed in the country as a whole.

## (9) Traditions of Accommodation

Is the consociation model a set of 'Western' ideas advanced by a group of western scholars and unsuitable for non-Western societies? This has been argued (Nolutshungu, 1982: 26), but there are also counter-arguments. There are examples of consociational political systems developing independently in non-Western countries such as Lebanon and Malaysia, non-Western scholars advanced similar ideas prior to Lijphart (Lewis, 1965; Ake, 1967). And non-Western leaders have stated that 'majority rule violates native traditions of trying to arrive at consensus through lengthy deliberations — traditions that closely fit the consociational idea' (Lijphart, 1985: 97).

What about traditions of accommodation in South Africa? Several scholars have commented upon traditions of consensual decision-making in the African community, and also in the tradition and ideology of the ANC (Schlemmer, 1978; Sparks, 1990). But there is also the long history of white domination and black exclusion, and a long tradition of majoritarian, Westminster style government in the white community. Lijphart regards this condition to be neither favourable nor unfavourable in South Africa.

The above conditions are held by Lijphart to be merely favourable, not decisive for successful consociation, 'the really crucial factor is the commitment and skill of the political leaders' (Lijphart, 1985: 127).

## The Role of the Elites

It is a recognised problem that, particularly in divided societies, it may be easier to retain mass support if no compromise with the opposition is attempted. This counteracts incentives for political leaders to compromise. Leaders may have grave problems maintaining both inter-segmental cooperation and intra-segmental support (Adam, 1983c). Even where leaders are committed to compromise, consociational democracy may break down as a result of disaffection of the rank and file of each community with its own established elite. Lijphart admits that if segmental leaders are unable or unwilling to manage the inherently difficult inter- and intra-segmental balancing act, consociationalism will not work (Lijphart, 1985: 100). But he seems to overemphasise the importance of the leaders' will, and, correspondingly, underestimates the strain under which leaders operate.

Even if there were willingness on part of the elites — would this be sufficient for successful consociation? Do conditions in South Africa facilitate the form of elite-cooperation required for the consociational model to operate? The initial phases of negotiations between the NP government and the ANC, seemed to correlate with a growth in the support of the Conservative Party (CP), capturing sections of the traditional NP constituency.[9] There were also indications of growing discontent on the grass-root level in the ANC. This was, however, not reflected in voter support. The 1994 election was a show of strength for both the ANC and the NP. The CP, on the other hand, who boycotted the 1994 elections and remained outside parliamentary politics, seem to have been all but wiped out, judging from their results in local government elections. The PAC, to the left of the ANC is also totally marginalised. Willingness to cooperate and compromise does not at present seem to be a liability for political parties in South Africa.[10]

The fact that South Africa for decades has been a thoroughly politicised society is also a potential problem for consociation style politics. Since politics are based on compromise between autonomous elites, a relatively depoliticised electorate is advantageous. In South Africa 'rolling mass action' has been a feature of political life for decades, and forms an important part of the organisational culture, particularly in the ANC, where it is also coupled with the ideology of participatory democracy. This could pose problems for the workings of the consociational model. The position of elites in the respective organisations are, however, strengthened by certain clientelist features (traditionally important particularly in the IFP and the NP), and organisational capabilities (particularly in the NP and the ANC).

Whether the leadership of current — or future — conflict groups/parties would have sufficient autonomy to enable conflict-regulation according to the consociational model is difficult to know, but so far it has been possible for the elite to walk a considerable distance without stirring up rebellion at grass-roots level.

Lijphart's ninth favourable condition, the positive impact of traditions of accommodation, reflects an assumption explicitly underscored by Nordlinger (1972): the willingness and ability of the elite to cooperate is largely a product of learning. Mutual confidence among elites are developed gradually through experience (Nordlinger, 1972).

Prior to the democratic transition, the conditions for mutual confidence seemed poor indeed, due to both the long tradition of white domination and repression, third force campaigns and violence between various black groups, continuing far beyond the point when such activities allegedly had ended and negotiations had begun. This served to undermine trust and confidence, and was all but conducive to elite cooperation.

Looking at the transition period and the two years of government of national unity, there are, however, some grounds for optimism. There has been a willingness to cooperate that is rare among long-standing enemies. Through this process, experience in cooperation, and a certain amount of mutual trust, has been built up in broad sections of the parties' leadership.

While the past few years have seen South African elites both able and willing to cooperate, doubts are often expressed as to whether this will last. The personality and authority of President Mandela, and his persistent focus on reconciliation is cited as a decisive factor. When he steps back in 1999, changes in leadership style might affect relations between the parties.

With regard to the conditions pertaining to the elite for consociation to be possible — an ability and willingness to cooperate, and a certain autonomy *vis-à-vis* their respective electorates — these seem to be reasonably positive in South Africa. But that the ability to cooperate and even compromise, is present, does not mean that there is a willingness to enter into formal power-sharing arrangements — or even that the material basis for such arrangements is present.

Contrary to what Lijphart assumes will be the case — the party system in South Africa has (at least so far) not followed predominantly along ethnic lines. And, even more important, a majority party has emerged. Whether this is seen as a sign of voting on the basis of racial identity or on the basis of class, it is clearly not a favourable basis for consociation. Power-sharing is very difficult where there is a clear majority party or segment.

## Restating the Argument

Are the models valid generalisations? Is the justice model a valid generalisation applicable to South Africa? Rawls specifies that his theory (and by implication Sachs' model) is developed for societies in which the moral sentiments are characterised by liberal individualism — where there is an overlapping consensus on a conception of persons as morally free and equal. Whether this can be said to be the case in South Africa was questioned, and tentatively answered in the affirmative.

In addition, Rawls' material condition was considered, concluding that South Africa may reasonably be regarded as a society characterised by 'moderate scarcity', and thus within the range wherein the theory is considered valid. Although no definite answers are available, this inquiry gave no basis on which to dismiss the justice model as a valid normative model for South Africa.

What about the consociational model? Should it be considered as a basically valid empirical theory, explaining democratic stability in plural societies? Is it a valid generalisation, and a normative model applicable to all plural societies, including South Africa?

In spite of plentiful critique over the three decades the model has been advocated — and disputed — there are no obvious answers. Part of the critique is convincingly refuted by Lijphart and other consociational theorists, some of it has lead to revisions of the theory, while some criticisms are difficult to dismiss. But none of these is a knock-down argument.

A major objection against applying the consociational model to South Africa is that, contrary to Lijphart's assumptions on segment number and size, a clear majority party has emerged, and, as it now looks, this situation is likely to persist for the foreseeable future. Another major obstacle to consociation is the vast socioeconomic inequalities in South African society, which run along party lines. The possibility of achieving substantial redistribution in a consociational South Africa will be further discussed in Chapter 8, as will the likelihood of democratic stability without redistribution. At this point it is sufficient to note that socioeconomic inequality, particularly between segments, constitutes a major problem for consociationalism even according to Lijphart's own theory. On balance, Lijphart estimates the conditions for consociationalism in South Africa to be more favourable than I find grounds to support. His overall assessment does not pay respect to the different weights of the various conditions, and their combined effects.

All things considered, I do not find reason to conclude that consociationalism should be dismissed as an empirically valid theory on the basis of methodological inadequacy. I do have serious doubts about whether the conditions in South Africa are such that the model is applicable.

The relevance of consociationalism hinges fundamentally on the accuracy of the diagnosis. The most fundamental problem concerns the general interpretation of South Africa as a basically plural and ethnically divided society. Differences in perception of reality in part due to methodological differences.[11] As previously noted, the justice model is fundamentally individualistic while consociational models assume that in severely divided societies the relative position of groups is of greater importance to group members than their position as individuals.

That ethnicity will take precedence over other cleavages in South Africa, such as class, or the black/white divide, is absolutely crucial for the consociational model to be applicable. And, as will be clear from previous discussions, this has so far not materialised. On the other hand, the 'new South Africa' is young and there is still disagreement on the significance of ethnicity for South African politics, now and in the future.

## Notes

1.   This is a difficult point in Rawls' theory. Policies and institutions sacrificing the liberty of current members of society for (hopes of) greater social welfare for future generations, are here justified, violating the fundamental premise that 'each person possesses an inviolability founded on justice that even the welfare of society as a whole cannot override' (Rawls, 1971: 3).

This 'exemption' jeopardises the priority of the first principle altogether. It is difficult to see why rational parties in the original position would choose the lexical ordering, requiring a total priority of the first principle, if it is possible (as assumed by Rawls) to get considerable increases in the level of welfare by sacrificing certain political rights — which in any case only open for marginal influence on political decisions (Rawls, 1971: 63).

Barry (1973) claims that Rawls' reasoning at this point is flawed, but that he arrives at the correct conclusion: (at least) over a certain level of economic development it is not rational to give up civil and political rights in order to promote economic growth. The premise that such a trade-off is possible does not hold. Civil and political rights are preconditions for economic growth, rather than obstacles. Instead of operating with a strict lexical ordering, limiting the range of his theory to societies of a certain level of economic development, it suffices with a 'conditional lexical priority' — in the cases where a liberty/development trade-off is at all possible (which is by no means certain at any level of development) it would be at a level of well-being where Rawls begins.

2.　There are, however, examples of authoritarian industrialised countries with redistribution and a high level of growth (e.g. South Korea and Taiwan).

3.　Nor is there agreement on the extent to which this is the case in western liberal democracies, but this is left aside for now.

4.　In recent years the level of political tension in Belgium has been rising to a point where the unity of the state is under siege.

5.　See Table 2.1.

6.　Source: Central Statistical Service 1997, Census 1996, Preliminary estimates. The results of the census indicate that the South African population is around 10 per cent lover than previously estimated.

7.　But none of the four European countries constituting the basis of Lijphart's theory, has ever been anywhere close to the South African situation in terms of inequality. In Malaysia, the consociational country most closely resembling South Africa in this respect, there has been some reduction in absolute poverty among the Malays but '(i)nequality in terms of income as well as assets remains large in Malaysia compared to other developing countries in the region and beyond ... there are very marked differences between ethnic groups which today, as in 1969, are matters of great concern' (Faaland, *et al.* 1990: 214).

8.　Other consociational theorists regard this as less favourable, fearing that geographically concentrated segments may demand secession and thus ultimately cause civil war (see Section 5.2.2).

9.　This trend has turned somewhat after the referendum in March 1992.

10.　Despite regular critiques of diminishing grass-root contact in the ANC, they seem to have a firm grasp on their constituency. For the NP, for whom compromise increasingly became a trade-mark, the costs seem somewhat higher; they have lost ground among their traditional core voters (the mantle of Afrikaner Nationalism is now carried by the Freedom Front). They have made up by drawing increasing support from other white groups and coloured Afrikaans-speakers, but they struggle to get beyond this numerically limited, and internally diverse, support base.

11.　It is, however, obviously also a matter of differences in political outlook.

# 7 Normative Acceptability

The objective of this chapter is to consider the normative acceptability of the constitutional models.

We have seen that the justice model and the consociational model diverge on a number of dimensions, and how this is in part a result of methodological differences and rivalling interpretations of the conflict structure of South African society. We have also seen how each of the positions corresponds with philosophical theories and traditions, adding a normative foundation and coherence. The justice model may be seen as Rawls' theory of justice applied to South Africa, while communitarian philosophy justifies the consociational approach.

In this chapter the models are considered in relation to external normative standards. Do they satisfy the criteria set by democracy and human rights norms?

The question of whether there are external normative standards that constitutions should meet is in itself controversial. Value-pluralism is overwhelming, both in the world at large and internally in most countries. No norms are universal in the sense of being self-evident, universally agreed to, or incontestably justified by philosophical first principles. But if the universality of the standards cannot be ascertained, why bother about normative standards at all?

As reflected throughout the thesis, I believe that the link between normative acceptability, the legitimacy of the constitution and the conflict-regulating potential of the constitutional structure, is significant. A constitution's normative acceptability — in the sense that the fundamental norms of the constitution correspond with moral sentiments in society — is of major importance for the ability of the constitution to establish itself and gain authority, and thus for its ability to serve as a conflict regulating instrument. This motivates the analysis in this chapter, but which standards are to be employed? To whom must the constitutional structure be acceptable?

The choice of *democracy* and *human rights* as normative standards for the South African constitution is hardly surprising. The 'ideological time' is massively pro these ideals, at least at the level of rhetoric. And the choice of normative standards in this analysis is partly a consequence of their current ideological hegemony. Not that this renders them true, but as long as no 'gold standard' for truth is available as far as norms and values are concerned, the norms upon which there seem to be a general consensus, internationally as well as in South Africa itself, are the best candidates.

Both models — and their political counterparts — also claim to be democratic and in accordance with human rights norms (Lijphart, 1985: 109, Sachs, 1990: 196). That they claim these qualities for themselves is obviously not independent of the ideological hegemony of these ideals, but for the purposes of this analysis it constitutes an independent reason for evaluating the proposals in light of them. It becomes a question of whether the models measure up to their own standards.

While democracy and human rights norms seem, at a superficial level, to enjoy almost universal acceptance, the consensus stops at the level of semantics. Which conception of democracy is to be employed when assessing the models? Whose interpretation of basic human rights is to be counted as valid? These are crucial questions.

To define a single normative standard necessarily implies a bias. The elasticity of the concepts, and the controversies surrounding them, preclude clear-cut conclusions as to whether or not the constitutional models in question 'measure up to the standard'. Rather, different elements and aspects of *democracy* and *human rights* have to be separated, and the constitutional models seen in the light of each element. This chapter is thus as much a discussion of the concepts as an assessment of the constitutional models. The tasks cannot be separated if each constitutional model is to be given a 'fair trial'.

## Democracy Defined — and Redefined

*Democracy* is the subject of a vast body of literature. Unfortunately, there is no guarantee that clarity will increase with the number of conceptual clarifications. Democracy — the Greek term translating into 'government by the people' — is one of the foremost words of honour in the political vocabulary, and consequently it has an array of interpretations. This discussion is no quest for 'real' democracy. The aim is primarily to clarify the ideals of democracy to which each of the constitutional models adhere. For the sake of a balanced discussion, the initial stance should be as open as possible, so as not to exclude any relevant definition. A simple definition of standards or criteria would render at least one of the models irrelevant.

In the following paragraphs 'democracy' will be addressed from different angles, delineating the most important dimensions of the concept, and clarifying the views implicit in the two models in relation to each of them.

## Democracy and Majority Rule

Common sense definitions of democracy tend to identify 'majority rule' as the essence of democracy. When there is disagreement, the most 'natural' way to resolve questions is to go along with what the majority wants. This definition is echoed in much of the literature on democracy: 'Democracy I shall understand as a simple majority rule, based on the principle "One person one vote"' (Elster, 1988: 1). And majority rule is central to the idea of democracy that has been, and largely still is, prevailing in South Africa's black opposition (Horowitz, 1991: 91–100).

But the principle of 'majority rule' is not as simple as it might seem. Public choice theory has brought out internal problems inherent in majoritarianism, hindering accurate aggregation of preferences. Preferences are likely to be distorted through cycling problems, strategic and manipulative behaviour as well as sheer chance (Offe, 1985; Sen, 1970). In addition there are transaction cost barriers to the exercise of political influence, preventing numbers and intensities of preferences from being accurately reflected in legislative outcomes (Sunstein, 1988: 335).

The attraction of the principle of majority rule lies in the claim that the majority 'naturally' is entitled to act for the whole (Barry, 1979: 172). Is this necessarily true? Is permanent exclusion of minorities compatible with democracy? Is a majoritarian decision democratic even if the vital interests of (ethnic) minorities, are overrun? Should a minority, in the name of democracy, be expected to acquiesce in the majority's trampling on its vital interests? When confronted with such implications, few democrats sustain the claim that democracy is unrestrained majority rule. Democracy is also associated with safeguarding certain interests and rights for all citizens.

Despite the shortcomings of pure majoritarianism, and the contra-intuitive consequences which may be derived from it — at the level of common sense it does not seem possible to detach democracy from the concept of majority rule. How do our two models come out according to this common sense definition of democracy?

It seems to fit the justice model rather well. Majority rule is a central concern of Albie Sachs: a democratic South Africa is one in which the majority, previously deprived of political power as well as resources and opportunities, may acquire political positions and power, and use this to change society in accordance with their needs and interests. Still, majority rule is by no means unrestrained. Although relying on majoritarian decision-making procedures, majoritarianism does not pertain to the electoral system. And democracy is restrained by the extensive Bill of Rights, safeguarding the individual rights of all citizens.

What about the consociational model? If democracy is taken to be synonymous with 'majority rule' the consociational model clearly does not qualify as democratic. The essence of this model is precisely to avoid ending up with what the majority wants. If the additional aspect — protection of the vital interests of all — is included, the model fares better. No group needs to fear that their vital interests will be invaded: all groups are given a share in political power, and a right to veto decisions. This model is undoubtedly further removed from the common sense notion of democracy, but does this necessarily make it less democratic? The proponents of consociationalism argue that it is not.

Consociationalists reject the premise that the majority is necessarily entitled to act for the whole, and hold the essence of democracy to be *to give all significant groups/interests in society a genuine opportunity to influence decision-making*. Or, in the words of Robert A. Dahl, democracy is seen to be 'the quality of being completely or almost completely responsive to all its citizens' (Dahl, 1971: 2).

The principle of majority rule may be compatible with this conception of democracy — in homogeneous societies where the composition of the majority shifts, or at least may be expected to shift, such that even those currently in minority imagine themselves as part of a future majority. This is, however, the exception rather than the rule. In plural societies majority rule is thoroughly undemocratic, according to consociational theory. Under such circumstances the principle of majority rule spells majority dictatorship, awarding some group(s) power infinitely, while sentencing others to minority status for life — without hopes of political influence.

According to consociational theory majoritarianism is merely one form of democracy, acceptable only in 'easy cases', that is, homogeneous societies. To write off plural societies as unfit for democracy, because majoritarianism cannot work, is to confuse the inadequacy of a particular map for the terrain in question, with the possibility of finding a suitable map at all. Deeply divided societies expose the shortcomings of majoritarianism, not of democracy. Democracy is still possible, but it requires mechanisms giving all groups an effective say in government — a consociational constitutional structure.

So far the models are taken at face value, and matched with democracy in the common sense meaning of the term. This is important. The perceived democratic qualities of a system are of utmost importance for its legitimacy. However, an examination of more theoretical distinctions clarifies each model's conception of democracy.

## Procedural and Material Definitions of Democracy

> Political theories can be 'democratic' in two different, although related, senses. Democratic theories in the narrower (and more traditional) sense speak to the question, what is the best form of government? Those in the broader sense ask, instead, what is the best society? (Beitz, 1989: ix)

An important distinction in definitions of democracy runs between those defining it solely by criteria applying to the procedures for decision-making, and those holding that in a truly democratic political system it is not enough that the decision-making procedures satisfy certain criteria, that the content of the outcome should also be taken into account. The former category may be labelled formal or procedural democracy, the latter material or substantial democracy.

Democracy, understood in procedural terms, may be defined as an institutional arrangement for reaching political decisions where individuals are empowered to rule after having competed for popular votes (Schumpeter, 1940), or as 'a method of determining the content of laws (and other legally binding decisions) such that the preferences of the citizens have some formal connection with the outcome in which each counts equally' (Barry, 1979: 156).

Even this procedural definition of democracy requires that certain substantial criteria are satisfied. Freedom of communication and organisation is necessary in order for political preferences to form and be aggregated. For the system to function and endure, civil liberties must be guaranteed, along with the system of contract and a principle of representation, guaranteeing all citizens basic political rights. Although these criteria are substantial they are directly related to the decision-making procedures themselves: the electoral institution, decision-making procedures in elected bodies, and relationships between the elected bodies and the executive. As long as the procedure is correct, the outcome is to be taken as authoritative, no criteria apply as to its content.

The relevance of procedural criteria to political democracy is seldom denied. However, it is commonly argued that the procedural definition is too limited. In addition to formal, institutional features, certain constraints should apply to the content of the outcome of the political process. These additional criteria for 'material democracy' range from substantive equality, concerns for the general welfare, respect for human rights, to personal liberty and the rule of law. The argument for including external, material criteria when assessing the democratic qualities of a political system is that only when (one or more of) these are satisfied do the formal institutions of democracy become significant — otherwise they merely provide unjust regimes with a democratic guise.

Those defending procedural democracy argue that it is superior to substantial democracy precisely because of its minimal and formal character. It is limited enough to be supported by a majority of citizens, and thus endure, while broad enough to secure a sufficient political basis from which organised groups and individuals can fight for their economic and social interests. This defence for a formal/procedural democracy is voiced by, among others, Agnes Heller (Rakner, 1992: 24–25). It is also the general idea of John Rawls' delimitation of the constitutional domain (see Chapter 4).

How do our two constitutional models place themselves on this dimension?

If democracy is understood as a political system ensuring equal opportunity of political influence for all significant groups, the consociational model specifies a decision-making procedure whereby this ideal may be achieved in deeply divided societies. Although the consociational model may be said to include a material concern for protection of minority rights, this is attended to through the design of the procedures themselves (PR electoral system, proportional executive, decisions by consensus, decentralisation). Consociational models do not rely on external standards judging the content of the outcome of the decision-making process.

Procedural criteria also figure prominently within the justice model. To argue that Sachs' proposal — with its comprehensive Bill of Rights, including social and economic rights, and extensive judicial review of legislation — is purely procedural, would be, however, to render the distinction completely useless. The very heart of the justice model is the creation and functioning of a Bill of Rights, that is, of an external standard that legislation and policies are required to meet. Criteria apply not only to the decision-making process itself, but also to the content of its outcome. Laws and policies must respect civil, political and cultural rights of citizens, be directed towards redistribution, and take environmental concerns into consideration.

On the other hand, even procedural democracy requires that laws and policies respect certain substantial criteria in order for the democratic decision-making procedures to function and endure. It is possible to defend the additional criteria included by Sachs in procedural terms — as necessary for democratic decision-making procedures to function according to their intentions under the particular circumstances prevailing in South Africa. Inequality is enormous, and the argument that such a highly unequal distribution of economic resources is detrimental to the effective exercise of democratic political rights, enjoys wide support (Krouse and McPherson, 1988).

We have seen that both the consociational model and the justice model restrain majority rule in the name of democracy: the former through institutionalisation of consensus-orientated procedures of decision-making. The latter, while relying on majoritarian decision-making procedures, checks the content of the outcome against external criteria, formulated in a Bill of Rights. After this clarification of the conceptions of democracy underlying the two models, I will now go on to consider how they fare according to three widely accepted criteria of political democracy.

## Polyarchy

Lijphart claims adherence to 'the clearest and most widely accepted definition' of democracy available, namely Robert A. Dahl's concept of 'polyarchy' (Lijphart, 1985: 87). Dahl defines polyarchy, the closest empirical approximation to the ideal of political democracy, in terms of three basic criteria (Dahl, 1971): (1) competition for all effective positions of government; (2) an inclusive level of political participation; and (3) protection of civil and political liberties.

Are these criteria in fact satisfied in the consociational model? This has been doubted by its critics. And what about the justice model, does it meet the requirements of polyarchy?

## (1) Competition for Political Positions

Democratic elections are the only method for picking out a unique set of rulers, compatible with the idea of the natural equality of all individuals. Another rationale for competition for political positions is to provide links between voter preferences and the content of the political outcome, through making the elected accountable to their electorate. This is institutionalised through elections with regular intervals for a legislative assembly, and a (direct or indirect) link between voter preferences and the executive branch of government. Do the constitutional proposals of Sachs and Lijphart satisfy the criterion of competition for all effective positions of government?

Democratic elections are central to both models. They even seem to agree considerably on the electoral procedures — a proportional electoral system for elections to the legislative assembly being acceptable to both. On closer scrutiny differences emerge. While both models provide elections based on the principle of 'one person one vote' whereby a unique set of leaders is picked out without violating the fundamental equality of all people, the dimension of accountability and direct links between preferences as they are revealed though elections and the outcome of the political process, is somewhat problematic in both models.

Proportional representation systems produces lines of accountability that are less clear, particularly at the level of individual members of parliament, than is the case with constituency based systems.

The link between voter preferences and political decisions is particularly weak in the consociational model where the relationship between the executive and voter preferences is complicated and indirect. With institutionalised grand coalition governments, proportionally elected executives, and decision-making by consensus, it difficult to express dissatisfaction with political decisions through voting.[1]

The justice model favours majoritarian decision-making procedures and a direct link between majority preferences and the executive branch of government. Apparently all is by the book: democratic election of leadership, satisfactory formal links between public preferences and the outcome of political decisions, and generally good accountability. However, one objection may be raised. The outcome of the political process is to be checked against a wide-ranging Bill of Rights. Although the Bill of Rights is envisioned as the outcome of a participatory process and democratically adopted, the process of determining whether legislation is in accordance with it, invariably involves judgement. The major responsibility for this control lies with the courts, ultimately the Constitutional Court. Major political matters are thus settled according to the judgement of officials who are not accountable to the public.[2]

## (2) Inclusive Political Participation

The second criterion of polyarchy is an inclusive level of political participation. The basic requirements are institutionalisation of elections with regular intervals, and the principle of 'one person one vote' within a wide franchise. Neither of the models in question violates these conditions. Both argue in favour of regular elections and universal suffrage. In this formal sense participation is guaranteed in both models.

But is this sufficient? It depends on why participation is seen to be important to democracy. If participation is seen only in functional terms, as an efficient way to select leaders and provide them with a certain amount of legitimacy, participation in the formal sense is all that is needed. If, however, political participation is seen to have intrinsic value, is a way to satisfy an existential human desire (Arendt, 1958), participation in the sense of voting in elections every fourth year, clearly will not do. It does not satisfy the qualitative aspect of participation. That the political system contains opportunities for democratic practice for the majority of citizens may also be a criterion when evaluating its democratic qualities (Pateman, 1970). Consociationalism, as well as most forms of liberal democracy may be criticised for being elitist and neglecting the participatory aspect of democracy.

The justice model, on the other hand, places considerable emphasis on the value of popular participation. Participation is assumed to give better decisions and to increase the legitimacy of legislation and policies, thus enhancing political stability. The justice model recommends various institutions to increase civil society involvement in decision-making. Decentralisation is also favoured as a means to increase participation. While consociationalism favours decentralisation as a method for protecting the segments from undue intrusion, the rationale for decentralisation in the justice model is first and foremost to involve larger sections of the population in decision-making.

The consociational model's heavy reliance on the elite as political actors and the high degree of secrecy it entails, have made critics characterise the model as government by elite cartel.[3] This criticism is refuted by Lijphart who argues that a substantial degree of oligarchy and secrecy is a common and probably unavoidable characteristic of democratic politics everywhere (Lijphart, 1985: 111). He also argues that the extensive decentralisation and devolution of power integral to the model increases participation through multiplying the number of political arenas.

The limited emphasis on participation in consociational models is related to what is regarded as an internal tension between representation of interests and individual participation in plural societies. According to their definition of democracy, it is more important to democracy that all significant (group) interests are effectively represented than to increase the scope for individual participation. A certain level of political participation is a precondition for a representative democracy — and participation in elections should under no circumstances be denied. Above this level, to the extent that the considerations of representation and participation conflict, the latter has to yield. In plural societies, minority interests are effectively represented only in a political system based on consensus politics. Leaders' autonomy *vis-à-vis* their electorate increases their ability to reach compromise. And this autonomy is inversely related to the political activism of the population. Increased participation implies less chance of effective representation of all interests in decision-making.

To sum up this discussion, the relative importance and function of political participation varies between the models. If the criterion of inclusive political participation is interpreted in a limited, formal sense, both models qualify. Both satisfy the 'technical' aspects of selection of a legitimate leadership and representation of interests. Participation may, however, also be seen to be of existential value, and a goal in itself. If democracy is seen to be important mainly due to the opportunities it contains for democratic practice for the majority of citizens, the justice model is clearly the most adequate answer, Consociationalism should be rejected, along with many forms of liberal democracy.

## (3) Protection of Civil and Political Liberties

The third criterion for regarding a political system as a polyarchy is that civil and political rights are protected. The models' capacity for rights-protection and their human-rights compliance will be more thoroughly addressed later in this chapter. The question is therefore only briefly addressed at this stage.

Critique against the models on account of this third criterion is mainly directed against the lack of *effective* political rights. The consociational model is criticised for lack of political rights due to the 'missing link' between citizens' preferences — expressed when they exercise their political rights by voting — and the outcome of politics.

The problematic point of the justice model is the extensive constitutional domain, limiting the domain of politics. A system where 'the dead rule the living' through constitutional pre-commitment limits the domain of the political. By placing so much power in the hands of the judiciary, questions of how this power is to be checked arise. Citizens' possibility for influencing decision-making through the democratic process is limited, and thus too, in a sense, their political rights. If the requirements for altering the constitutional provisions are such as virtually to block constitutional change, this may be considered an important problem.[4] On the other hand, the model opens for a variety of ways in which citizens may influence decision-making — even in the constitutional domain itself.

## Are the Models Polyarchies?

On balance, should the models be regarded as democratic, that is, as polyarchies, according to Dahl's three criteria?

The legitimacy of labelling the consociational model 'democratic' have been questioned. Van den Berghe (1981), Nolutshungu (1982) and Huntington (1981) all write off consociationalism as oligarchy, elite conspiracy and facade democracy, and argue that the model does not measure up to the standard of polyarchy, given by Dahl. Lijphart himself rejects this criticism by referring to Dahl's own classification of countries according to degree of democracy. Of the eight countries in the world that Dahl considers to be most democratic, four are consociational. And all the consociational countries are considered to be polyarchies, save two cases of 'near-polyarchies'[5] (Dahl, 1971, cited Lijphart, 1985: 110, see also Dahl, 1991).

Unlike the consociational model, derived inductively from empirical cases, Sachs' justice model has no direct empirical counterparts which are 'tested' by Dahl. However, there is little reason to doubt that a political system constructed according to the specifications of the justice model would qualify as a polyarchy.

## Are the Models Acceptable in Light of Central Human Rights Norms?

Protection of civil and political rights is a criterion for being regarded as a political democracy or polyarchy. And we have seen that even formal or procedural definitions of democracy contain elements of human rights protection. Certain civil and political liberties are necessary for a democratic system to function. And material definitions of democracy often embrace concerns for social and economic rights as well. We have also seen that both the models under scrutiny are constitutional democracies, safeguarding certain important rights from majoritarian control.

Although constitutional democracy and human rights protection are not synonymous concepts, neither are they completely independent. Regardless of how the concepts are defined there is considerable overlap. It is thus almost a matter of course when empirical studies conclude that human rights are best protected in democratic regimes (Linz, 1992). But all categories of human rights are not equally well protected in constitutional democracies — and all forms of constitutional democracies do not protect human rights equally well.

A Bill of Rights formally protecting all categories of human rights is no guarantee of a flawless human rights record. Human rights protection is both a matter of enacting the rules, of compliance, and of capacity. But even though constitutional protection of rights does not guarantee that the rights will be protected or respected by the state, the formal framework is important. The ways in which power are legitimised and organised, and the relationship between those who govern and those who are governed, are decisive for human-rights respect. In general it is the state that possesses the power to protect rights. The constitutional structure regulates the political process, influences governments' accountability, limits the legitimate use of state power and affects governments' capacity for action as well as their resources. All this in turn influences the extent to which different rights will be protected.

I will not go into lengthy discussions about different conceptions of rights but simply take as my point of departure what is often referred to as 'The International Bill of Human Rights'. This term includes the most central international human rights instruments: the UN Universal Declaration of Human Rights (1948); the International Covenant on Civil and Political Rights (1966); and the International Covenant on Social, Economic and Cultural Rights (1966).[6] This is the crux of the 'international human-rights culture' to which Sachs' refers (Sachs, 1990). This is a yardstick against which the acceptability of a new South African constitution will be measured in the international milieu, and by the internal opposition. But although this may be taken as a relatively uncontested point of departure, the interpretation of the rights and their relative weight is disputable.

## Civil Rights

The central civil liberties — to life, personal liberty and integrity of the person, administration of justice and freedom of movement — seem to be adequately handled in both the constitutional models.[7] The consociational model treats these matters only in passing. Sachs, on the other hand devotes much attention to, for example dilemmas concerning the administration of justice. Questions such as the role of common and customary law within the legal system are relevant, not only to the protection of civil rights, but also with respect to cultural rights and the rights of equality and non-discrimination.

Internationally, and particularly in the UN-system, the interdependence of different categories of rights is increasingly emphasised. The UN Human Rights Committee, interpreting obligations of States under the *International Covenant on Civil and Political Rights*, have for instance 'included the obligation of States to undertake measures to decrease infant mortality into definitions of obligations to safeguard the right to life' (Tomasevski, 1990: 84).

When civil rights, such as the right to life, are interpreted as above, requiring some form of public welfare policies, the observance of these rights by the models is less a matter of course. While the justice model is directed towards safeguarding the right to life in a material sense, involving public obligation to welfare measures, this is not as clearly the case for the consociational model. The incentive structure of consociational governments, as well as the limited capability of the state to provide for general social policies, involving redistribution, detracts from the observance of 'material' rights. However, also a consociational South African government could be capable of undertaking the limited requirements to 'undertake measures to decrease infant mortality'.

## Political Rights

Political rights relate directly to the system of governance and the central right is the right to participation in the political decision-making process. This aspect is thoroughly discussed in the first part of this chapter, concluding that a question-mark remains as to whether the consociational model pays due respect to the political rights of citizens. Although Lijphart argues in favour of universal suffrage and regular elections, there is a very limited possibility for voters to influence the political course: grand coalition governments, decisions by consensus and minority vetoes obfuscate the parties' responsibility for actual decisions as well as for the general political direction. In addition, devolution of power and segmental autonomy removes important issues from the central political arena. In South Africa, where material wealth follows segmental lines, this also limits the possibility of citizens to use their political rights to fight for their economic interests.

The respect for political rights within the justice model is also questioned. We have seen that the domain of politics is limited. The general direction is laid down in the constitution, as a form of pre-commitment. The constitutional process itself respects political rights, but, particularly *vis-à-vis* later generations, problems arise. Still, at least as long as the constitution is not too difficult to alter, this cannot be considered as illegitimate infringement of political rights.

## Social and Economic Rights

The notion of social rights is relatively new. During the last hundred years the notion of charity has been replaced by that of social justice as the underlying assumption of social rights. International human rights instruments encompass a wide range of socioeconomic rights, and to address the likelihood of observance of each one under the alternative constitutional schemes, is beyond the limits of this analysis.

The right to an adequate standard of living and freedom from hunger is the most basic socioeconomic right. Other key rights are the rights to work, health, education and shelter. The core notion of social rights is access to social services and social protection, and its realisation is conceived as a gradual increase in entitlement and scope in accordance with the society's level of development. Their progressive realisation is a component of development as well as a yardstick against which development can be measured. Privatisation of public services for education, health, nutrition and housing makes the realisation subject to the financial capability of each person, household or family, hence denying their nature of human rights (Tomasevski, 1990: 98).

This conception of the character of social rights and the demands they place on governments corresponds closely to the views of the justice model. And the idea of 'progressive realisation' of rights is reflected in Sachs' affirmative action approach and the central idea of an 'expanding minimum floor of social rights'. The intentions are impeccable. The wisdom of addressing such matters in the constitution, and the capacity of achieving them within the framework proposed by Sachs, is, however, a different matter, which will be considered in the following chapter.

The consociational model also recommends some form of redistribution given the enormous inequalities within South Africa. There are, however, strong forces within the model counteracting redistribution. Concern for the material conditions of individuals, central to the idea of social and economic rights, is not significant in consociationalism. Socio-economic rights may be safeguarded within a consociational framework — at least where differences between groups are limited and resources not too scarce.[8] Under the circumstances prevailing in South Africa, it is more doubtful whether consociationalism would be able to do so.

Social rights are often criticised for being neither enforceable nor affordable. The need for public health, social services and educational facilities for large and increasing numbers of people, exceeds the capacity of most developing countries. Human rights obligations related to social rights necessitate public investment.

The International Covenant on Economic, Social and Cultural Rights states, in Article 2(1), that parties to the Covenant are committed to invest in human rights 'to the utmost of (their) available resources'. This implies that human rights should be accorded a priority in public expenditure. It has been interpreted as follows. 'The obligation of progressive achievement exists independently of the increase in resources; it requires effective use of resources available' (United Nations, par. 23, in Tomasevski, 1990: 96–97).

Again, Sachs' constitutional solution echoes the international human rights documents. When faced with charges of not taking economic capacity into consideration, he replies that affordability has to be built into the characterisation of social rights in the same way that reasonableness enters into the definition of negligence, or proportionality into the concept of self-defence. It involves a relationship between the duty to spend on the one hand

and the obligation to pay on the others. Some entitlement will be free, others have to be paid for. Some are based on general tax revenue, some on payment, some on contribution (Sachs, 1992: 112).

*Equality and Non-discrimination*

The rights to equality and non-discrimination has several dimensions. It does not only pertain to 'negative' rights and formal barriers. The principle of discrimination also encompasses equality of treatment in social security (Tomasevski, 1990: 84).

In South Africa, observance of the principles of non-discrimination and equality is not only a matter of changing the structures of racial discrimination. It is also a matter of gender — women enjoy far from equal status and equal opportunities. And it is a matter of urban-rural inequalities since the burden of poverty falls disproportionally on the rural population. In addition there are the questions of ethnic, linguistic and religious divisions giving rise to similar concerns.

Generally, the justice model tends to focus primarily on the existing socioeconomic inequalities and racial discrimination and measures to abate and overcome them. The consociational model, on the other hand, tends to focus almost solely on the potential for future discrimination along other (ethnic) lines. The justice model addresses the questions of inequality and discrimination at the level of individuals, while the consociational model takes groups as the relevant units for comparison. While certain aspects of inequality and discrimination may be taken care of within both models, the consociational model seems to be insensitive to, for example the problems of inequality due to gender discrimination.

The justice model faces a dilemma when striving to reconcile the concerns for equal rights and non-discrimination with the comprehensive programme of affirmative action, involving racial and gender preferences and quotas. However, as Sachs convincingly argues, as long as the criteria for affirmative action (excluding quotas for admission to higher education) are such that none is excluded from consideration, preferential treatment of disadvantaged groups are, according to international human rights standards, not considered as violation of the principles of equality and non-discrimination (Sachs, 1992; Tomasevski, 1990). But the issue is truly complicated, as the following quote illustrates.

If all citizens are to be treated equally, then cultural minorities are disqualified because their particular skills are ignored. But if citizens are treated unequally on the basis of cultural difference, then cultural minorities suffer discrimination because they lack certain rights granted to the rest of the population. (Eriksen, 1991: 273)

## Cultural Rights, Rights of Peoples and Minorities

This category of rights raises the question of whether human rights are necessarily rights of individuals or whether they also apply to collectives, such as ethnic groups.

The justice model is exclusively formulated in the language of individual rights. But individuals of various cultural groups have rights directly related to preserving their cultural identity. Rights often referred to as collective, such as the right to speak one's language or practice one's religion, are formulated as universal rights for all individuals: 'Human rights are indivisible and universal, but they are all human rights for specific persons' (Sachs, 1992b: 60). Disadvantaged groups may, as noted above, have the right to a favourable treatment/affirmative action, but the groups are then only defined according to the traits of the individual members that make them disadvantaged, so that when a certain degree of equity or equality is achieved the right to special treatment terminates.

What the justice model strives to avoid is that provisions for protection of minorities from discrimination, turn into mechanisms protecting minority privileges. Group rights, entrenched in the constitution are regarded as a form of not very well hidden apartheid. But individual rights may also have this effect. An apparently race-free right such as the right not to be deprived of one's property without full compensation in freely convertible currency, could in practice be a means of using the law to keep alive in perpetuity social distinction on the basis of race (Sachs, 1986: 207).

The individual rights approach to the protection of minorities is rejected by consociationalists, and even more explicitly by communitarian thinkers. It is argued that the different groups, due to religious or cultural differences, have different conceptions of the good, and of the relationship between individuals and the community. If the state articulates one particular set of values (e.g. a liberal conception of justice) and sets out to transform society in accordance with this view, some groups may feel their culture threatened, even if their individual rights to culture, religion etc. are safeguarded. The reason is that the standing of the individual in the community is an integral part of the culture, and that the communal character of culture is neglected.[9]

A concrete problem with collective rights is that inevitably some have to demand them in the name of others. When this happens, chances are always that some of these 'others' do not feel represented by the leader or group presenting the claim. There are always dissidents — and what happen to these? A fundamental paradox in multi-cultural ideology such as consociationalism is that it assumes that 'cultures' are homogeneous and 'have values', ignoring that there are conflicting interests and values *within* every 'culture'. The fact that the leaders of an ethnic group claim certain values and traditions, does not necessarily mean that all the group members support them. It may thus be risky to assign *groups* rights, groups inevitably consist of persons — old, young, rich and poor, men and women — who often have different interests and values (Eriksen, 1992: 230).

Both the justice model and the consociational model protect, in different ways, cultural and minority rights; while the justice model stresses equal rights, the consociational model emphasises the right to be different. And the conclusion seems to be that both equal rights and the right to be different may lead to discrimination and injustice.

## *Are the Models Acceptable in Light of Central Human Rights Norms?*

Jack Donnelly and Rhoda Howard (1986) have evaluated human rights protection within different categories of regimes, based on a definition of human rights explicitly including all categories of rights included in the International Bill of Human Rights.

They distinguish, first of all, between communitarian and individualistic regimes. Individualistic regimes are sub-divided into liberal and minimal regimes, while communitarian regimes are divided into four sub-groups: communist, corporatist, traditional and developmental.

The degree of permissable inequality is the basic difference within the category of individualistic regimes. Liberal regimes have as their central value that the state should treat each individual as morally and politically equal. 'Inequality is not objectionable to the liberal, but the principle of equal concern and respect does imply a floor of basic economic welfare, degrading inequalities cannot be permitted' (Donnelly and Howard, 1986: 805). The minimal state emphasises liberty and down-plays the concern for equality. The state is only required to protect the individual against violations of personal liberties. Minimal regimes, according to Donnelly and Howard, allow degrading inequalities, and are thus not in accordance with the requirements for human rights respect.

Communitarian regimes give priority to the community, both ideologically and in practice. This often implies priority of the state over the individual. Individuals are entitled to respect only as members of the group or society, in accordance with the duties and roles ascribed to them. According to Donnelly and Howard, all forms of communitarian regimes are incompatible with the idea of human rights because they preclude individual autonomy.

In communist regimes the collectively defined goal of building a society based on a particular idea of the good, conflicts with the civil and political rights of individuals. Similarly, corporatist regimes, structured around interest-group representation and divided into non-competitive hierarchical structures, violate basic political rights by not permitting political conflicts (such as labour conflicts). Traditional societies — societies based on a harmonious, organic conception of unity between individual and society — are also incompatible with respect for human rights, as defined by Donnelly and Howard. The reason for this is that individual goods can only be attained to the extent that the individual is a part of a larger collective — the family or the tribe. Developmental regimes govern by force, justifying repression as a necessary element in a strategy for economic development. Individual rights, in particular *vis-à-vis* the state, are set aside, thus violating the concern for basic human rights.

According to this classification only liberal democracies that provide a certain level of material well-being to their citizens, protect human rights adequately.

Where does this leave our two models? It could be reasonable to characterise Lijphart's consociational model as a form of communitarian regime which, according to Donnelly and Howard, does not provide sufficient individual autonomy to be compatible with human rights respect.[10]

The argument (implicit in consociationalism) that in plural societies the collective human rights of ethnic minorities are in some cases more important than the individual political rights of individuals, is rejected by Donnelly and Howard. They argue that this is not a competing view of human rights but rather a competing view of human dignity, incompatible with the idea of human rights. It denies 'both the centrality of the individual in political society and the human rights of men and women to make, and have enforced, equal and inalienable civil, political, economic and social claims on the state' (Donnelly and Howard, 1986: 816). This is, however, no undisputed assessment. Besides, the form of consociation recommended for South Africa by Lijphart, based on civil liberties, universal suffrage, regular elections, and spontaneous formation of groups, seem more acceptable with regard to individual autonomy. Consociationalism may also have problems with the criterion of not allowing degrading inequalities.

The findings of Donnelly and Howard support the previous conclusions with regard to human rights. All categories of rights, save the collective ones, fit very neatly with the justice model, while the consociational model has several difficulties, most of them stemming from the focus on groups rather than individuals.


## Concluding Remarks: Are the Models Acceptable?

From the above discussion it is clear that the answer to this question depends upon which definition of democracy is taken as the point of departure, and how human rights compliance is interpreted.

Both models take care of important democratic values and satisfy basic human rights requirements — and both may be criticised on the basis of other aspects of democracy and human rights.

Sachs' justice model places considerable emphasis on being *visibly* democratic. If a new South African regime is to gain legitimacy it must be clear to all that the basic rules are fair, and the system genuinely democratic. The constitutional structure should thus be uncomplicated. 'Simple democracy' is required, meaning basically 'majority rule' — 'one person, one vote, one value' on a common voters' roll. The emphasis on 'majority rule' is, however, deceptive. Although the model provides for majoritarian modes of decision-making, and a majoritarian base for the executive, there are several limits to majority rule. The constitution is the highest norm, and the extensive constitutional domain envisaged in this model limits the effect of majority rule. Thus, while majority rule is an important element in the justice model, it is not *the* important element. The conception of political democracy underlying this constitutional strategy also includes important aspects of rights protection. A comprehensive Bill of Rights, safeguarding the individual against abuse from the majority, occupies a central position. And it requires protection, not only of civil and political rights, but of social, economic, cultural and environmental rights as well.

The major challenge the justice model faces from democratic theory is not that it does not include all the democratic criteria, but rather that it includes too much. While a constitution is perfectly compatible with democracy, the extensive constitutional domain proposed by the justice model intrudes on the domain of politics, restricting the freedom of choice for voters and elected representatives. The constitutional provisions for comprehensive affirmative action leaves little room for future democratic decisions. In addition, when the constitutional domain is so extensive there is also much room for rational disagreement — and this may politicise the constitution and damage the legitimacy of the constitution as such. A related problem is that the constitutionalism proposed by Sachs relies heavily on judicial review by the supreme court, and thus of the judgement of non-elected officials. The courts' lack of accountability excludes the citizenry from important political processes.

Thirdly, the extensive pre-commitment that the justice model prescribes, raises the problem of 'the dead ruling the living'. Although Sachs envisages and suggests arrangements for civil society participation in the constitutional process ('participatory formulation of rights') — thus justifying the constitution as pre-commitment, it does not solve the problem of why later generations, who had no possibility of participating, should be bound by the constitution. How difficult it is to change various parts of the constitution is important in this respect.[11]

All things considered, the justice model cannot be regarded as undemocratic, nor to conflict with basic human rights. It fits well with the criteria for constitutional democracy. What about consociationalism?

In early writings Lijphart himself pointed at democratic defects of the consociational model (Lijphart, 1968: 131–34, 177–80; 1977: 47–45). It was advocated as an imperfect — but the only realistic — democratic option for plural societies. His argument was, in the words of Theodor Hanf, that while many people prefer the champagne of majority-rule democracy to the mere water of consociationalism, only a few prefer to die of thirst if champagne is not available. In later writings he maintains that consociationalism is the only democratic option of plural societies, but he is far less modest about the democratic qualities of consociationalism.

> There is nothing in consociationalism that true democrats have to be ashamed of. It is fully democratic — to the extent that any real-world democracy can approximate the democratic ideal — and it is just as democratic as majoritarianism. (Lijphart, 1985: 109)

However, all his critics do not agree. The feature of consociationalism most frequently called in doubt for lack of democratic qualities is the high degree of secrecy, and lack of clear lines of accountability providing a formal link between the preferences expressed by voters and the outcome of the political process (Barry, 1979).[12] This is also a problem in terms of human rights, infringing on the political rights of citizens. Consociationalism also faces charges for failing to take into consideration the social and economic rights of citizens.

Judged against the normative standards of democracy and human rights neither of the models is flawless. The consociational model meets, however, with more criticism than the justice model. This is hardly surprising in light of the fact that the justice model is an application of general principles to South African conditions, while the consociational model is derived from the experiences of countries troubled by ethnic, religious and linguistic conflicts. And the justice model springs from the same source as the ideas of democracy and human rights: liberalism and the idea of 'natural rights'. It relies on the same normative foundation, the fundamental equality of all human beings. Because all are born free and with equal moral worth, each individual is entitled to a special protection which not even the welfare of society as a whole can legitimately override.

Lijphart's general argument that democracy requires different measures under different circumstances, seems valid. He may also be right in his argument that in deeply (ethnically) divided societies a political system, in order to be democratic, must provide all with a genuine opportunity to have their interests taken into consideration. But this does not necessarily make consociationalism the most democratic system for the circumstances of South Africa. Again, the base line appears to be which interpretation of the South African situation is regarded as valid.

After this discussion of the models' normative acceptability, I want to return briefly to why acceptability is important. That the basic norms of society are acceptable is not only a matter of ideals, it is also important for stability. In an open, democratic, form of government the stability of a regime depends to a large extent on its legitimacy. 'The steering capacity of a given state will to a large extent depend on whether vital interest groups in society regard its power-base as legitimate' (Rakner, 1992: 28). The legitimacy of a constitution is, among other factors, a function of the acceptability of its basic norms, that is, the extent to which it reflects moral sentiments in the population. But the relationship works both ways — acceptability must be seen in relation to performance. To consider the likely performance of the models, given that they had been adopted in their pure form, is the — somewhat speculative — task of the following chapter.

# Notes

1.  It has been argued that consociationalism may provide stability to plural societies — where democracy is difficult — precisely because it is only superficially democratic: *'if* the trick can be brought off, the combination in divided societies of elections and elite collusion is superior to either elections without collusion or collusion without elections, because it satisfies both the value of peace and stability and the value of freedom of speech and organisation' (Barry, 1979: 191).

2.  Given the importance of the constitutional court judges, the procedure of appointment is of considerable political importance.

3.  For instance List PR, the electoral system favoured by Lijphart for South Africa, is held to be undemocratic because it gives too much power to party hierarchies (Rabushka and Shepsle, 1972; Dutter, 1978).

4.  The details of constitutional entrenchment are, to my knowledge, not discussed in Sachs' work.

5.  And, as Lijphart underscores, the near-polyarchies, Cyprus and Malaysia, are placed in this category due to the incidence of violence, not because of defects in their democratic character.

6.  For a full list of Human Rights instruments relevant to South Africa see Andreassen and Swinehart (1991: x)

7.  I follow generally the framework for rights-assessment in the Yearbooks on *Human Rights in Developing Countries*, 1989–91.

8.  Empirical evidence shows that consociational countries are capable observing the social and economic rights of its citizens. This is seen, for example in the case of the Netherlands.

9.  In this context it is interesting to note that one of the very last problems to be overcome in the constitutional negotiations were over the right to single-language schools (see Chapter 9).

10. Unlike Dahl, Donnelly and Howard do not classify actual regimes according to their standard, and it is thus not possible to check how they would categorise the actual regimes that Lijphart takes as his point of departure.

11. The entrenchment of constitutional provisions is also a practical problem. If the constitution is very detailed and comprehensive, and amendment is difficult, this might negatively affect constitutional stability.

12. While recognising that consociationalism may be technically superior when it comes to achieving stability of divided societies, he argues that this does not render the model democratic. The democratic guise of consociationalism is, however, seen to be valuable. Democratic elections, although not effectively influencing the outcome of political decision-making, take care of important civil and political liberties and provide an acceptable method for election of leadership. The *appearance* of democracy is what really counts from the point of view of stability — and stability is the most important goal of consociationalism.

# 8 Practical Feasibility

Having analysed the methodological and normative qualities of the constitutional models most central to the South African constitutional debate, we now go on to consider their feasibility in the circumstances of South African society. Would the models have functioned as intended if they had been adopted in their pure form? Are they suitable frameworks within which the problems of South African society could have been addressed?

The suitability of the models are considered both within each model's own interpretation understanding of what constitutes the basic conflict structure of South African society, and within the inverse horizon of problems.

The structural problems of inequality and poverty, are focused upon in the first section of the chapter. To what extent is a more equitable distribution of resources necessary for political stability? And how is redistribution conceived in the two constitutional schemes? What is the likelihood of redistribution within each of the constitutional frameworks?

The second part of the chapter is devoted to the ethnic question. Which model seems the most capable in terms of facilitating peaceful co-existence in the South African context? Again the differences in interpretation are vital to the assessment.

Definite answers cannot be given to the questions addressed here. The issues are complex and depend on a host of factors, economic as well as political. The constitutional structure is only one, albeit important, factor affecting political performance. Still, the exercise carried out here is valuable in that it provides both a critical consideration of each model's reading of the South African reality, and an assessment of the models' strengths and weaknesses for South African circumstances. This in turn highlights potentials and limitations of the actual constitution, which is moulded in the conflict between these constitutional ideals.

**Inequality and Poverty: Responding to the Apartheid Legacy**

The questions addressed in this section are: is stability possible in South Africa without redistribution? And how do the constitutional models influence the prospects for redistribution and reduction of poverty?

To determine how the models, if implemented, would affect the different sectors of South African society and economy is an impossible task, and the ambition of this analysis is not to make predictions. Based on the presentation of the models in Chapters 4 and 5, and the analyses in the two previous chapters, an evaluation can, however, be made of the tools by which the two constitutional schemes attempt to come to grips with the problems of inequality and ethnic tension, as outlined in Chapter 2.

*Is Democratic Stability Possible in South Africa without Redistribution?*

The justice model answers this question with a blunt 'no'. Democratic stability is not possible in South Africa without redistribution. The inequalities in South Africa are not only massively unjust, they also threaten political stability. Eradication of poverty and inequality are the primary objectives that the justice model is constructed to accomplish. And the chief means are affirmative action measures of different varieties.

What about the consociational model? Although focus is on the importance of ethnicity, the problems of socioeconomic inequality are not entirely bypassed. Lijphart, when advocating his model for South Africa, recognises that the huge inequalities in South African society represent grave problems to successful consociation. It is not, however, regarded as an insuperable obstacle (Lijphart, 1985: 125). Whereas democratic stability is unlikely in a situation characterised by massive inequality, it may still be possible through appropriately devised consociational institutions. But the likelihood of successful consociation in South Africa would improve considerably if inequalities between the segments were reduced. Lijphart maintains that socio-economic problems, contrary to the problems of ethnic conflict, may be overcome by deliberate political action, and recommends a strong commitment to reduction of inequality between the segments.

Both strategies thus involve redistribution as part of their constitutional 'solution' for South Africa. And in the following paragraphs the likelihood of a more equal distribution within the proposed frameworks will be considered.

*Three Conditions for Successful Redistribution*

Socio-economic inequalities tend to be persistent. It seems clear that in order to move towards a less unequal distribution of wealth and income focused government action and careful targeting of policies are requried.

There is a general agreement among experts that with a marginal tax rate of 45 per cent, there is little room for increases in revenue from taxation. Nor is the South African economy in such a shape that a boost in GNP per capita can be expected. Moderately optimistic forecasts operate with growth rates of around 3 per cent (RSA, 1996b). This is little more than the estimated population growth rate of 2 per cent.[1] Redistributive strategies based on automatic 'trickle down effects' of economic growth through the market, or solely on allocation of the surplus of economic growth, are not likely to achieve significant redistributive results. At least not in the short and medium term so crucial to a new democratic regime.[2] To reduce inequality and improve living conditions for the poorest sections of the South African population, active government policies are required.[3]

Three factors in particular appear to be important for redistribution and reduction of poverty. Firstly, redistribution seems to require a potent government. Secondly, it is of vital importance that the government is capable of resisting the temptations of macroeconomic populism and heavy deficit spending. And thirdly, long term development depends on an adequate general economic policy and restructuring of the economy.

These factors are influenced by the constitutional set-up, although far from determined by it. The aim of the following analysis is to evaluate how the constitutional models affect government capacity for action, and the ability and motivation for re-structuring the economy. A crucial factor is the scope allowed for political organisation and resistance by the rich. In order to assess the prospects for long term development it is also necessary to take into consideration the dangers of macroeconomic populism. In some institutional set-ups, governments rely more precariously on short-term majority support, and are thus more vulnerable to popular pressure.

It should be kept in mind that this is a discussion of the likely effects of the institutional mechanisms of the consociational model and the justice model, respectively, rather than an analysis of the actual economic performance of the South African economy.

### The Justice Model and Redistribution

Distributive concerns are at the very heart of the justice model as a constitutional model for South Africa. It proposes to promote poverty reduction and a more equal distribution of resources through two channels. In addition to the most conventional instrument of change associated with democracy — namely transforming popular demands (electoral preferences) into political action through majoritarian modes of decision-making and a potent central government — it proposes a redistribution through constitutional pre-commitment. Within this framework the legal system becomes a major instrument of redistribution.

#### Government Potential for Action

The political institutions of the justice model are designed to provide strong governments. Furthermore, and this is of special importance with regard to redistribution, it is designed to produce governments with the capacity to intervene in the economy. A majoritarian mode of decision-making, a legal framework designed to encourage rather than hamper redistribution, and structures to strengthen the relationship between the state and civil society, are measures designed to promote the redistributive potential of governments.

Although much depends on the extent to which the government in position is committed to redistribution, even 'reactionary' governments will be — at least formally — obligated towards redistribution through constitutional precommitment.[4] The scope for resistance by the wealthy sections of society is relatively limited. They do, however, have the exit option. 'Brain drain' and capital flight are challenges that could adversely affect economic performance, and the fear of which add to the bargaining strength of the privileged sections of society.

#### The Dangers of Macroeconomic Populism

With regard to redistribution and general economic performance, a potential problem pertaining to the justice model is that there are few mechanisms restraining governments tempted to engage in 'macroeconomic populism' and heavy deficit spending. The constitutional programme for a new economic policy envisioned in the justice model is prone to boost expectations (see below). And majoritarian governments are more clearly accountable, and more in need of being able to deliver in the short-term than consociational governments. While the justice model seems vulnerable to macroeconomic populism, this is in the last instance a matter of political skill. External conditions also affect deficit spending, such as the enactment of constitutional requirements for balanced budgets, implicit or explicit requirements from domestic and foreign investors, or from financial institutions such as the World Bank.

The constitutional framework of the justice model is also likely to affect the economy in other ways. Although the financial consequences of affirmative action measures, taxes etc., are difficult to determine ahead of the actual development, they will undoubtedly affect incentive structures in different sectors of the economy. This — and the uncertainty generally associated with redistributive policies — could have considerable impact on financial markets and on the enterprise establishment. It might negatively influence the willingness to invest in South Africa, which in turn, could have consequences for the growth rate.

## An Alternative Economic Policy?

'Affirmative action in the wide sense' is the framework for an alternative economic policy or developmental path outlined in Sachs' constitutional proposal. Sachs proposes that the main principles of the new economic policy should be laid down in the constitution itself, rather than left for the political process. The actual policies and measures should be left for governments to decide, but given the legacy of apartheid, the path towards a more just distribution of resources should be a pre-commitment, enshrined in the constitution and guarded through the legal system.

Redistribution through constitutional constraints is paradoxical, bills of rights and judicial review are institutions normally associated with maintaining the status quo. Here they are converted into instruments of progressive change by:

- providing a legal basis for affirmative action;
- committing future governments to redistribution through constitutional guarantees for 'an expanding minimum floor' of social and economic rights;
- structures to encourage civil society participation (to ensure that rights are in accordance with needs, and to increase accountability and legitimacy);

- structures to monitor and enforce the rights (constitutional court, human/ social rights commissions, ombud-institution, etc.).

Redistribution through constitutional pre-commitment has the advantage of predictability. It is conceived to proceed in an orderly fashion, balancing the demands for rapid change against the need for a predictable political and economic environment. Institutionalisation of materially just 'basic rules of the game' responds to the legitimate claims of the disadvantaged for a greater share of the total resources in society, and, simultaneously, to the legitimate fears of the currently privileged minority.

Is the justice model's affirmative action approach likely to achieve substantial redistribution and reduction of poverty in South Africa?

A wide spectre of redistributive strategies may be conceived within this development path: redistribution may be sought through taxation, as well as through various forms of government spending programmes. Particularly in the areas of education, health and housing/infrastructure, where constitutional guarantees are to be given for 'an expanding minimum floor of rights', governmental affirmative action programmes will not only be an option, they will be virtually mandatory.[5]

There are openings for asset redistribution in Sachs' proposal. Land reform is considered as particularly important. This must be done in an ordered and principled manner balancing the rights of the various stakeholders. Also in other respects there are limits to asset redistribution within the framework of this model. Total nationalisation of industry is ruled out by constitutional provisions for a mixed economy, presupposing an important role for the private sector in the economy. And the Bill of Rights guarantees all citizens certain rights to property and a private sphere of non-interference.

There are, however, grounds for scepticism and critique. While the justice model is conducive to redistribution in the sense that it removes obstacles to redistributive policies, and limits the scope for resistance from the rich, there are no guarantees that the policies will succeed. The social impact of redistributive measures, as well as their consequences for the general economy, is difficult to determine. This constitutional framework, providing considerable scope and push for change, entails correspondingly great risks of failure. If the distributive goals of the justice model are to be achieved a variety of policies and programmes must be set in motion simultaneously. While it is possible to make fairly reliable predictions about the short-term impact of each measure viewed in isolation, it is virtually impossible to estimate the aggregate effects of all the different policies.

Choices have to be made under a considerable degree of uncertainty, with the risks that this implies. The active role of the state in transforming the social structure places heavy strains on the administrative apparatus, and it does so in a period of transformation of the apartheid state system.

Another important critique of the justice model is that it relies too heavily on the capacities of the legal system. In addition to all the ordinary tasks of the courts, they are entrusted — or burdened — with the ultimate responsibility for protecting all citizens against discrimination, ensuring that legislation and policies are sufficiently directed towards redistribution, and with overseeing their implementation. Attempts to solve the problems of severely divided societies through the entrenchment of guarantees puts a heavy load on constitutional law and the judiciary, rather than on constitutional practice, evolved through elected politicians.

> It is doubtful that a rights and requirements approach to divided societies can survive the fragile state of judiciaries in these societies. All it is likely to do, when politicians are opposed to the claims, is to put undue pressure on a nascent institution that might otherwise evolve traditions of genuine and useful inter-dependence. (Horowitz, 1991: 159–60)

Although the justice model presupposes the setting up of quasi-legal bodies — such as the ombud, the human rights commission, a social rights commission, and regionally based bodies for solving disputes by conciliation — the danger of overloading the legal system appears very real.

Capacity problems are not the only difficulty associated with this extensive 'legalisation' of politics. To tilt the load of redistribution heavily on the legal system implies that fewer issues are left for politics. Constitutionalism crowds out democracy.

Conferring so much political power in judges and other non-elected personnel gives rise to serious problems of accountability. The procedures for appointment of these bodies, the length of their terms, and the possibilities for checking their power, become crucial questions in the context of the justice model.

There is the obvious danger of excessive politicisation of the courts and of the consitution.The extensive constitutional domain and the narrowing of the domain of politics may threaten the stability of the constitution. The constitution is to serve as a common set of rules, facilitating orderly political struggle. A very comprehensive constitution, embracing too many elements on which there is room for rational disagreement, is likely to turn the constitution itself into an object of political conflict, rather than a means to structure it. There will always be ample room for disagreement on what a just distribution in practice implies. If this disagreement becomes a matter of legal interpretation of the constitution rather than a matter of politics, disagreement may endanger the stability of the political system as such.

On balance, I find that a South African constitution constructed according to the justice model would have considerable potential for advancing distributive justice. The proposal definitely provides a framework for addressing social and economic change. There are, however, problems associated with the justice model's 'legalisation' or 'constitutionalisation' of distributive matters. In addition, substantial change — however well planned — always implies risks. A threat to long term development within this framework lies also in the dangers of macroeconomic populism, undermining prospects for long-term growth, which is an important condition for succeeding within the framework of this model.

## The Consociational Model and Redistribution

Proponents of consociationalism admit that consociational models are most adequate for countries where the socioeconomic resources are evenly distributed between the groups. Where it is still advocated as the solution for South Africa this is partly due to lack of acceptable alternatives, and partly because the unfavourable factor of socioeconomic inequality is seen to be outweighed by other, favourable, factors. It is, however, also argued that inequality may be overcome within a consociational framework.

Recognising that inequality between the groups threatens accommodation and political stability, state action to redistribute resources between the groups is recommended, mainly in the form of affirmative action programmes and proportional allocation of resources between the groups.

But is redistribution possible in a political system constructed to insulate the various groups from interfering with each other?

### Consociational Governments' Potential for Action

Minimising inter-group competition at the central political level is a key idea of consociational theory. Ideally the central government is a neutral 'mediator. 'Hard decisions' concerning distribution are to be decentralised, delegated to intra-group political bodies, or else to the market.

Representation of all groups in legislative and executive political bodies (institutionalised coalition governments) and decision-making by consensus, leave all significant groups with (stronger or weaker) veto powers. Is redistribution feasible when all measures have to be agreed to by 'haves' and 'have-nots' alike? Policies aimed at substantial redistribution are obviously more difficult to enact when those who are adversely affected by the reforms are given the political power to obstruct redistributive efforts. The scope allowed for political organisation and resistance by the rich, detracts from the likelihood of substantial redistribution within a consociational constitutional framework. Although redistribution is not rendered impossible, consociationalism implies a strong bias towards the status quo. To resist change is easy, to bring it about is very difficult. In South Africa, where socioeconomic differences are likely to follow segmental divisions, the consociational approach to redistribution is not likely to do much for the problems of poverty and inequality.

In a consociational South Africa there are likely to be vast differences between groups, both with respect to the level of material well-being and numerical strength. Presumably, (at least some of) the poorer segments will be far stronger, numerically, than the wealthy segments.[6] What the consociational model does is to go a long way towards neutralising the bargaining power that democratic systems normally award to numerically strong groups. In some countries this may be necessary to increase the bargaining powers of otherwise weak minorities. In South Africa these measures serve largely to strengthen the strong and weaken the weak. The main weakness of the rich segments — their lack of electoral strength — is neutralised, while the poor segments are in effect deprived of their main power-base. Their numerical/electoral strength is not convertible into governmental power. These conservative traits of consociationalism have been strongly criticised in the South African context:

> Any participation in political decision-making by formerly excluded groups becomes meaningful only if it allows for actual or at least potential impacts on the existing distributive mechanisms of the state apparatus. Meaningful democratic participation aims at influencing the stakes in scarce resources according to institutionalised trials of strength ... So long as constitutional designs do not address themselves to this fundamental problem of agreed-upon mechanisms for redistribution, they remain futile exercises. (Adam and Giliomee, 1979: 297)

The major bargaining-power left to the deprived groups is their blackmail potential. Although the numerical and electoral strength of the poor are not directly converted into political power through control over the central government, it may work indirectly. Advantaged minorities may be willing to concede to certain redistributive policies — such as the affirmative action schemes suggested by Lijphart — if they believe the measures to be necessary in order to maintain stability. The gains for the strong group then outweigh its losses.

## *Ability to Resist Pressure for Macroeconomic Populism*

What about the impact of consociationalism, and the redistributive measures it proposes, on the overall performance of the South African economy?

The consociational model is often criticised for lack of efficiency. Decisions by consensus in broad coalition governments are slow and cumbersome processes. There is no strong executive, capable of reaching the swift and hard decisions deemed necessary to create a climate favourable to economic growth.

There is, however, little empirical evidence to support these claims. Countries with apparently weak governments and unstable political systems, such as Italy, and countries with consociational systems, such as Switzerland, have performed better in terms of economic growth than the economy of, for example, Great Britain, the archetypical majoritarian democracy with a strong executive. Although these differences in economic performance may be in spite of, or largely independent of, the mode of political decisions-making, a relationship is also conceivable: swift radical decisions are not necessarily good decisions. Stability and gradual change at a slow pace provide a more predictable environment which seems favourable to the economy. Consensus-orientated coalition governments tend to leave the economic forces more to their own working. Apparently weak or even unstable political systems, may thus create surprisingly stable frameworks for economic activity (Lijphart 1992).

A consociational solution for South Africa thus cannot be dismissed on grounds of economic inefficiency. Redistributive policies implemented in a consociational system are unlikely to have severe disruptive effects on the economy. With all measures being (at least implicitly) approved of by all parties, the rate of change is likely to be slow. Thus it is likely to affect investors' confidence positively, and limit capital flight.

The redistributive potential of consociational governments seems, however, to be rather weak. If redistribution is insufficient to maintain political stability, this may in turn threaten the economy.

*An Alternative Economic Policy?*

Although Lijphart recognises the need for redistribution, the matter is given a rather brief treatment (in his 1985 book on power-sharing in South Africa roughly one page is devoted to the question of socioeconomic inequality). Nevertheless, from what he does say, it seems clear that redistribution is envisioned within a context of rapid economic growth. Surplus from growth will facilitate a 'painless' reduction of inequality between the segments if supported by 'deliberate political action, including preferential treatment for the disadvantaged segments' (Lijphart, 1985: 125). He cites, and seems to concur with, proposals for the institutionalisation of proportional revenue sharing and equalisation payments for less developed regions and institutional sectors, put forward by Heribert Adam (1983: 142) and seems to envisage an affirmative action programme somewhat akin to what Sachs terms 'affirmative action in the narrow sense'. However, there is an important difference: Lijphart's concern is for the distribution of resources between the segments, not within them. As a consequence of the collectivist methodological focus of consociational models, the group is the relevant unit for determining distributive justice. The question of inequality between individuals is not addressed.

In consociational theory redistribution is motivated differently than in the justice model: allocation of resources by the state should be done out of consideration for the relative strength of the groups.[7] Socioeconomic inequality only requires state action in cases where stability is threatened.[8] In South Africa this is considered to be the case, and redistribution is recommended for the sake of democratic stability.

Given that a consociational South African government recognises the need for redistributive measures, what is the likelihood of success?

Successful redistribution seem to require ground-level participation. This poses difficulties in consociational systems: a central consociational idea is that, while hostility runs deep within the rank and file of each segment, their elites have the willingness and ability to reach agreement. Consociational models depend on the elites as largely autonomous policy-makers, and rely on the loyalty of the constituencies towards their politicians. Active civil society participation in policy formation implies that citizens are encouraged to engage directly in political activity. Civil society participation that is channelled into intra-group political forums, may be more compatible with consociationalism. However, even in this context it presents problems by reducing the relative autonomy of the political elite (see Chapter 6).

Redistribution within a consociational framework depends heavily on a favourable economic climate. The willingness of the economically privileged groups to concede to redistributive measures is likely to vary with the general economic situation. In a rapidly growing economy, where concessions imply relatively small losses in their present standard of living, redistribution is much easier to bring about than in a stagnating economy where the level of material well-being is jeopardised even without redistributive policies. Lijphart himself acknowledges this, in stating that redistribution 'obviously requires that sufficient economic resources be available' (Lijphart, 1985: 125).

Doubts about the realism in Lijphart's economic forecasts have already been voiced. Lijphart's confidence concerning the availability of sufficient resources for redistribution is backed by two premises, both of which are disputable: (1) that South Africa is basically a wealthy country; and (2) that the transition from apartheid to a consociational democratic government would spur international investment on a scale that increase economic growth sufficiently to facilitate substantial redistribution.

South Africa does have vast natural resources. Compared with other countries in the region it is a relatively wealthy country, and a middle income country by world standards. On average, that is. With the extremely unequal distribution it has one very wealthy segment and a huge poor majority. If radical distribution is ruled out, as it is in consociational models, it means that something near the current standard of living of the white minority is the base line for comparison. In this perspective 'growing' out of the problems is inconceivable. There has been an increase in foreign investments in South Africa with the breakdown of the apartheid system (and also a significant inflow of development aid), but at the same time the South African economy is experiencing problems with relatively low productivity. Although there is growth potential in the economy, it is wishful thinking to expect a boost in economic growth sufficient to transform South Africa into a fast growing economy, and sufficient to create a surplus for 'painless' redistribution.

Adding to the problems is the high population growth and, with a young population profile, a high number of new entries into the labour market. The potential for curbing unemployment through increased economic growth, is limited. Even with optimistic prognoses, economic growth by itself will barely be able to take care of the addition to the labour force, and will by no means solve the country's vast unemployment problems. The structure of the economy and the increasing capital-deepening imply that economic growth is not necessarily reflected in employment at all.

The situation with regard to education reinforces the problems on the labour market. Education has been of grossly unequal quality for the different groups, which is reflected in labour skills and labour-market value. Redistribution between groups, in order to be effective in the long term, will have to address the problems of inequalities in education.[9] Inequalities between (racial/ethnic) groups are also very visible in areas such as the distribution of land, housing, health and infrastructure.

All these factors add to feelings of relative deprivation among the underprivileged and are potent sources of unrest and political instability — and of the rocketing crime rate. Within each area substantial redistribution is an overwhelming task, let alone all of them taken together. Against this backdrop, there is little ground for optimism regarding the possibilities for substantial redistribution solely or mainly through allocation of surplus from economic growth. Redistribution premised on a fast growing economy seems to be wishful thinking in the case of South Africa.

Although ample factors within consociationalism work against substantial redistribution, it is likely that a certain amount of redistribution would take place in a consociational South Africa, both as a consequence of the blackmail potential of the poor segments, and because it is in the rational self-interest of the privileged groups to make some concessions in order to enhance the legitimacy of the system. If the privileged groups are convinced that their interests are best served by consociation, and that a successful consociation and political stability depends on a less striking racial distribution of resources, a limited redistribution is the rational response.

The crucial question is whether these mechanisms are sufficient to reduce inequality between segments sufficiently for all groups to regard the system as legitimate, and thus facilitate successful consociation. While consociationalism is unlikely to bring about substantial redistribution in South Africa, it is not impossible that it may accomplish sufficient redistribution between the segments to facilitate stability. Given that groups form along ethnic lines, 'restitution in the symbolic realm ... (may) be almost as decisive as real equality in achieving the goal of reconciled coexistence' (Adam and Giliomee, 1979: 294). Without doing much for the vast majority, removal of the worst proofs of racial/ethnic injustice may create an impression of change. Given that ethnicity over time proves to be the most important cleavage, the creation of an elite and a middle class within each segment may suffice. This is a process that has already been under way for many years and which has grown in speed with the democratic transition. Although the vast majority of blacks remain as poor, or poorer, than before, there is a visible and growing black elite and middle class.

If Sachs is correct in assuming that groups form along class lines, and that poverty and inequality become the major political issues, then it is doubtful whether a consociational government would be capable of sufficient redistribution for it to be regarded as legitimate by the majority of South Africans in the longer term. Under these circumstances a constitution along the lines of the justice model appears to be a more feasible alternative.

But what if Lijphart's diagnosis is right, and over time ethnicity establishes itself as the most pervasive source of conflict — could the justice model answer to these problems?

## Ethnicity

Regardless of the relative importance ascribed to ethnic conflict, South Africa is indisputably a heterogeneous society. Linguistic, religious and ethnic diversities are ample, both between and within the racial categories of the apartheid regime. Cultural variety abounds. Just as it is impossible to ignore the fact of socioeconomic inequality in South African society, it is similarly far-fetched to deny its multi-ethnic character. The significance and political importance of these phenomena may be contested, but their existence is beyond dispute.

Both models do address the challenges posed by the plural character of South African society. Are their answers adequate? Do they provide suitable strategies for curbing ethnic conflict?

### Ethnicity and the Justice Model

We have so far concentrated on the justice model as a framework for distribution of resources and opportunities. It is, however, constructed as an answer to the problems posed by pluralism. A fundamental objective is to solve the problems of creating a common political framework in societies characterised by fundamental value-pluralism. Both the model as applied to

South African conditions by Sachs, and the more abstract versions set out in the writings of John Rawls and others, have this as a primary goal.

Although the justice model is reluctant to recognise ethnic groups as politically relevant units, ethnic loyalties and cultural differences are not overlooked. They are, however, viewed in a basically individualistic perspective and treated on a par with other forms of value pluralism. The response of liberalism to the existence of such differences — insoluble even in principle — is for the state to aim at impartiality. The basic institutions of society should strive for equal opportunity to pursue their ideal of the good.

Concern for cultural differences and ethnic identities figures prominently in the justice model, but only in the form of guaranteeing individual cultural rights. Culture, language and religion are important social phenomena — because they are important to individuals. The state should guarantee the individual rights of all citizens to engage freely in religious and cultural activities, pass on their traditions and beliefs, learn and use their own languages, etc. The rights may, of course, be exercised by individuals collectively, but should not be given to groups as groups. Individuals are the only bearers of rights.

While one may conceive of a system where in principle individuals can opt out of their group (as Lijphart in fact suggests), membership of ethnic groups is restricted in the sense that one cannot join at will. Ethnic groups by definition have an ascriptive element. According to the justice model, to give certain rights or privileges to such groups as groups would violate the principle of non-discrimination. Ethnic identities, while recognised as important for individuals, should be regarded as a private matter. The state should not take action to extinguish such social bonds, nor should they be the source of special treatment — favourable or non-favourable — by the state.

To the extent that ethnicity becomes a political issue, and a source of political mobilisation, the justice model recommends a strategy of 'benign neglect'. If ethnic differences are publicly recognised as politically relevant, and institutionalised in the political system, the conflicts will be cemented. Hence, within a framework of guarantees for, and protection of, the cultural rights of all on an individualistic basis, the state should be 'colour blind', that is, overlook ethnic differences and treat all citizens equally, regardless of ethnic affiliation.

Sachs seems to run into contradictions when faced with the dangers of politicised ethnicity. While generally speaking in favour of toleration, and advocating a constitutional structure where 'living with differences' is a key theme, he strongly underscores the importance of nation-building. There are certain assimiliationist traits in his proposal. What is advocated is an inclusive nationalism, the promotion of feelings of 'South African-ness'. Rather than being a strategy for swamping minorities into the culture of a majority, the metaphor is that of many small streams joining together in a flood. This tension between toleration and nation-building is in itself not objectionable, but Sachs also seems to envisage governmental action to prevent political mobilisation along ethnic lines, 'attempts to restore apartheid by political mobilisation based on setting group against group' should not be permitted (Sachs, 1990a: 25). Such a ban is problematic both on normative and practical accounts, and is in many ways an anomaly within Sachs' otherwise liberal framework, strongly emphasising toleration and equal civil, political, and cultural rights.

The ambivalence is understandable in light of South Africa's long (and also very recent) history of 'divide and rule' through manipulation and ignition of ethnic tension. And it exposes a general problem of self-reference inherent in liberalism: to what extent should the intolerant be tolerated?

**Ethnicity and the Consociational Model**

The justice model's answer to the problems of pluralism is regarded as insufficient by adherents of consociational theory. It does not take adequate care of the 'communal nature' of the cultural ties that render ethnic loyalties particularly salient, and which turn ethnic groups into important political units.[10]

The fundamental problem of liberalism — of the open, tolerant and value neutral society — is that people do not only seek freedom of choice and material well-being. They also seem to seek — and even more vigorously so — meaning, truth and a direction for their lives; ultimate and non-negotiable values which only deep, more or less ascriptive, social bonds, religion, tradition and cultural/ethnic identification, seem able to provide. Thus the strengths of liberalism, its tolerance, value-neutrality and fundamentally secular character, also become its weaknesses.

Consociational models propose a method for taking care of the 'meaningful' structures of ethnicity, while simultaneously providing mechanisms for containment of ethnic conflict. Based on the assumption that 'high fences make good neighbours' decentralisation, segmental autonomy, mutual vetoes and consensus-orientated modes of decision-making are institutionalised. The groups are not to interfere in each other's affairs.

A central assumption of consociationalism is that considerable autonomy is needed in order to preserve and develop the cultures of the different segments. To safeguard the continuation of the culture as such, collective or group rights will, in some cases, have to take precedence over individual rights. If the individual is given the right to choose freely in a 'cultural supermarket' the distinctiveness of minor ethnic groups is likely to weaken and eventually disappear. This leaves the current and future members of these groups culturally poorer than they would otherwise be. Culture is a matter transcending the individual, an essentially common experience. This communal nature of culture, and thus of cultural rights, is not possible to attain within the individual rights approach of liberal justice theory. Liberalism renders ethnicity meaningless through reducing it to a property of individuals. Consociationalism is able to grasp ethnicity more adequately, as an essentially intra-subjective or collective matter, according to communitarians and (implicitly) proponents of consociational theory.

Lijphart and other consociationalists do not ignore the impact of the apartheid system on ethnicity in South Africa. Certain consociational devices — for instance measures implying pre-definition of segments — which on purely 'technical' grounds would seem suitable, are rejected due to the psychological impact of the apartheid experience. Neither is it denied that attempts have been made by the white minority governments to stimulate ethnic conflict in the African population. However, Lijphart argues that this worked contrary to its intentions, and 'artificially' united the black population. Once the unifying effect of apartheid and white domination is gone, the African population is bound to split in its constituent — ethnic — units. This prediction is based on South Africa's diverse ethnic make-up as well as on comparative 'evidence'. The consociational solution is to be prepared for this development by setting up a constitutional structure which acknowledges ethnic groups as the relevant political units of society.

In this perspective the consociational value-hierarchy is necessarily different from that of individualistic liberalism. It becomes more important that all groups share in the political power — retaining a protected domain within which each can develop according to its own culture — and how the vote of individual citizens influences the outcome of the political process becomes less so. As long as basic democratic requirements are satisfied (i.e. that all citizens have the right to vote and their civil rights are protected), the social organisation of all groups should be allowed to proceed according to their own moral standards in a consociational framework where inter-segmental conflicts are settled by consensus, and no group has to fear domination.

## Which Model Answers Most Adequately to the Problems of Pluralism and Ethnicity in South Africa?

The judgement as to whether consociationalism or the justice model would have been the most promising approach for South Africa inevitably depends on the political significance of ethnicity. So far there has been a considerable overlap between racial divisions and voting patterns, but with the exception of the IFP, the FF and minor extra-parliamentary parties, political mobilisation has not followed along ethnic lines, and the parties that mobilise on an ethnic basis receive limited support from their own segment. It is, however, far too early to draw conclusions. The 1994 election, as a 'freedom poll' was very special, and even though the tendencies in the 1995/96 local government elections point in the same direction this does not mean that ethnicity will not be an important basis for political mobilisation in the future. President Mandela has put his political weight behind the project of national reconciliation. He is a symbol of freedom for all black South Africans and has gone out of his way to win the confidence of conservative Afrikaners and to allay fears in the coloured population. Although this is ANC policy, it is also very much a personal project, and it will be very interesting to see what happens when Mandela leaves the South African political scene.

Given that Lijphart's collectivist assumptions regarding the strength and role of ethnic identity in South Africa is correct, preservation of cultural distinctiveness through consociation could be more effective in containing ethnic conflict than the majoritarian framework proposed by the justice model. On the other hand, if Sachs and his like-minded are correct in their diagnosis — that what today takes the form of ethnic and racial tension to a large extent stem from the 'divide and rule' strategy applied by the apartheid state, combined with the problems of poverty and socioeconomic inequality — then consociational solutions could exacerbate conflicts rather than reduce them, due to their limited redistributive potential.

In certain sections of the South African population there appears to be a potential for ethnic mobilisation. This is reflected first of all by the IFP's mobilisation of rural Zulus and the support of Afrikaner parties to the right of the NP.[11] Still — and even if this trend is strengthened — it is not clear that the best response is to institutionalise ethnicity in the political system. While fencing groups off from one another may in some social contexts give rise to valuable cultivation of cultural diversity, to the benefit of all groups, there are reasons to doubt that this will be the case in South Africa.

First and foremost, fundamental structural inequalities between ethnic groups in South Africa detract from the suitability of consociationalism. And this is not only a matter of income and wealth. Large sections of society are literally uprooted: millions have been evicted to 'homelands', with or without the direct use of force. Family structures are broken by the system of labour migration. Modernisation processes, industrialisation and urbanisation, have left many black South Africans without direct access to traditional sources of cultural distinctness and social ties through which their heritage is passed on. While uprooting seem to nourish discontent, and leave the grounds open for ethnic mobilisation, it does not necessarily facilitate cultural development in a meaningful sense. The infrastructure (such as schools and organisational networks) required for cultural development in a modern context are unevenly distributed within South African society. While the Afrikaners fit the description of ethnic group/segment implicit in consociationalism, and to a certain extent also the Zulu nation, few other *ethnics* have the cohesion, self-consciousness and infrastructure needed to function adequately within, and benefit from, a consociational system.

This is not only a moral problem. It also presents problems to the function of the system itself. Consociationalism with its elite focus, grand coalition governments, consensus orientation, and high degree of secrecy, presupposes representative leaders who 'retain the support and loyalty of their followers' (Lijphart, 1977a: 53). This may to some extent be the case with Afrikaner nationalists.[12] In the black population there is widespread respect for traditional authorities, but this will not necessarily result in loyal support to the political elite. It may be politically significant, particularly in rural areas of KwaZulu-Natal, and in rural areas in other parts of the country (such as the Eastern Cape and Northern Province). But the support that coloured, Indian, or urban black leaders receive is generally not due to communal attachments. 'They are "leaders" because they articulate grievances ... They can hardly guarantee loyal, unquestioned support if they would enter into a controversial elite cartel' (Adam and Giliomee, 1979: 290).

A consociational South Africa would almost certainly lead to an increase in ethnically based political mobilisation. If the underlying assumption about the role of ethnicity and the character of ethnic groups turns out to be correct, it is not unlikely that the power-sharing mechanisms of this model could produce political stability. If, however, the interpretation turns out to be mistaken, if there is a stable majority segment, or if socioeconomic divisions (class) prove more salient than ethnicity, the political situation could become very unstable.

Even if it does succeed in producing stability, the implementation of this system in South Africa would imply a strong bias in favour of the privileged minority, working to institutionalise and entrench inequalities. The cultural relativism and collective focus embodied in consociationalism are valuable ideals to counterbalance the individualist liberalism of the justice model. South Africa is, however, a case in which cultural relativism leads to conservatism (Van Diepen, 1988: 7). This, coupled with the poor redistributive force of consociationalism, could well undermine the legitimacy of a consociational constitutional structure in the longer term.

There are, as we have seen, problems also when it comes to the justice model's handling of the ethnicity problem. The argument that a Bill of Rights does not cater sufficiently for minorities as cultural entities, may be valid. From the point of view of the white minority their interests may be insufficiently protected within this liberal framework. However, the most important problem with this form of protection, from the point of view of the privileged minority in South Africa, is probably not that it does not cater for their legitimate need to preserve and develop their culture, but rather that it does not protect their way of life, in the sense of standard of living. And while the wish to defend material resources is perfectly understandable, it cannot — given the inequalities in South Africa and their history — be regarded as a legitimate minority right.

A main argument against minority protection through constitutionally guaranteed individual rights is that this — at the end of the day — leaves the minorities at the peril of majority rule. Although the Bill of Rights protects vital minority interests, it does so only by placing external constraints on the majority. This, it may be argued, is a vulnerable defence. Politics is a matter of power, and unless the minorities have a share in power their interests will be threatened. The majority will, over time, through interpreting and amending the constitution — or by circumventing it — get their way. This argument is highly relevant. There are numerous examples of constitutions theoretically protecting all kinds of rights, but without any bearing whatsoever on practical politics. On the other hand there is never any guarantee against abuse of power. In consociational systems some parties may also decide not to play by the rules if they deem that their interests are better advanced through extra-legal means. Politics in ethnically divided societies is always a walk on a tight-rope. The case of former Yugoslavia illustrates both the possibilies of establishing institutions that accommodate the interests of different ethnic groups within the same state, and how rapidly and effectively such a system is undermined.

## Restating the Argument

I have now presented and evaluated Arend Lijphart's consociationalism and what I have termed Albie Sachs' justice model. These two constitutional models have been chosen because they articulate the rivalling positions in the battle over a post-apartheid constitution in South Africa. Their validity and applicability to the South African context have been questioned on methodological grounds. Their normative qualities have been considered, as has their feasibility in light of the ethnic diversity and socioeconomic inequality in South African society.

The models differ on a number of dimensions, and both may be criticised on methodological as well as normative accounts, but neither can be rejected as unsuitable for the South African context on the grounds of this critique. Each model addresses important social problems and gives a relatively coherent answer to the problems it sets out to solve — as it is interpreted here. On the basis of the inverse interpretation of South African society, both approaches appear utterly misplaced. In the end, the question of whether the models are valid generalisations, as well as whether they are acceptable on normative grounds, comes down to a matter of interpretation. Is South Africa 'really' a deeply divided society where ethnicity is the single most relevant political factor, or is it basically a class society, where socioeconomic inequality is the most acute obstacle to peace and democracy? There are both empirical evidence and political views supporting each interpretation, although so far ethnic divisions seem to be less salient than race and class in the 'new' South Africa.

The justice model, with its focus on individual rights and distributive justice, is founded on and justified by liberal contractarian theories. Within this interpretation injustice between individuals is the main problem. And the logical solution is to design the basic structure of society in such a manner that it results in a more equal and just distribution of resources and opportunities. From the point of view of liberal theories of justice the consociational approach is totally unacceptable. Its collective methodological focus — regarding groups rather than individuals as the basic units of South

African society, is dismissed, along with its emphasis on the political significance of ethnic loyalties.

The consociational approach is, however, justified by another influential school of contemporary normative political philosophy. *The communitarians* argue for the primacy of society and of deep structures of belonging, such as ethnic loyalties. The individual is partially constituted by society and norms are seen to vary fundamentally between cultures. This ontology implies that social conflicts cannot be overcome by creating common norms of material justice — a goal towards which the basic structure of society is directed. In multi-ethnic societies the state should thus aim at mediation only, protecting the groups from one another. Conflicts arising from diverging norms should be resolved in intra-segmental political bodies. In this perspective, the justice model's concern for justice as the primary virtue of social institutions invariably means illegitimate imposition of one specific group's norms.

Having acknowledged that both models may be provided with an internal justification, we went on to consider their coherence with external 'universal' standards: the acceptability of the constitutional proposals were considered in the light of democracy and human rights norms. This analysis concluded that although both models on an overall account may be considered acceptable, the consociational model, in particular, has important deficiencies.

The consociational model lacks clear lines of accountability. The opportunity for popular participation is limited, as is voter influence on the outcome of politics. This detracts from its democratic qualities, and is also a problem in terms of political human rights. The lack of concern for socioeconomic rights is another inadequacy — particularly acute in the South African context, given the apartheid legacy. This could hinder a consociational model from gaining the support needed for stability.

The justice model is clearly more satisfactory in terms of democratic and human rights criteria (save collective rights and the rights of minorities). This is not surprising as the model draws its roots from the same philosophical tradition as do democracy and individual human rights norms. The main danger is that of 'overdoing it'. The tension inherent in constitutional democracy, between democracy and the domain of politics on the one hand and the constitutional domain on the other, becomes acute. Enshrining all forms of human rights in the constitution constricts the room for democratic political decisions and limits the effect of political rights.

Given the circumstances of South Africa, there seems to be a better chance of the justice model being supported by moral sentiment in civil society, setting in motion a process of 'constitutional patriotism' and thus gaining authority and stability. At least at the initial stage, the justice model seems more likely to provide governments with legitimacy. This could in turn, make them less dependent on current performance and provide space for pursuing long-term goals. In the longer perspective, political performance is crucial.

Are the models feasible 'solutions' in light of the problems and conflicts of South Africa? Neither ethnic conflict, nor (and even less so) problems of poverty, inequality and violence — are 'solved' by enacting a constitution, not even if the ideal constitution could be found. Some constitutional structures provide more adequate frameworks, however, within which these problems may be addressed.

Concerning the prospects for reducing inequality and alleviating poverty, it is argued that three factors are crucial. First of all, redistribution in the South African context seems to require focused government action, and *potent government* is thus a precondition. Secondly, long-term economic development is frustrated by irresponsible *macroeconomic populism*. Government ability to resist the pressure of popular expectations, and avoid heavy deficit spending is crucial. And thirdly, restructuring of the economy and an adequate *development path* is needed to cope with the legacy of apartheid.

Neither of these conditions is a direct function of the constitution. They all depend on external economic conditions as well as the political judgement capacity and skill of the leadership. Still, probabilities for potent governments, responsible macroeconomic policies, and the formulation of an adequate development path differs between the two models.

Consideration of the models against these criteria concluded tentatively that the justice model is the more likely to produce potent governments — and governments with better potential for developing a new alternative economic policy through which redistribution may be pursued. The justice model does, however, seem to render its governments vulnerable to popular demands for increases in welfare, and hence to the temptations of macro-economic populism.

As regards the consociational model, the opposite conclusion was drawn: governments are likely to be weaker and the privileged sections of society are provided with considerable scope for resisting redistribution. Given the mediator role of governments and the emphasis on de-politisation and foreclosure of conflicts between the segments of society, there is also little potential within this model for a new development path or economic policy. It seems that governments would have to rely mainly on redistribution with growth through the trickle-down effect of the market, and significant redistribution is not likely to occur. Consociational governments seem, however, less prone to enter into macroeconomic populism, thereby reducing the risks of severe long-term economic decay.

While the justice model, on a total score, appears better fit for taking on the legacy of apartheid, in the sense of promoting significant increases in welfare for the black majority, this is also the strategy running the greatest risk of failure. It may result in a more just society and thus promote stability, but it may also end in economic chaos.

Regarding the models' capabilities for providing answers to the problems of societal pluralism, that is the ethnic diversity and conflict in South African society, the suitability of their solutions rely precariously on the adequacy of their interpretations. If ethnic loyalties have the qualities assumed by consociationalists — that is, if they are deep structures providing a sense of meaning, to the effect that the relative standing of cultural groups are more important to their members than their relative standing as individual citizens — then the justice model does not seem as adequate an approach. Protecting the cultural rights of individuals within a common political sphere will not suffice. Meaningful development of cultural identity and tradition requires segmental autonomy and the safeguarding of each group against intrusion by others. But is this a reasonable interpretation of the role of ethnicity in South Africa?

There is no neutral ground from where the accuracy of the respective interpretations may be assessed. Considering the nature of the political transition and the two years of democratic politics under the government of national unity, I so far lean towards accepting the interpretation underlying the justice model as the more appropriate. The model's strategy for safeguarding 'the right to be different and the right to be the same' through guaranteeing individual cultural rights, seems adequate — provided that the rights of association and freedom of expression are not significantly restricted.

In my view the failure of consociationalism to include concerns for the social and economic legacy of apartheid is critical. Although the model may function according to its intentions, and be superior to the justice model in other divided societies, it is, given the circumstances of South Africa, likely to preserve the unjust inequalities created by apartheid. This in turn, could undermine its legitimacy and lead to regime break-down. Given that sufficient obfuscation of the racial structure of inequality had been achieved a consociational system could, however, have turned out to be stable.

A question flowing from the consideration of the two constitutional models is whether it is possible to 'get the best of the two worlds' — or perhaps rather to avoid the worst problems associated with the justice and the consociational models respectively? Could a combination of promising elements from each of them yield a constitution with better potential for solving the problems of South Africa? And is the new South African constitution such a fruitful synthesis? This is a central question in the remaining chapters.

## Notes

1.  Source: Central Statistical Service 1997. The annual compound population growth rates for the period 1991-1995 is estimated at 2.06 per cent. This estimate may, however, be too high. The census conducted in 1996 indicate that the South African population is only 37,9 million and not 42 million as previously estimated.

2.  The 'trickle down effect' refers to the stylised relationships between economic growth and income in which income inequalities narrow only when a relatively high level of industrialisation has been achieved and the labour surplus of the economy has been absorbed into employment in the industrial sector. For a period — as long as there is a labour surplus — rapid economic growth will widen income inequalities, but growth is also a precondition for the later narrowing. The theory originates from the works of Kuznets (1955) and has for decades been popular within development economics. Critique is, however, also widespread (see McGrath, 1990: 96).

3.  The particular policies through which redistribution may be sought, cannot be inferred from constitutional models, but the scope allowed for various forms of policies vary between the models.

4.  As long as 'intolerable inequality' exists, the institutions installed to guard the constitution and the Bill of Rights (courts, Social Rights Commission and the Ombud), work to ensure that legislation and policies work to 'expand the floor of basic social rights'.

5.  The Reconstruction and Development Programme (RDP) adopted by the ANC before the 1994 elections, and subsequently made the official policy of the ANC-led Government of National Unity, is in important respects a policy framework along the lines prescribed by the justice model.

6.  Especially if we go along with Adam's (1983) prognostication, where three 'cultural heritage groups' are envisioned — Afrikaner, English and African. The African group is expected to split along Zulu-Xhosa lines, leaving us with four groups instead of 14, as predicted by Lijphart. On the basis of the current situation, Adam's diagnosis seems more correct, at least for the initial phase.

7.  For instance, civil service appointments may be distributed to achieve proportionality in the bureaucracy, or to give some over-representation to (numerically) weaker groups.

8.  Since the groups are the units for comparison, different factors contributing to their power and relative standing add up. Numerical strength, reflected in political representation, may compensate for socioeconomic weakness. In spite of great socioeconomic inequality, there may still exist an equilibrium between the ethnic groups

constituting society. The collectivist methodological focus of consociational models thus contributes to their propensity to down-play the role socioeconomic factors.

9.  The many years of unrest have also interfered with the formal education of a whole generation of African youth — leaving many of those most active in the struggle for change, unfit for peace. Unless active steps are taken to meet the expectations of this highly politicised group, it is likely to undermine the legitimacy of the new regime and threaten political stability in the longer term. The crime rate is already extremely high and rising, and constitutes a major threat to political stability as well as economic growth (see Chapter 2).

10. This critique of the individualistic foundation of liberal theories of justice, is only implicit with Lijphart — and in most consociational theory. It is, however, formulated more explicitly by the communitarians who share the same collectivist preconditions. This is discussed at length in Chapter 4.

11. The Minority Front, with a basis in the Indian community also did surprisingly well in the local governments elections in Durban in June 1996, while the nationalist coloured parties, who have attracted considerable attention in the Western Cape, remain insignificant.

12. Although the NP, by going into negotiations with the ANC and later with the Government of National Unity, lost significant support among Afrikaner nationalists.

# PART IV
# THE 'FINAL' CONSTITUTION

# 9 Constitutional Compromises

Having analysed the main contenders in the battle over the South African constitution, we now embark upon the examination of the 'final' constitution and the process leading up to its adoption.

The interim constitution of 1993 stands as a major landmark in the South African constitution-making process. It is the 'truce' that ended the first round of the battle for a democratic constitution in South Africa, by enabling the transition from *apartheid* rule in the April 1994 elections. The interim constitution laid the foundation for a second phase of negotiations and included a set of entrenched constitutional principles that defined limits for the 'final' text. Knowledge of the interim constitution and its constitutional principles is crucial to understand the character of the 'final' constitution.

After two years of negotiations 'the birth certificate of a nation' was passed by the Constitutional Assembly on 8 May 1996. According to the rules of the interim constitution it was submitted to the Constitutional Court for certification. The task of the court was to test its consistency with the constitutional principles. Judgement was handed down on 6 October. A number of sections were rejected and the text was referred back to the Constitutional Assembly. New negotiations were needed for the 'final' constitution finally to be 'final'.

This chapter presents both the 1993 interim constitution, the text that was adopted on 8 May 1996 and the amendments that were made in order to comply with the requirements of the Constitutional Court.[1] The presentation is guided by the framework of analysis developed in Chapter 3 and seeks to clarify the character of the constitutional texts on dimensions that are crucial from the perspective of democratic consolidation. This also emphasises how the 'final' South African constitution has been formed by the models presented in previous chapters, in some cases leading to an outcome that differs from both.

**Constitutional Talks**

When did the process towards a post-apartheid constitution for South Africa start? Lines could be drawn to the adoption of the Freedom Charter in 1955 or even to the founding of the ANC in 1912. Organised and articulated struggle against the foundations of the apartheid state goes a long way back. The struggle has been directed towards creating a new political order, and thus constitutional change, but the explicit focus on constitutionalism is of recent date. The predominant ANC ideology has traditionally been one of 'popular democracy' or unchecked majority rule. Interest in constitutional government emerged as a significant force only in the latter part of the 1980s. Albie Sachs himself, as a 'convert to constitutionalism' was instrumental in starting the process that brought about a growing acceptance within the ANC for the values of human rights protection through a justiciable Bill of Rights (Judicial Service Commission, 1994).

Constitutionalism has remained a controversial issue within the organisation. The increased embracing of constitutionalism by central parts of the ANC coincided with the process of secret talks between the ANC and the apartheid regime, starting in 1986 (Maphai, 1994: 43). This has lead critics to see the ANC adoption of a position of liberal constitutional democracy as a concession to the NP government, and constitutional experts involved in the negotiation process, and as a betrayal of their traditional ideals of participatory democracy and social justice (van Huyssteen, 1996).

The fact that the NP government also displayed an increasing interest in constitutionalism during the 1980s seems to support this interpretation. As the realities of a multi-racial *demos* became a question of when, rather than if, they reworked their position away from the majoritarian, Westminster-style government of the day, where parliament rather than the constitution is the highest authority, towards a state form based on constitutionalism, federalism and power-sharing, as presented in Chapter 4 above.

As we have seen throughout this book, the notions of constitutionalism that the two parties embrace is rather different. The NP has primarily seen constitutionalism as a method for foreclosure of issues, a way to lift as many issues as possible out of the political domain, or at least away from the arena of the central state, and into intra-segmental fora. The primary role of the constitution is to limit conflicts between groups through diffusion and division of political power, and by ensuring that no group is capable of threatening the central interests of any other group.

The conception of constitutionalism reflected in the ANC position is different. It is that of constitutionalism as pre-commitment. Like Ulysses binding himself to avoid succumbing to the temptation of the sirens' song (Elster, 1979). Here constitutionalism is about commitment to certain values. It seeks to ensure that long-term goals are not compromised by short-sighted decisions, but otherwise acknowledges the need for a strong political force to facilitate development. It implies a certain distrust of political power, but not to the extent reflected by the NP position.

In the light of these differences in the conceptions of constitutionalism there is little reason to assume that the ANC conversion to constitutionalism was a direct result of influence or pressure from the National Party. On the other hand both parties' positions are influenced by the negotiation process and the need to reach a settlement.[2]

## Codesa

The formalised constitutional process started with 'talks about talks' in May 1990. A year and a half later, in December 1991, the first formal negotiations started at the World Trade Centre, Kempton Park, outside Johannesburg. This was the first session of *Codesa* — the Convention for a Democratic South Africa. The second session, which took place in May 1992, ultimately broke down over the issues of federalism, the composition and role of the senate, the status of the interim constitution and the majority needed for adoption of the 'final' constitution. In light of the analysis in the preceding chapters this is hardly surprising. These are central matters affecting the very core of the rivalling constitutional models, namely the conflict between the 'acquisition of power by the oppressed majority' and the 'protection of the minorities against the majority' (Maphai, 1994: 80).

After a period of 'rolling mass action' and escalating political violence, talks resumed again in April 1993, this time in the context of a Multiparty Negotiating Process. A conservative alliance (COSAG) led by the Inkatha Freedom Party (IFP) and the Conservative Party (CP), were dissatisfied with the lack of progress on the issue of federalism, as well as with the interim status of the document under negotiation, and walked out of the negotiations. Despite problems the interim constitution was adopted with 'sufficient consensus' on 18 November 1993, clearing the path for elections to be held on 27 April 1994. Shortly before the elections, constitutional amendments securing the powers of the provinces, the possibility of a *Volkstaat*, a constitutional role for the Zulu monarch, and promises of post-election international mediation, brought parts of the Afrikaner right-wing (the Freedom Front (FF)), and finally also the IFP into the electoral process.

## The Interim Constitution

The interim constitution is an intriguing document, marked by the bargaining that brought it about.

Elements of institutionalised power-sharing figure prominently: a coalition government of national unity (GNU) with secured participation for all parties with more than 5 per cent of the vote; the creation of nine provinces with their own elected parliaments and provincial constitutions; a two-chamber parliament with provincial representation in the Senate; and institutionalisation of proportional representation (PR) elections for the legislatures at national and provincial level. Significant for the sitting regime, jobs of civil servants were guaranteed for five years. Most consequential, however, were the 34 constitutional principles, fully entrenched, with which the 'final' constitution was required to comply.

### The Constitutional Principles

What is referred to as 34 constitutional principles (CPs) is in fact a much higher number of requirements as many of them have several parts (see appendix for full text). The CPs fall into three different categories.

The first ten principles are provisions for democratic, constitutional government with regular elections, universal suffrage, a common voters roll and proportional representation. It is a commitment to basic human rights, equality before the law, non-discrimination and a constitutional basis for affirmative action. It is stated that the 'final' constitution must provide for a separation of power between the branches of government,[3] appropriate checks and balances, an independent judiciary and freedom of information. A related concern is expressed in principle XXIX which states that '[t]he independence and impartiality of a Public Service Commission, a Reserve Bank, an Auditor General, and a Public Protector shall be provided for and safeguarded'.

The second category of principles may be seen as concessions to consociationalism (CPs XI–XXVII and XXXIV). It is stated that 'provision shall be made for participation of minority political parties in the legislative process' (CP XIV), and that constitutional amendments shall require special procedures and special majorities. Protection must be given to the diversity of language and culture, 'collective rights of self-determination in forming, joining and maintaining organs of civil society, including linguistic, cultural and religious associations' (CP XII); recognition of and protection for traditional leadership, indigenous law and common law. The constitution shall not preclude 'the right to self-determination of any community sharing a common cultural and language heritage' (CP XXXIV).[4]

Even more important from a consociational perspective are the principles concerning federal arrangements (CPs XVI–XXVII). They state that government 'shall be structured at national, provincial and local levels' (CP XVI), with democratic representation at each level. The constitution must define and protect provincial powers and boundaries, and amendments require approval of 'a special majority of the legislatures of the provinces, alternatively ... a two-thirds majority of a chamber of Parliament composed of by special representatives' (CP XVIII.4). Amendments concerning special provinces must be approved by the relevant provincial legislature. National and provincial levels of government shall each have 'exclusive and concurrent powers' (CP XIX), and 'appropriate and adequate legislative and executive powers and functions that will enable each level to function effectively' (CP X).

CP XXI sets out how powers shall be allocated to each level of government. Generally, decision-making power should be placed where such decisions can be taken most effectively in terms of rendering of services. Powers must be allocated at national level where 'one voice' or national uniformity is required; or where necessary for national economic policies or protection of the common market. Concurrent powers should be given *inter alia* for the purposes of provincial planning and development; the rendering of services; socioeconomic and cultural matters; and where necessary to guarantee equal opportunity or access to a government service. Even where the provinces have exclusive powers there is a number of conditions under which the national level of government should be given authority to intervene (among others maintenance of national standards; economic unity; national security).

This amounts to a substantial power of the national government to override provincial legislation, but there are limits. 'The national government shall not exercise its powers ... so as to encroach upon the geographical, functional or institutional integrity of the provinces' (CP XXII). Furthermore, all levels of government shall have constitutionally defined fiscal powers and functions and 'a constitutional right to an equitable share of revenue collected nationally' (CP XXVI). The shares shall be recommended by a Financial and Fiscal Commission where all provinces are represented. In addition to these specific requirements CP XVIII.2 adds the more general — and very significant — condition that 'the present powers and functions of provinces in terms of the constitution may not be substantially diminished in the new constitutional text'.

The constitution must also set out 'a framework for local government powers, function and structures' (CP XXIV), while the details of local government are to be left to ordinary legislation at parliamentary and/or provincial level.

The principles regarding federal arrangements are open to various interpretations and leave scope for bargaining, and this is where much of the hard negotiations took place in the second phase of the constitution-writing process. As we shall see, these are also what caused the most trouble for the Constitutional Court during the certification process.

The last category of constitutional principles deals with more specific issues: the right to join and form unions; the rights of collective bargaining and fair labour practices. Another specifies that the constitution must provide for a non-partisan, career-orientated public service broadly representative of the community; yet another that the security forces must be non-partisan. There are also provisions guaranteeing the working of a Government of National Unity, and the present Parliament, until April 1999.

## Who Won the Battle of the Interim Constitution?

The end of *apartheid* and the introduction of a democratic political order is a tremendous victory for the liberation movement and the ANC. The interim constitution and the constitutional principles represent, however, significant deviations from the favoured constitutional model of the ANC. There are concessions that bear proof of the bargaining strength of the sitting regime, as well as the blackmail potential of the IFP and the white right wing parties.

On the other hand, the concessions fall short of the NP government's proposals, let alone the aspirations of the IFP and other conservative parties, fighting the battle from outside the arena of the negotiations. Despite a federal structure, the interim constitution grants relatively limited powers to the provinces,[5] and although minority parties may participate in the Government of National Unity they are not given any veto powers.

The greatest defeat from the perspective of the NP government was the failure to secure a long-term share in executive power. The interim constitution is a 'sunset arrangement' valid for only five years. Beyond this period the only secured terrain is that covered by the 34 constitutional principles, and they do not include a share in executive power for minority parties. This was to be one of the major battles of the second stage of the constitution-making process.

The two-stage process itself is a compromise between the NP government's demand for a negotiated settlement safeguarding their position before they surrendered power, and the ANC's position that the constitution of a post-apartheid South African democracy could only be legitimate if drawn up by a democratically elected body.

Prominent characteristics of the interim constitution are summarised in the table below. There are compromises on a number of issues, resulting in mixed or 'quasi' arrangements that cannot easily be fitted into the typology of the bipolar analytical framework. On most dimensions the interim constitution reflects an attempt to accommodate both views, either by striking a compromise, or, in some cases, by endorsing both (often seemingly contradictory) concerns. This is reflected in the table where, on some of the dimensions, both positions are put in bold types. With regard to the last dimension, normative justification, relatively strict coherence is required. I have not found sufficient coherence between this mixed constitutional structure and either of the philosophical positions that underlie the constitutional models presented earlier. Some of the choices of labels may be open to dispute, e.g. whether this is a unitary, decentralised form of state or a centralised federal arrangement, but the table conveys the overall impression of a mixed constitution, leaning toward consociationalism. There is more detailed discussion of the arrangements of the interim constitution in relation to the presentation of the 'final' constitution later in the chapter.

## Second phase of Constitution-making: the Constitutional Assembly

The second phase of constitution-making started on the 27 April 1994: a Constitutional Assembly of 490 members was elected by proportional representation. The ANC won 312 seats, just short of the two thirds required to single-handedly adopt a new constitution. The Constitutional Assembly consisted of the two chambers of Parliament in joint session.

### Table 9.1 The Interim Constitution of 1993

| Dimension | The Interim Constitution<br>position within the range of variation | |
|---|---|---|
| **(i) Institutional Set-sup** | | |
| institutional focus | **legal system** | political system |
| electoral system | majoritarian | **proportional** |
| legislature-executive rel. | presidentialism/**quasi-presidentialism**/parliamentarism | |
| compos. of legislature | uni-cameral | **(quasi) bi-cameral** |
| compos. of executive | one party | **coalition** |
| | **single executive** | collective executive body |
| decentralisation | unitary state | **federal state** |
| | **centralised** | highly decentralised |
| decision-making mode | adversarial | **consensual** |
| | **majoritarian** | minority vetoes |
| **(ii) Interpretation of Reality** | | |
| methodological focus | **individual** | collective |
| problem focus | **structural** | cultural |
| | **inequality, poverty** | ethnicity |
| **(iii) Central Value** | **justice** | stability,<br>cultural autonomy |
| | **positive liberty** | **negative liberty** |
| **(iv) Objective** | **transformation** | regulation |
| **(v) Response to Pluralism**<br>(the nation-building dimension) | assimilation / **non-interference** / separation | |
| **(vi) State-Society Rel.** | participation | representation |
| **(vii) The Constitutional Domain** | democracy | **constitutionalism** |
| | Rule of law | **Rechtsstaat** |
| | **precommitment** | foreclosure of issues |
| **(viii) Normative Foundation/ Justification** | liberalism | communitarian |
| | contractarian philos. | philosophy |

The central co-ordinating body and main negotiating forum was the 46 member multi-party Constitutional Committee. The other main structures were the 12 member Management Committee and six Theme Committees.

The work of the Constitutional Assembly set off to a slow start. A busy schedule in Parliament caused delays as did logistical problems involved in coordinating two administrative structures.[6] What really hampered the process, and caused concern, was, however, the decision of the IFP to boycott the constitutional negotiations.

*Inkatha Freedom Party — Playing from Outside the Field*

The IFP walk-out from the Constitutional Assembly in March 1995 came after months of disagreement over international mediation. International mediation on 'outstanding issues' was part of the Agreement for Reconciliation signed by the IFP, the ANC and the NP on 19 April 1994, in order to bring the IFP into the elections.

After the elections, the parties failed to agree on what role international mediation should have in the process. The ANC argued that mediation would only be relevant once a deadlock had occurred, and only in relation to issues specified in the agreement (i.e. outstanding issues in the 1993 interim constitution and issues relating to the role of the Zulu monarchy.) The IFP, on the other hand, wanted mediation to pertain also to the 'final' constitution, and seemed to opt for mediation as an alternative process to the negotiations in the Constitutional Assembly (Kotze, 1996: 145–50).

The electoral performance of the IFP was relatively weak. Although they ended up as the third largest party, and were awarded a majority in KwaZulu-Natal,[7] their share of the national vote was only 10.5%. With 48 representatives in the Constitutional Assembly, Inkatha's influence in the multi-party forum was likely to be limited. Their blackmail potential was on the other hand considerable, due both to their strength in KwaZulu-Natal and their apparent ability to generate political instability and violence. In this perspective the alternative route of international mediation must have seemed advantageous to the IFP compared with participation in the formal constitution-writing process. This was particularly so since the first phase of constitution-making had shown that concessions could be drawn through a boycott strategy and the establishment of a dual process of negotiations (Kotze, 1996: 135).

It should, however, become clear that the post-election situation was different. The new democratic structures, struggling to build legitimacy, could not afford to be sidelined. The ANC, strengthened by their solid electoral victory, stood firm on the decision that international mediation was out of the question until specific outstanding issues appropriate for such mediation were identified. The IFP on their part stood by their decision not to return to the Constitutional Assembly, although they continued to participate in Parliament and in the Government of National Unity.

The obvious problem with regard to the IFP boycott is, of course, the negative effect on the legitimacy of the constitution. This aside, are there reasons to believe that their participation would have made a difference to the product? There are signs that the IFP might have gained more in terms of federalism and provincial autonomy if they had participated. The party's position is radically federal, bordering on confederalism. Although it goes further than the other parties represented in the Constitutional Assembly, all parties except the ANC and the PAC were united in their support for greater provincial powers. This is also an issue where there seemed to be differences of opinion within the ANC, with voices suggesting further concessions in terms of provincial autonomy if this could bring the IFP on board. (A clear statement to this effect was made by Mpumalanga premier Matthews Phosa, cited in the *Daily Star* on 26 February 1996.) But the IFP did not join and, as it were, the second stage of negotiations, like the first, was finalised with the ANC and the NP as the main players.

The DP, with a mere 7 seats in the Constitutional Assembly, drew attention to their core concerns due to principled argumentation and stamina. While their arguments regarding liberal freedom, the need for checks and balances, and the dangers of horizontal application of rights, were not always successful, the party yielded an influence disproportionate to its size.

The Freedom Front consists mainly of and for conservative Afrikaners. Despite the ideological distance from the ANC, the party was generally cooperative throughout the negotiation process.[8] In return, the door was kept open for a *Volkstaat* Council and a potential right of minorities to self-determination within the framework of the South African state. And a commission is to protect the cultural and other rights of minorities. Despite the concessions the FF abstained from the Constitution Bill vote, citing protection of the Afrikaans language in education as the main reason.

*Last-minute Compromises*

The deadline for the constitution-making process was within two years of the first session of Parliament, that is, 10 May 1996. On most clauses agreement was reached well ahead of the deadline, but some major issues were under debate until weeks, and even days of the scheduled date. The question of minority influence in the executive arm of government was among these, along with other issues affecting 'the heart of the constitution' — and the core of the constitutional models discussed previously: the powers of the provinces; the role of the National Council of Provinces; the balance of power between Parliament and the executive.

The very last outstanding issues concerned aspects of the Bill of Rights. They may seem as details compared with the broader issues above, but are matters of both practical and symbolic significance. The contentious issues were, first, the formulation of the property clause, and the limitations in the right to property (particularly in relation to land reform); second, language in education, that is whether there should be a right to receive education in single-language schools; and, last, whether the right to strike should be balanced by a constitutional right to lock-out.

Failure to reach a compromise would ultimately result in a referendum on the ANC constitutional proposal.[9] Neither party welcomed a referendum or new elections, but the ANC seemed to use the referendum-spectre as a bargaining chip in the last phase, bolstered by a good showing in the November 1995 local government elections.[10] Pressure from the labour movement reinforced the ANC position.[11]

The single most important issue from the perspective of the NP, with their consociational position, was that of minority party influence in the executive, and this became the party's most obvious defeat. That this battle was lost, and that the party had realised it, became clear during a private *bosberaad* between senior constitutional negotiators from all parties at Arniston in early April 1996, where the NP indicated that they could accept a constitution without provisions for a government of national unity in its existing form. They continued to negotiate for an alternative arrangement to secure minority influence in executive decisions, but in this matter the ANC did not concede. Failure to secure even a token share of executive power was a serious defeat for the NP, and was cited as the main reason for their decision to resign from the GNU, three years before its mandate expired. With no prospects of a share in power it became vital for the party to build its credibility as the leader of the opposition.

With regard to the powers of the provinces, the role of the Council of Provinces, and the separation of powers, agreements were reached through mutual adjustment. Major gains from the perspective of the opposition were the retention of legislative review, and recognition of the Council of Provinces as part of Parliament, which remained bi-cameral.

Compared with the 1993 interim constitution, the text that was adopted on 8 May is less consociational and more in line with the justice model and the ANC's negotiating position. This reflects the fact that the ANC, with an overwhelming victory at the polls, had almost two thirds of the members in the Constitutional Assembly, and thus were in a better bargaining position than prior to the transition.

But the 'final' constitution is not a complete victory for the ANC. While the party won most of the constitutional battles between May 1994 and May 1996, the interim constitution and the 'final' constitution are surprisingly similar. Concessions were made during the first phase of the constitution-making process that set the premises for the negotiations, particularly so those that were entrenched in the 34 constitutional principles. And the constitutional principles not only set the premises for the negotiations, they also made sure that the Constitutional Assembly's adoption of a 'final' constitution did not end the constitutional battle.

## To Certify or not to Certify ...

The interim constitution requires that before a new constitution can take effect, the Constitutional Court must certify that the text is consistent with the 34 constitutional principles (IC, Section 73(2)). For four months after the adoption of the Constitution of South Africa Bill the question was whether the 'final' constitution would be certified and become law, or whether the Court would refer it back to the Constitutional Assembly for new negotiations.

For the Constitutional Court the task was difficult. Judicial certification of a national constitution is unprecedented. The interim constitution gives no details of the procedure, only states that the outcome is final and binding. Thus the Court first had to define its approach (Constitutional Court, CCT 23/96 [1][12]). Should the constitution be judged as a whole or section by section? Should it be matched against each individual principle, or should the constitutional principles be taken *en bloc?* There are also problems of interpretation. What the CPs require and what the constitutional text implies, involves a measure of judgement. Formulations are ambiguous, as will often be the case were compromise must be found between fundamentally different political positions. The judges faced the difficult task of giving substance to these formulations without sidelining the democratic political process and choosing sides in the long-standing political controversy.

The position adopted by the Constitutional Court is carefully spelled out in the judgement (CCT 23/96). The constitutional text was judged first with regard to the structure as a whole, and then section by section. An integrated, holistic approach was taken with regard to the constitutional principles. The CPs were regarded as guidelines and boundaries. As such they were not interpreted with technical rigidity, but seen as 'broad constitutional strokes' to be applied 'purposively and teleologically' to create a new democratic constitutional state. Each principle was considered on its own terms, but in light of the total set of CPs, 'no CP should be interpreted in a manner which involves conflict with another' (CCT 23/96 [32–43]). The constitutional principles define a scope of permissible options, and the Court emphasised that it should not do the work of the Constitutional Assembly by favouring one permissible option over others. Similarly, in cases where a constitutional provision can be reasonably interpreted in more than one way, and where some interpretations violate the principles while others do not, a 'benign' approach was taken. That is, the Court interpreted the text so that it would be compatible with the requirements of the CPs. The judgement made in each case clear which interpretation formed the basis of its decision, and this is the authoritative interpretation for later evaluations of constitutionality (CCT 23/96 [42–43]).

Apart from the complexity of the task, the matter was also complicated by the potentially grave consequences of sending the carefully stitched compromise back to the Constitutional Assembly. In principle the entire constitution would be open for re-negotiation. And even if an agreement were made that only the rejected parts should be renegotiated, there would be a host of related issues that needed to be reconsidered. That the NP had left the Government of National Unity and was in the process of establishing itself as an opposition party could make it more difficult to reach a new agreement. On the practical side, the secretariat of the Constitution Assembly had been scaled down to only a few people and the former staff had gone to new positions (*Mail & Guardian*, 5 July 1996). A number of the most senior constitutional negotiators both of the ANC and the NP had also left Parliament after the 'final' constitution was adopted. Among them were the Chairman of the Constitutional Assembly, Cyril Ramaphosa of the ANC and his deputy Leon Wessels of the NP.[13]

These factors suggest that there were reasons for the Court not to 'rock the boat', but there were also incentives working in the opposite direction. The certification of the 'final' constitution is the most important and prestigious decision the Constitutional Court will ever make, and a questionable certification could seriously harm the reputation of the Court itself. The Court also has a special interest in the constitution as it is the very basis of its existence and determines the scope of its authority.

As part of the certification process, political parties, organisations and the general public were invited to send in submissions setting out how the text violated one or more of the CPs. Some objectors were invited to give additional oral statements so that the court could inquire more fully into the issues that were raised.[14] Hearings were held in the first two weeks of July 1996, and most of the political parties used the opportunity to present arguments.[15] The most notable exception was the ANC.[16]

The ANC gave notice that it identified with the position of the Constitutional Assembly, in whose name the application for certification was made, and hence would not present a separate argument. This unequivocal backing blurred the distinction between the Constitutional Assembly and the ANC, and made the constitutional text appear as an ANC document rather than the product of inter-party negotiations. This runs counter to what otherwise stand out as a primary aim of the constitution-making process — namely to create a sense of shared ownership in the constitution and thereby promote nation building.

The 'partisan' image of the constitutional text also added to the task of the Constitutional Court. The Court needed to be extra careful as any ruling was bound to be political, in the sense of supporting the ANC or the opposition. The independence of the Court had also previously been questioned (O'Malley, 1996).

The combined weight of all these factors add up to a heavy burden on the shoulders of the eleven Constitutional Court judges.

## Judgement Day

Judgement was handed down on 6 September. 'Not certified'. The overall structure, and the vast majority of regulations in the constitutional text were found to satisfy the constitutional principles, but the Court pointed to the following problem areas as the reason for their judgement (summarised in CCT 23/96 [482]):

- the powers and functions of the provinces were found to be substantially less than and inferior to those of the interim constitution (the text did not comply with CP XVII.2);

- the constitutional text did not provide the required 'framework for the structures' of local government, nor 'appropriate fiscal powers and functions' (NT Chapter 7, on local government, was dismissed as a whole, along with NT Section 229, as inconsistent with CPs X, XXIV and XXV);
- the text failed to provide for the independence and impartiality of the Public Service Commission and to specify its powers and functions (NT Section 196, in breach of CPs XX and XXIX);
- the independence and impartiality of the Public Protector and the Attorney General were not sufficiently provided for (NT Section 194 failed to comply with CP XXIX);
- the entrenchment of fundamental rights were deemed insufficient and the Court also found a lack of special procedures for constitutional change (NT Section 74 failed to comply with CP II and XV);
- the section on states of emergency (NT Section 37(5)) 'attempt to render derogable what can in practice never be justified' (CCT 23/96 [94]);
- there was an impermissible immunisation of certain statutes from constitutional review (NT Sections 241(1) and Schedule 6, Section 22(1)(b), violates CP IV and VII); and finally
- the text failed to recognise the right of individual employers to engage in collective bargaining (NT Section 23 violates CP XXVIII).

Rumours had been that the draft constitutional text would be referred back to the Constitutional Assembly, but still there was an atmosphere of shock when it actually happened. The battle was on again. The new context had strengthened the opposition, and there was also pressure to re-open issues that the Constitutional Court had accepted (*Mail & Guardian,* 4 October 1996). The demands in this direction were particularly clear from the IFP, who, somewhat surprisingly, joined the amendment process.[17] The ANC on their part, struggled to restrict this round of negotiations to a minimum.

The compromise was that the Constitutional Assembly would concentrate on the issues that the Court referred back, but with 'elasticity' for related concerns. Significantly, the constitution would not be adopted anew. The changes would be tabled as amendments and adoption day would still be 8 May. As agreement was about to be finalised, the IFP pulled out of the negotiations again. The amended constitution was passed by the Constitutional Assembly on 11 October, resubmitted to the Constitutional Court and finally certified on 4 December 1996.

## Table 9.2   The 'Final' South African Constitution*

| | Dimension | The 'final' constitution<br>position within the range of variation | |
|---|---|---|---|
| (i) | **Institutional Set-up** | | |
| | institutional focus | legal system | **political system** |
| | electoral system | majoritarian | **proportional** |
| | legislature-executive rel. | presidentialism/**quasi-presidentialism**/parliamentarism | |
| | compos. of legislature | uni-cameral | **bi-cameral** |
| | compos. of executive | **one party** | coalition |
| | | **single executive** | collective executive body |
| | decentralisation | unitary state | **federal state** |
| | | **centralised** | highly decentralised |
| | decision-making mode | adversarial | **consensual** |
| | | **majoritarian** | minority vetoes |
| (ii) | **Interpretation of Reality** | | |
| | methodological focus | **individual** | collective |
| | problem focus | **structural** | cultural |
| | | **inequality, poverty** | ethnicity |
| (iii) | **Central Value** | **justice** | stability,<br>cultural autonomy |
| | | **positive liberty** | **negative liberty** |
| (iv) | **Objective** | **transformation** | regulation |
| (v) | **Response to Pluralism**<br>(the nation-building dimension) | assimilation / **non-interference** / separation | |
| (vi) | **State-Society Rel.** | participation | **representation** |
| (vii) | **The Constitutional**<br>**Domain** | democracy | **constitutionalism** |
| | | Rule of law | **Rechtsstaat** |
| | | **precommitment** | foreclosure of issues |
| (viii) | **Normative Foundation/**<br>**Justification** | **liberalism** | communitarian |
| | | **contractarian philos.** | philosophy |

\*   Although important changes were made as a result of the Constitutional Court's judgement they do
   not affect the position of the 'final' constitution for any of the dimension of this framework.

In the remaining part of this chapter the 'final' constitution is scrutinised.
The starting point is the 'new text' that was adopted on 8 May 1996, with
due notice of amendments made in the negotiations following the
Constitutional Court judgement. The central characteristics of the 'final'

constitution are laid out in Table 6.2 above. The discussion concentrates on these dimensions, highlighting the 'final' constitution's relationship to the rivalling constitutional models as well as the interim constitution.

## The 'Final' South African Constitution

*The Institutional Set-up*

The overall structure of the 'final' South African constitution resembles what we have referred to as Albie Sachs' 'justice model' (see Chapter 4), with a basically centralist and majoritarian political structure, no grand coalition requirements, and a strong reliance on the legal system, both in terms of balancing the powers of the government through judicial review and in terms of facilitating social change.

There are differences, however, most of which can be seen as concessions to the consociational views opposing this position throughout the process. Most significant are the elements of federalism. There are, as in the 1993 constitution, nine provinces, each with a provincial legislature with legislative as well as executive powers. The provinces may adopt their own provincial constitutions and establish provincial monarchs. Their boundaries, powers and functions are constitutionally entrenched.

A National Council of Provinces (NCoP) replaces the Senate, and contrary to the justice model — and the wishes of the ANC — Parliament remains bi-cameral. The constitution contains special majority requirements in matters affecting the provinces, and a set of rules governing relationships between the tiers of government (cooperative government).

The 'final' constitution (like the interim constitution) also resembles consociational models in that the National Assembly (and provincial legislatures) are required to elect their members through a system that results in proportional representation (Section 46).

A central feature of consociationalism is that (ethnic) groups are recognised and protected as collective units. This is not explicitly done in the 'final' constitution, but Section 235 opens in principle for the recognition of a right of communities to self-determination. Legislation can be passed to this effect, providing it is within the framework of the right of the South African people as a whole to self determination. This — although only a possibility, not a requirement — is nevertheless significant as it allows for cultural councils, such as a *Volkstaat* council, to have some form of autonomy.

Elements of collective rights for ethnic groups are also implicit in the recognition of traditional leaders.

## Form of Government — Presidential or Parliamentary?

The form of government in the 'final' constitution are best characterised as *quasi-presidentialism*. As in the interim constitution the President is elected by the legislature (Section 86).[18] The National Assembly can remove the President (and/or the Cabinet) through a vote of no confidence supported by a majority of its members (Section 102).[19] In this sense the South African President is in the same position as a prime minister of a parliamentary democracy. On the other hand, the South African President's double role as Head of State and Head of Government, and the powers vested in the presidency, place him or her in a powerful position compared with the norm for the executive in parliamentary systems of government (Sections 83 through 85).

Criticism has been voiced against this 'hybrid' form of government. One argument is that the dual role of the President is unfortunate because it prevents the Head of State from rising above party politics (Harber and Ludman, 1995: 310). In all political systems the extent to which a president is able to rise above party politics is due to personal as much as institutional factors. The South African system is not particularly conducive in this respect, but it clearly does not prevent it. President Mandela has to a considerable extent succeeded in rising above party politics, concentrating on issues of national reconciliation. Most of the tasks as head of the executive has been left to his deputy Thabo Mbeki, who is often portrayed as *de facto* prime minister. Whether this pattern will be carried over into the reign of Mandela's successors in the presidency, will depend on personal factors as well as the parliamentary situation.

Another criticism has been that the dual position as Head of Government and Head of State renders the South African President too powerful, as one scholar put it, 'like the American President and the British Prime Minister rolled into one'.[20] To me this is a misinterpretation.

That the President is elected by the National Assembly does, as long as there is a clear majority party, create a monolithic power structure enhancing the powers of the majority. The distinction between the legislative and executive arm of government is to some extent obfuscated, as it is in parliamentary systems of government. While this in some cases may strengthen the executive, it is also a weakness. The fact that the South African President may be removed from office by a (simple majority) vote of no confidence in Parliament leaves him or her much more vulnerable than, say, the US President.

Save the symbolic value of being Head of State, the position of the South African President is much more similar to that of the Prime Minister in Britain (and other monarchies where the monarch has little or no actual political power). While the regent may formally have important powers (such as to sign or veto bills), these will in practice lie within the domain of the Cabinet, rendering the power map similar to that of the 'final' South African Constitution.[21]

In some respects the South African President is in a weaker position than the British Prime Minister. The South African system is not only parliamentary in structure, but also contains significant checks and balances: South Africa is a constitutional state and the Constitutional Court has extensive powers. The parliamentary opposition also has wider powers than in the purely majoritarian Westminster system. In addition, the federal arrangements in South Africa leaves the provinces as a potential source of opposition.

*Why not a Directly Elected President?*

From the assumption that the South African system vests extraordinary powers in the presidency, flows the argument that such a powerful position should at least be directly elected.[22] Arguments for direct presidential elections are also made from the opposite perception, that the presidency is too weak under this dispensation. Direct election enhances the powers of the President by providing democratic legitimacy and a personal power base. It tends to produce a strong executive and a clearer separation of powers, and is the arrangement most consistent with the justice model.[23]

From a consociational perspective, the disadvantages of direct presidential elections are clear. In divided societies a directly elected executive president will generally represent one segment of the population, and it is very difficult for minority parties to get a share in executive power. Arrangements where the executive is elected by parliament is more conducive to formal and informal power sharing arrangements. Even without grand coalition requirements, minority parties can influence the choice of president and the composition of the cabinet, particularly when there is no clear parliamentary majority.

That this unique form of 'parliamentary presidentialism' was agreed upon in South Africa should be seen in light of the nature of the rivalling constitutional positions, and the fact that the main battle was fought over power sharing in the executive arm of government.

At the centre of the 1993 compromise over the interim constitution, is the GNU, a grand coalition government along the lines of Lijphart's consociational model — save that there are no minority veto (see Chapter 5). In this context parliamentarianism is a logical choice. The functioning of a grand coalition government requires that members are able to negotiate and make binding decisions. Strict separation of powers and strong legislative checks on executive decisions are detrimental to the consensus politics that is the core of this arrangement.

The absence of minority vetoes made the GNU an acceptable transitional arrangement for the ANC, but with a comfortable parliamentary majority, the party could not accept a permanent forced coalition government. From the perspective of the justice model, a strong executive is a priority as it is seen as the main driving force of social change. The GNU-arrangement left the opposition with too much power to hamper executive efficiency. There was less reason for the ANC to get rid of the 'parliamentary presidentialism' of the interim constitution. For a majority party the arrangement has clear advantages as long as it is not combined with a forced coalition arrangement; it secures control over the executive, and also tends to be more conducive to party cohesion than a system of direct presidential election.[24]

The justice model and consociational models limit power through different dynamics. The justice model relies on separation of powers and a system of checks and balances where the Constitutional Court has the main responsibility for keeping the government within the limits of the Constitution. Consociational models rely on executive power to be shared among the parties and diffused between the levels of government. Under the 'final' constitution — and as long as there is a majority party in parliament — there is neither much diffusion and sharing, nor a clear separation of powers.

The arrangement in the 'final' constitution is an example of how a compromise between two constitutional positions, in combination with the parties' strategic interests, has resulted in a system where neither model's 'safety mechanisms' are fully operative. In this perspective the NP's focus on power-sharing may in fact have enhanced the powers of the majority. The negotiations for a share in executive power (which they in the end did not achieve), presuppose diffusion of power along the lines of the consociational model, shifting the perspective from 'external' checks on executive power. Characteristically, when issues of separation of powers and checks and balances were brought into focus, they were often introduced by the DP.

What does check the powers of the executive in the 'final' constitution? Possible sources of opposition are Parliament, the provinces, the Constitutional Court and the various watchdog bodies created specifically to keep the government within the bounds of the constitution. In the following we will look at the potential of these bodies to check the power of the national executive and parliamentary majority effectively.

## Bi-cameral Legislature

The 'final' constitution, like the interim constitution, provides for a bi-cameral Parliament. The first chamber, the National Assembly, is elected directly in party list PR elections. The Senate of the interim constitution is substituted by a National Council of Provinces (NCoP), consisting of ten representatives from each of the nine provinces. To include the NCoP in the definition of Parliament was one of the concessions that the ANC made during the second stage of the negotiation process. The electoral base of the NCoP differs from that of the National Assembly, and a President backed by a majority in the National Assembly does not automatically have a majority in the NCoP. This strengthens the distinction between the legislature and the executive and increases the potential for opposition.

The National Assembly is, however, by far the most important of the two chambers. The NCoP is mainly relevant with regard to legislation affecting the provinces, and even in such cases they may be over-ruled.

## The National Assembly

Most decisions in the National Assembly require only a simple majority vote. Constitutional changes require heightened majorities (normally a two thirds majority of all members, in some cases a three quarters majority (Section 74)[25]). Special procedures are also prescribed for constitutional amendments. In the 8 May text these are limited to involving the NCoP when amendments affect the provinces or the NCoP itself (NT Section 74b). The Constitutional

Court ruled, however, that the CPs demand special procedures for all constitutional changes, in addition to super-majorities (CCT 23/96 [156]). The provisions for constitutional change in the amended text give special protection to Chapter 2 (the bill of rights) (AT Section 74(b)). The NCoP and provincial legislatures are involved to a greater extent, and the amendment-process are opened to the public. 30 days' notification are required before an amendment bill can be tabled in the National Assembly (to allow for public comments, debate in the provincial legislatures and the NCoP). An additional 30 day period are required after tabling in the National Assembly before the bill is put to vote (AT Section 74(5)).

Besides constitutional change, a two thirds majority is required for the National Assembly to overrule the NCoP on issues where national and provincial legislatures have concurrent powers (Schedule 4). This is a potentially important source of minority influence, since Schedule 4 includes vital matters such as education, health, welfare services, housing, cultural matters, agriculture, environment, tourism, trade and development. But the heightened majority clause only comes into effect when a bill is rejected by the NCoP.

Even where no special majority requirements come into operation the opposition parties have a means to check the powers of the majority: they may refer legislation to the Constitutional Court (Section 80). This not only prevents the majority from passing unconstitutional legislation, but may also delay legislation from taking effect.[26] This right is, however, not unlimited. One third of all members have to support the application. The Court may also order applicants to pay costs 'if the application did not have a reasonable prospect of success' (this 'deterrent' was not in the 'interim' constitution). The ANC wanted to limit this power of the opposition to hamper the legislation process, and it was a significant victory for the opposition that the legislative review was retained.

In sum, with the powers that the 'final' constitution places with the opposition parties in the National Assembly, substantial checks are in place to keep the majority, and the executive, within the bounds of the constitution — provided that no party controls two thirds of the votes.[27] In addition opposition parties are free to influence legislation the way minority parties normally do in democratic systems, that is, through participation in the debates and parliamentary committees.

The role of the National Assembly under the 'final' constitution depends crucially on the balance of power between the parties. So far the assumption has been that the ANC will remain in control of an absolute majority of the seats in the National Assembly. If this is not the case, the picture changes completely. Under this scenario the position of the executive in South Africa is unusually weak. The president will either lead a majority coalition, or a minority cabinet trying to forge shifting majorities in parliament on a case-to-case basis. Many bills require special majorities, and a majority in the National Assembly may at any time remove the president and/or the Cabinet by a vote of no confidence (Section 102). The opposition can also hamper the legislative process by referring bills to the Constitutional Court. The President cannot veto bills passed by the National Assembly. He or she may delay legislation by having its constitutionality considered, but ultimately has to assent.

In this context the 'final' constitution renders the National Assembly strong indeed. It has the powers that flow from a parliamentary system of government (ultimately a vote of no confidence), and in addition there is a set of checks and balances: legislative review, special majority requirements, and special procedures involving a second chamber of Parliament.

## *The 'Floor-crossing' Clause*

A controversial regulation in the interim constitution require MPs and Senators to vacate their seats if they cease to be a member of the party that nominated them (1993 Constitution, Sections 43 and 51). This so-called anti-defection or floor-crossing clause strengthens the party whip and prevents MPs not only from joining other parties, but also to some extent from voting against their party's position. The clause may be supported on different grounds. Theoretically the floor-crossing clause is consistent with the conception of representation that underlies the party-list PR system, where voters vote for parties, not individual representatives in their private capacities. From a consociational perspective it has the advantage of strengthening party cohesion. It allows party elites to enter into deals knowing they will be able to bring their parliamentarians along, which is a condition for workable power-sharing arrangements. On the other hand, in a context where one party has a large majority, its role in preventing splits and party proliferation is highly negative for successful consociation.

The anti-defection clause has also been seen as useful in preventing (ambitious and/or corrupt) MPs from joining other parties. With the NP as the governing party of the past and the ANC as the (perceived) governing party of the long-term future, the clause could be seen to cater to the NP in particular. But while the ANC might gain from an exodus, the clause is extremely useful to the party in terms of preventing splits, silencing dissident voices and keeping together its very broad church. While the clause initially appeared to favour minority parties, the ANC currently stand to gain the most. Preventing splits is an absolute priority for the ANC. Without a split the party is likely to retain its clear majority for a very long time. It is thus not surprising that the ANC was set on retaining the clause.

The anti-defection clause came under increasing criticism as undemocratic, and it was dropped from the text of the 'final' constitution shortly before it was adopted in May 1996 — dropped from the main text, that is. It was retained in terms of Schedule 6 until the second general election under the new constitution, in approximately 2004.[28] The clause was challenged during the certification process, as contrary to universally accepted fundamental rights, freedoms and civil liberties and not accepted in the democratic world. The Constitutional Court dismissed the complaint, emphasising that the clause increases the accountability of legislators to their parties. Under a party-list PR system, it is the party that is accountable to the voters. Besides, the Court noted, anti-defection clauses are found in democracies such as Namibia and India (CCT 23/96 [180–88]).

## The National Council of Provinces

Like the Senate of the interim constitution, the members of the Council of Provinces are elected by the provincial legislatures in proportion to party strength, but with the difference that each provincial delegation carries only one vote. Each delegation is headed by the premier of the province (or his designate) and consists of ten members, six permanent members and four floating members appointed by the provincial legislature (Section 60). The arrangement favours the majority party in each province. Compared to the Senate, this is a second chamber with a more genuinely separate status in terms of its composition.[29]

All legislation passed by the National Assembly must be referred to the NCoP, but the procedure and the status of the Council's rejection of a Bill vary depending on the nature of the matter. If it is a constitutional amendment dealing with the NCoP, with provincial matters, or with Chapter 2 (the Bill of Rights), the Bill lapses unless the NCoP passes it by a two thirds majority (AT Section 74).

In other cases the National Assembly can overrule the NCoP, with or without special majority requirements. If the Bill falls within the area of concurrent national and provincial competence (Schedule 4),[30] rejection by the NCoP (i.e. by a majority of the provincial delegations) is followed by a mediation procedure, involving a multi-party Mediation Committee.[31] If no agreement is forged the Bill goes to a new vote in the National Assembly, where it lapses unless it is passed by a two thirds majority of all members (Section 76). In relation to matters of concurrent national and provincial competence the NCoP has substantial powers.

With regard to other national legislation the Council has far less influence. The representatives cast individual votes and if the Bill fails to get a majority it is referred back to the National Assembly for new consideration, but no heightened majority is required. Bills may also be introduced in the NCoP, but their status is weak. If the National Assembly does not pass the Bill, it ultimately lapses.

It is not immediately easy to see whether the Council of Provinces has more or less power than the Senate.[32] Nor is it straightforward to determine whether the parliament of the 'final' constitution would operate more according to the logic of the justice model than that of the interim constitution. Both depend on the parliamentary situation. If the governing party, that is the majority party in the National Assembly, no longer effectively controls a majority of the provincial delegations (as the ANC does at present) the Council of Provinces may provide a significant source of opposition influence in national politics.

## Powerful Centre

Despite federal structures the 'final' constitution paints the picture of a relatively centralised state. The powers granted to provincial legislatures are limited, and the overriding powers of the national legislature considerable.

The most vital matters affecting the provinces are those listed in Schedule 4 as 'concurrent national and provincial legislative competencies'. In these matters the central government provide framework legislation, while the specific content is left for the provinces. In case of a dispute the national level of government has considerable overriding powers (even though they are somewhat reduced in the amended text) (Section 146). Also in what is defined as 'exclusive provincial matters' (Schedule 5) the central government has the right to intervene on a number of grounds (Section 44(2)). And the residual powers — 'the silence of the law' — lies with the centre (Section 148). The fiscal powers of the provinces are limited and subject to regulation by the national Parliament (Section 228), but each province (as well as each municipality at local level) is entitled to an 'equitable share' of revenue raised nationally.[33]

The powers of the provinces *vis-à-vis* the centre were hotly debated throughout the negotiation process, and was arguably the most significant of the issues that were re-opened in the amendment process. The Constitutional Court's ruling was that, although no particular clause was in breach of any particular constitutional principle, the text adopted on 8 May substantially reduced the sum of provincial powers compared with the interim constitution (CCT 23/96, Chapter VII, particularly [479–81]). The Constitutional Assembly had two options: they could reduce the scope of the national override (the favoured option of the ANC), or they could add to the list of provincial powers. The result was a combination of the two. The most significant change was arguably the reintroduction of certain provincial controls over policing (AT Sections 205-208). Were these changes sufficient to meet the Constitutional Court's requirements? This was the main question when the amended text was submitted for certification. The Court's judgement is telling: 'the powers and functions of the provinces in terms of the amended constitution are still less than or inferior compared to those accorded to the provinces in terms of the interim constitution, but not substantially so' (CCT 37/96 [204]).

The provinces' authority over local government matters is limited as local government is defined as an independent tier of government with its own constitutionally guaranteed legislative powers (concurrent with national and/or provincial legislatures), a guaranteed share of fiscal resources, and a certain representation at the national level.[34] The relative independence of local government, with direct links between the national and local level, diminishes the powers of provincial governments and can be seen as a strategy from the ANC for reducing the provinces' potential as loci of opposition towards policies enacted at national level.

Local government was neglected in the interim constitution, and new legislation for local government was far from finalized when the 'final' constitution was adopted in May 1996. The government (the ANC) thus wanted to keep the constitution vague on these issues not to exclude potentially promising options. The Constitutional Court ruled, however, that the CPs required that a framework for different forms of local government and their fiscal powers and functions be set out in the constitution. The amended text does this to the Court's satisfaction, while leaving considerable scope for national legislation in the actual design of types of municipalities (AT Sections 151-164). The IFP, when rejoining the negotiations in October 1996, put forth demands for a decisive role for traditional leaders in rural local government. Failure to get this demand accepted was cited as a main reason for their subsequent decision to pull out again.

All in all, the 'final' constitution vests considerable powers at the national level of government. The actual scope of provincial powers will depend for a large part on the ability of the National Council of Provinces to represent the interests of the provinces. The NCoP is, however, run along majoritarian lines and does not enable individual provinces run by opposition parties to buck the centre.

*Cooperative Government*

The constitution states that national, provincial and local spheres of government are 'distinctive, interdependent and interrelated' (Section 40). The arrangement is not described as 'federal' (which is a highly politicised term, particularly within the ANC), but rather as 'cooperative government'. It is an arrangement where the provinces and local levels of government are envisioned to perform extensive functions, but with relatively limited legislative powers and limited access to instigate court action against the central government. Chapter 3 of the 'final' constitution, specifies a relationship between the tiers of government where differences are ironed out in inter-governmental fora and through special procedures, and with court action only as a last recourse.

This reads like a formulation of the relationship between the centre, provincial and local tiers of government envisaged in the justice model. Local government should be encouraged, not as competing centres of political power, but in a manner harmonising its workings with national political goals (Sachs, 1990: 153). In matters of policy the central government should have the upper hand.

It is a rather different notion of federalism and decentralisation that underlies Lijphart's consociationalism (see Chapter 5). Here decentralisation is a means to defuse power and de-link national and provincial decision-making in order to prevent the national government from impacting on the 'own affairs' of provinces or segments. If the establishment of cooperative mechanisms to iron out differences between the provinces and the centre, has the effect of lowering the 'fences' protecting the autonomy of the provinces, it is clearly contrary to the rationale of the consociational model of government, although in and by themselves the arrangement seem to echo the consociational model's ideal of decision-making through bargaining and elite cooperation rather than confrontation.

The powers of provincial legislatures are protected by the constitution, and provincial legislatures can veto constitutional amendments affecting specific provinces, but otherwise the provinces have to rely on the NCoP to advance and protect their interests, and given the way the NCoP operates, this requires concerted action. A majority of the provinces can veto constitutional change that affect provinces and block important legislation, but once the NCoP has approved a Bill overriding provincial powers, there is little individual provinces can do, although, as a result of the certification process, the scope for court action in such cases is somewhat widened (AT Section 146 (4)). Court practice in such cases will be significant for the actual powers of 'dissident' provinces.

How the system of 'cooperative government' will work over time depends on how provincial politics develop and whether there are effective mechanisms to facilitate cooperation and harmonisation of national and provincial interests and goals.

As long as the present political configuration persists — in which the ANC not only is in majority in the National Assembly, but also in most of the provincial legislatures and hence in the Council of Provinces — the judiciary will have to bear the brunt of the responsibility for keeping the government/ruling party within the bounds of the constitution.

## The Guardians of the Constitution

The 'final' constitution places a heavy burden on the legal system. Given the relatively weak separation of powers between the legislative and executive arms of government, the Constitutional Court together with the other 'watchdog' bodies provided for in the constitution, are left with most of the responsibility for keeping the majority in line, at least as long as there is a clear parliamentary majority.

The Constitutional Court is given extensive powers and is set to be a very important body in South African politics. It can rule on all constitutional matters and all matters relevant to the constitution, and has the power to determine whether a matter is of such relevance. It is the ultimate authority on whether national and provincial legislation is un-constitutional. It is given the authority to decide that Parliament or the President has failed to comply with a constitutional duty, to decide disputes between organs of state and to certify provincial constitutions (Section 167). Given the character of the 'final' constitution, and of the Bill of Rights in particular — the Constitutional Court could end up with what amounts to significant legislative powers.

The 11 judges are appointed for a non-renewable period of 12 years (Section 176).[35] Given the long terms and extensive powers of this non-elected — and non-accountable — body the question of its impartiality becomes acute. This calls for a focus on the appointment of the judges.

The executive is 'the engine of the political system of the modern state' (Schrire, 1996: 172) and the body that the Constitutional Court needs to watch particularly closely. In most countries with a constitutional court, procedures are in place to limit the influence of the executive over the appointment of judges. '(T)he power of appointment is not left exclusively in the hands of any one branch of government, and in particular not the executive' (O'Malley, 1996: 183).

The South African President has significant powers of appointment, both under the interim and the 'final' constitution. The President, 'after consulting the Judicial Service Commission (JSC) and the leaders of parties represented in the National Assembly', appoints the President and Deputy President of the Constitutional Court (Section 167). The remaining judges are appointed by the President from a list of nominees prepared by the JSC. (If too few of the nominees are acceptable, the President can require a supplementary list.)

The President also plays an important role in the composition of the nominating body.[36] The composition of the JSC is such that the majority in the National Assembly could effectively control it (O'Malley, 1996: 185).[37] The President's role — direct and indirect — in the appointment of the Constitutional Court could be seen to weaken its independence.

With the politically crucial role of the South African Constitutional Court, the independence of the Court is crucial — not only in real terms, but also the perception of independence. If the Court is perceived as biased in favour of the ruling party, it could add to political tension, rather than serve the function of a neutral umpire. A desire to demonstrate an independence from the government could, on the other hand, lead to a bias in the opposite direction, which, from a democratic perspective, is a problem since is means unduly diminishing the right of the majority to rule. Either way the court is likely to be seen by parts of the population as overtly political. The more controversial and politically important the cases are, the more likely they are to be affected by such considerations.

In addition to the Constitutional Court and the judiciary, the 'final' constitution establishes a number of other watchdog bodies or 'state institutions supporting constitutional democracy'. These include the Public Protector; the Human Rights Commission; the Commission for the Promotion and Protection of the Rights of Cultural, Religious and Linguistic Communities; the Commission for Gender Equality; the Auditor General; and the Electoral Commission (Section 181). These are independent bodies appointed by the President on the recommendation of the National Assembly. Nominations are made by a committee of the Assembly proportionally composed of all parties, and the list of nominees is required to 'reflect broadly the race and gender composition of South Africa' (Section 193).

Criticism has also been voiced with regard to these bodies, due to lack of independence, particularly with respect to the Public Protector (ombudsman) and the Auditor General, arguably the two most powerful in terms of watchdog functions. Both the Auditor General and the Public Protector could, according to the constitutional text as adopted on 8 May, be dismissed by a simple majority in Parliament (NT Section 194). This leaves them vulnerable to political pressure. As Judge Mahomed, deputy president of the Constitutional Court remarked, the independence of such offices has to be built in properly 'not by the mere catechism of independence' (*Sunday Times*, 7 July 1996). In the subsequent negotiations the threshold for dismissing the Auditor General and the Public Protector was raised to a two thirds majority in the National Assembly (AT Section 194).

The effectiveness of these 'watchdog' bodies depend on a host of factors. The resources put at their disposal is obviously an important factor. Security for tenure and salaries of those appointed, contribute to their independence. As with the Constitutional Court, the appointment procedure is also important. To secure the independence and impartiality of such bodies without tilting the balance too much in favour of the minority is a profound dilemma.

There are different strategies to create 'impartial' or 'independent' bodies. One can seek 'neutral' candidates through special majority requirements or aim at some form of political balance by securing different parties' representation, either directly or in the appointment process. Nomination and appointment can also be divided among different bodies, e.g. nomination by the executive, approval by the legislature or vice versa (but this is only effective to the extent that these bodies are truly independent of each other, which is questionable in the South African situation).

To ensure that the majority cannot tailor the watchdog bodies to their liking would, in the current parliamentary situation, require appointments by a special majority in Parliament. Such an arrangement would, however, be prone to result in deadlock. Too heavy checks on the ability of the majority to get their candidates appointed also tilts the balance overwhelmingly in favour of the minority and of the status quo.

The 'final' constitution adopts a mixed approach: nomination of candidates by a multi-party committee or commission, and the final word with the executive. The representation of various parties and interests in the nomination process reflects the ideal of impartiality as political balance rather than 'neutrality', while the decisive influence of the ruling party at the last stage reduces the significance of this balance.

Thus, while the 'final' constitution provide the Constitutional Court and other watchdog bodies with substantial powers to check the legislative and executive branches of government, the independence of these bodies have been questioned, due to the ruling party's influence over appointments, and in some cases also dismissals.

That these — in some perspectives flawed — appointment procedures were agreed upon, should be seen in the light of the different conceptions of constitutional limitation of power that underlie the rivalling constitutional positions, and of the fact that the primary aim of the National Party was for a share in executive power, and other arrangements were negotiated on the premise that this would be the case.

In a fully-fledged consociational system with a grand coalition government and mutual veto powers the appointment procedures outlined above would secure minority parties influence over appointments. When the Constitutional Court appointments were discussed during the 1993 negotiations for the interim constitution, the NP, negotiating on the presumption that there would be some form of minority veto in the cabinet, settled for an arrangement where all the judges would be appointed by the President on the advice of the Cabinet. When it became clear that there would not be minority vetoes the Democratic Party insisted that the appointment procedures had to be renegotiated to lessen the impact of the executive (O'Malley, 1996: 184). This was done, and the checks are further strengthened in the 'final' constitution, but, the impact of the executive/parliamentary majority remain substantial.

Even with the Government of National Unity arrangement of the interim constitution — without minority vetoes — the arrangement that was adopted facilitated input from minority parties at all stages of the process. Had the NP achieved its primary objective — a share in executive power — the appointment procedure specified in the 'final' constitution would have been a logical corollary. Under the 'final' constitution, the opposition participates in the nomination process, but with no secured share in executive power it is left with little say over the composition of watchdog bodies.

From the perspective of the justice model, and the ANC as governing party, this path, involving 'independent' and multi-party bodies in the process, is more comfortable than special majority requirements. Apart from the possibility of deadlock-situations, heightened majorities are prone to produce conservative watchdog bodies. This would not only make it more difficult for the majority to govern, it would also run contrary to the second function that these bodies are seen to fulfil in the justice model, namely as agent of transformation and change.

## The Guardians of the Constitution as Agents of Social Transformation

The 'final' constitution is much like Sachs' justice model in the sense that the legal system and the Constitutional Court is cast in the role of main guardian against state abuse. At the same time it is to function as an agent of social change.

The Bill of Rights, Chapter 2 of the new constitution, includes a number of basic social and economic rights: Sections 26 and 27 states that everyone has the right to have access to adequate housing; health care services, including reproductive health care; sufficient food and water; social security, including, if they are unable to support themselves and their dependants, appropriate social assistance.

These rights impose on the state the duty to 'take reasonable legislative and other measures, within its available resources, to achieve the progressive realisation of each of these rights'. This formulation is made in a manner that places obligations on the state, while taking the scarcity of resources into account. This echoes the justice model's conception of 'progressive realisation of a minimum floor' of social and economic rights.

Certain social rights appear to apply unconditionally, namely the right to a basic education, including adult basic education (Section 29(a)), the right not to be refused emergency medical treatment (Section 27(3)), and the rights of children (Section 28). The rights of children include the right of every child to basic nutrition, shelter, basic health care services, and social services and to appropriate alternative care when removed from the family environment. Children are defined as persons under 18 years of age, and with South Africa's young population profile this amounts to around 43% of the population.[38] This is, in other words, a clause that could place heavy responsibilities on the state.

A crucial aspect of the Bill of Rights is the property clause. Sachs underscores how — particularly in South African circumstances of extreme inequality — a strong property clause might have the effect of turning the constitution into a safeguard of privileges (Sachs, 1990a, see also Chapter 4 above). This issue is important for all parties, both in symbolic and material terms, which is why the property clause was among the most difficult on which to reach an agreement. The clause, as it was adopted, is carefully worded to appease local as well as potential foreign investors, but without barring social reforms. While acknowledging the right not to be deprived of property, it allows expropriation for public purposes or in the public interest, subject to compensation reflecting an equitable balance between the public interest and the interests of those affected (Section 25).[39] The section on property rights also provides for restitution of property or equitable redress for persons or communities who were dispossessed of property as a result of racially discriminatory laws or practices in the past (Section 25(6)). It is explicitly stated that '(n)o provision of this section may impede the state from taking legislative and other measures to achieve land, water and related reform, in order to redress the results of past racial discrimination' (Section 25(8)).

The 'final' constitution is weaker than the justice model in terms of bodies to promote implementation of social and economic rights. Sachs argues that in order to go beyond simply setting out social rights as something to be aimed for, the principle of an expanding floor of rights should be backed by a special Social Rights Commission to 'supervise the implementation of social rights programmes, assist the courts on social rights questions, and be a resource of information for legislative authorities as well as for the public' (Sachs, 1992: 35). Neither the interim nor the 'final' constitution include provision for a Social Rights Commission, but the Human Rights Commission has some of its functions, namely the duty annually to 'require relevant organs of state to provide the Commission with information on the measures that they have taken towards the realisation of the rights in the Bill of Rights concerning housing, health care, food, water, social security, education and the environment' (Section 184(3)).

Otherwise the 'final' constitution closely resembles the justice model in its social rights' provisions. To the extent that these rights are justiciable — which at least some of them are formulated to be — they confer great powers on the courts in matters of social and economic policy. It is however an open question to what extent the Constitutional Court will choose to use these powers.

While the need for social justice is evident, there are profound difficulties with justiciable social and economic rights. Extensive litigation related to social and economic rights could lead to a substantial 'legalisation' of social policy, taking decisions, priority setting — and very substantial resources — out of the hands of politically elected representatives. This could erode the separation of legislative executive and judicial powers as significant and inherently controversial legislation in effect would be 'delegated' to judges who are neither elected, nor accountable. The Constitutional Court risks being placed as a party to political controversy, undermining its function as an umpire and guardian of 'the Truth'.

Social and economic rights leave even greater potential for disagreement on what 'justice' requires, than do other aspects of the Bill of Rights. In Chapter 4, it was argued that there are reasons to be careful when lifting these into the constitutional domain. The circumstances of South Africa where social and economic inequality is so closely related to the unjust legal order of the past, call for measures to prevent the constitution from safeguarding the existing pattern of distribution. On the other hand excessive legalisation of social and economic issues could erode the rationale of the constitution in modern plural societies, namely to create a limited consensus on the basis of which difficult issues can be solved.

The tightrope between the functions of the constitution — that of guardian of the rights of all South Africans on the one hand and that of agent of progressive change on the other — is a difficult one to walk. Problems also arise with respect to the right to equal treatment and not to be unfairly discriminated against.

Section 9 of the 'final' constitution states that 'Everyone is equal before the law and has the right to equal protection and benefit of the law', and that the state 'may not unfairly discriminate directly or indirectly against anyone on one or more grounds, including race, gender, sex, pregnancy, marital status, ethnic or social origin, colour, sexual orientation, age, disability, religion, conscience, belief, culture, language, and birth'.

From the perspective of social justice a serious problem with the right to non-discrimination is that it may be used to prevent affirmative action programmes. In line with Sachs' recommendation an explicit foundation for affirmative action is given to prevent the equal protection clauses from turning into an instrument for protection of privilege.[40]

The provisions in the 'final' Bill of Rights binds not only the State, but also natural and juristic persons 'if, and to the extent that, it is applicable, taking into account the nature of the right and the nature of any duty imposed by the right' (Section 8(2)). The duty not to discriminate unfairly explicitly applies horizontally (Section 9(4)). The right is special in another sense as well. Discrimination on the grounds listed in this clause is to be regarded as unfair unless it is established that it is fair. In other words there is a reverse onus (Section 9(5)).

Horizontal application of constitutional rights is controversial. It gives rise to rights and obligations between individuals, but at the same time allows the state to interfere directly in private relationships (Leon, 1996). In this way it enables rather than restrains the state, and thus runs counter to what is traditionally seen as the rationale of constitutional protection of rights. Horizontal rights also contradicts the view that '(c)onstitutionally entrenched fundamental rights should be a shield in the hands of individuals and not a sword' (Leon, 1996). Lastly, it challenges the existing common law, such as individual freedom of contract.

Proponents of the horizontal school, such as Albie Sachs, hold that if the constitution does *not* to some extent regulate private relationships — particularly with regard to discrimination — while guaranteeing rights such as freedom of association and freedom of contract, this would 'ensure constitutional protection for privatised apartheid' (Sachs, 1990a: 157). It would make it virtually impossible for the poor majority to use their democratic power to make material conditions more equal 'since the resources needed to bring about any major improvements would be constitutionally under white lock and key' (Sachs, 1990a: 157). Horizontal rights are aimed at preventing this. In this respect the 'final' constitution is in agreement with the justice model.

The horizontal rights provisions add to the workload of the courts in general, and the Constitutional Court in particular.[41] And, like the social rights clauses they add to the Court's potential 'legislative' powers. The demarcation of the Bill of Rights and various aspects of common law will have to be developed by the courts on a casuistic basis 'the reform of the law becomes delegated to judges who are unselected and unaccountable, and whose approach in devising new rules will not be easy to define' (Jeffrey, 1996). On the other hand, this is how the common law has always been developed.

In the 'final' constitution the judiciary has the double role of a 'neutral' watchdog keeping the majority within the bounds of the constitution, and a 'progressive' agent of social change. It is a question to what extent these roles are compatible. The second role could lead to a politicisation of the courts that may jeopardise their neutrality. Another question is whether South Africa's already overloaded legal system is capable of carrying this burden. Radical restructuring of the legal system in itself adds to the strain, and an increase in cases related to social rights, land restitution etc., has to be tackled amidst a rampant crime wave. In addition there is the problem of whether, in a democratic society, the judiciary should be given so extensive powers, and of how their independence can be secured.

*Interpretation of Reality:*
*Individualism and Collectivism, Culture and Structure*

The 'final' constitution not only combines elements from various constitutional models, but is also to some extent a compromise between diverging interpretations of reality.

The constitution is, like the justice model, formulated overwhelmingly in individualist terms. Each individual is due the same respect and rights protection, and the state should treat all citizens equally. The emphasis on social and economic rights reflects a view of South African society where poverty and structural inequality are the major obstacles to be overcome for South Africa to become a stable democracy.

The focus on structural factors does not preclude recognition of cultural rights and the need to protect cultural, religious and linguistic diversity. Eleven official languages are recognised (Section 6). The Bill of Rights states that everyone has the right to 'use the language and to participate in the cultural life' of their choice (Section 30), to enjoy their culture and practice their religion with other members of their community, to use their language, and to 'form, join and maintain cultural, religious and linguistic associations and other organs of civil society' (Section 31). Everyone has the right to 'receive education in the official language or languages of their choice in public educational institutions where that education is reasonably practicable' (Section 29), and the right to establish independent educational institutions, provided that they do not discriminate on the basis of race (Section 29). These rights are, however, formulated as rights for individuals.

Few concessions are given to the view central to consociational and communitarian thought, that culture transcends the individual and that (ethnic) groups should be recognised and protected as collective entities. A certain recognition of this conception can, however, be read into the clause enabling 'recognition of the notion of the right of self-determination of any community sharing a common cultural and language heritage' (Section 235),[42] and in the clause providing for a Commission for the Promotion and Protection of the Rights of Cultural, Religious and Linguistic Communities (Sections 181 and 185). These clauses respond to requests from the Freedom Front and other groups of conservative Afrikaners to provide a constitutional foundation for a Volkstaat Council with a degree of self-determination. They seem to give an opening for elements of non-territorial 'federalism' along consociational lines.

The recognition of traditional leaders, and the Zulu king as a provincial monarch for KwaZulu-Natal, are other elements that are difficult to reconcile with an individualist, dominantly structural world view. Depending on the perspective, these may be regarded either as anomalies, compromises weakening the constitutional framework, or as safety-mechanisms, in recognition of the existence, and potentially explosive nature, of culturally related (ethnic) conflicts.

## Values and Objectives: Justice or Stability? Transformation or Regulation?

Does the 'final' constitution reflect the traditional values and objectives of the liberation movement, that is, to transform society into a more just scheme of cooperation? Or does it reflect the more pragmatic aim of proponents of consociationalism: namely to regulate society to prevent the eruption of latent conflicts? Has stability in practice replaced justice as the primary 'good' at which to aim?

At this level of rhetoric, this is not the case. Like the justice model the 'final' constitution highlights two concerns: on the one hand, the need to facilitate a strong state that can be a powerful agent of social change and, on the other, the need to safeguard the fundamental rights and liberties of individuals. The former, the concerns for social justice and the positive rights of the majority to instigate change, is to some extent given precedence in the sense that care is taken to limit the possibilities for using the Bill of Rights as a bastion to protect minority privilege. Particular care has been taken to ensure that land reform will be possible within the constitution and to ensure that apartheid is not privatised by legalising unfair discrimination in private relationships.

But there are elements in the 'final' constitution that hamper radical change: the constitution protects property rights (although not unconditionally) as well as other prerequisites of a market economy, and a range of decision-making powers are given to provinces and local tiers of government. This places limits upon how society can be changed, both with respect to means and direction of change. Federal arrangements and emphasis on proportional representation and consultation reflect the consociational view of stability through mediation between groups and interests, and limit the power of the majority to change the social structure unilaterally. This is true, even though the federalism of the 'final' constitution falls short of the consociational idea, and the 'own affairs' of the provinces are insufficiently protected from this perspective.

Given the magnitude of the task of changing a society like South Africa into a more just scheme of social cooperation, is it conceivable that such a transformation could be achieved within the legal framework that the 'final' constitution provides?

This depends, among others, on the actual legal force of 'progressive' social rights clauses in relation to more 'conservative' rights. If the social rights turn out to be mainly aspirations, the rhetoric of social justice is at best a matter of appeasement, an attempt to maintain stability by creating legitimacy for the constitution and the new social order among the disadvantaged majority, while in effect offering few opportunities for actual change. A strategy for regulation or management of conflict, rather than transformation of the social structure.

*Response to Pluralism: Assimilation or Non-interference?*

On the nation-building dimension, the 'final' constitution echoes the justice model: the state is to be 'colour blind' in the sense that all individuals, regardless of ethnic or other group identity shall participate on equal terms on the same political arena. Political representation is conceived overwhelmingly in terms of representation of individual citizens, rather than groups. This individualism is strengthened in comparison with the interim constitution, which allowed all significant parties representation in the executive, and made provisions for participation of traditional leaders at all levels of government.[43] Within this individualist framework cultural pluralism, religious and linguistic diversity is tolerated and encouraged as individual rights and the cultural religious and linguistic rights of all citizens are given constitutional protection.

Differences in culture and ethnic identity are not reflected in the political system, but the freedom of association extends to ethnically based organisations (although discrimination on the basis of race etc. is not permitted) (Section 18). There are no barriers against formation of ethnic parties, as are found in other ethnically divided African countries (e.g. Tanzania). There are, however, limits as to how ethnic mobilisation can be conducted. 'Hate speech' is prohibited. Freedom of expression does not extend to '(a) propaganda for war; (b) incitement of imminent violence; or (c) advocacy of hatred that is based on race, ethnicity, gender or religion, and that constitutes incitement to cause harm' (Section 16.1).[44]

By recognising traditional leaders and not excluding cultural councils, the 'final' constitution recognises ethnic structures in the larger political community. But these structures are supplements to the democratically elected bodies, not alternative channels of government or of political representation. They must act in accordance with the constitution and other relevant national legislation. Unlike the interim constitution, the 'final' constitution does not provide traditional leaders with any formal role in the political decision-making process. Their role as local government in many rural areas is challenged, leaving them with mainly ceremonial functions.

The ambivalence noted in the justice model with regard to the nation-building dimension is even more pronounced in the 'final' constitution. There is a strong emphasis on nation-building, of equal citizenship, a common political arena for all, and of the constitution as 'one law for one nation'. On the other hand, the 'final' text goes further than the justice model in recognising the importance of cultural diversity, and even accepts separate culturally based political institutions (cultural councils, ethnically specific traditional leaders and provincial monarchs).

## State-society Relationship: Participation or Representation?

Democracy in modern mass society necessarily includes elements of representation, but the justice model, following ANC tradition, emphasises participation rather than representation of interests. Participation should be encouraged at all levels: in the electoral process, in legislation and implementation, and in the construction of the constitution itself. The electoral system should be easy to comprehend to facilitate meaningful participation by all. Participation should also be stimulated through institutionalising consultation processes whereby civil society organisations are drawn into decision-making.

These concerns are reflected in the interim constitution as well as in the 'final' constitution. National as well as provincial parliaments are required to 'facilitate public involvement in the legislative and other processes' and to allow the public access to their proceedings (subject to 'reasonable measures' to regulate such access) (Sections 59, 72 and 118).

Participation is a concern in the 'final' constitution, but compared with the justice model, the set-up is directed more towards representation of interests. Proportional representation has the explicit aim of ensuring the representation of different interests in the legislature, in various committees etc. The federal arrangements, with provincial representation in the Council of Provinces, serves the purpose of giving a voice to the specific interests of provinces. Traditional structures of leadership and (potentially) cultural councils may to some extent provide a voice for minority groups *vis-à-vis* the larger community.

These arrangements reflect not only an embracement of representative democracy, but can also be seen to grant a certain acceptance of the consociational conception of group representation. Central to this notion is the view that in plural societies, minority groups are likely to remain minorities. To include them in the political sphere special arrangements are called for, arrangements representing them as groups.[45]

## The Constitutional Domain

Although both the NP and the ANC increasingly came to embrace constitutionalism during the 1980s and early 1990s, the character of their constitutionalism differs. Both seek to regulate the power of the majority, but while the NP have sought to limit it through foreclosure of issues, the aim of the ANC has been to ensure that the will of the majority is 'steered' by constitutional pre-commitment. The 'final' constitution, reflects most clearly the latter notion.

It seeks to bind changing governments to the basic values underlying the constitution: commitment to changing society in a more just direction, and respect for the rights of individuals. These concerns are safeguarded so that they are not jeopardised by short-term considerations. This limits the political domain by transferring power to the Constitutional Court. The more comprehensive the constitution is, and the longer the list of justiciable rights, the less room is left for politics. The 'final' constitution with a Bill of Rights that includes social and economic rights as well as civil, political and cultural rights, opens for substantial 'legalisation' of politics. If the Constitutional Court adopts a politically active role, there is a vast number of issues where this constitutional pre-commitment could come into play. This would take potentially controversial issues out of the domain of democratically elected politicians and places them into the hands of non-elected, non-accountable judges. As noted above, this may undermine the impartiality of the Court.

Constitutional pre-commitment is not the only way that the 'final' constitution limits the domain of the political. There are also elements of foreclosure of issues and the removal of decision-making powers from the central political domain. The Bill of Rights demarcates several 'private' areas, outside the government domain, including important property rights. The federal arrangements could potentially channel controversial issues away from the national arena. In both cases there are, however, overriding powers and concerns that limit the extent to which this foreclosure of issues is able to serve the function that the consociational model envisages, namely to protect these interests and 'own affairs' from being encroached upon by the majority.

Taken at face value the scope and functioning of the constitutional domain under the 'final' constitution is close to the justice model. The actual balance will, however, depend on how the different aspects of the constitution is interpreted and manifested. Since the elements of foreclosure are by nature more 'conservative' and status-quo orientated these may prove more effective than they appear to be at first sight.

*Normative Foundation*

We have seen how the 'final' constitution on a number of dimensions incorporates elements from different constitutional approaches, sometimes accommodating seemingly contradictory positions. This is reflected also at the level of justification. Compared with the constitutional models discussed in Chapters 4 and 5, it is more difficult to tie the structure of the 'final' constitution to a particular philosophical position. From the perspective of normative philosophy, different aspects of the constitution seem to draw on different normative traditions.

The structure of the 'final' constitution is close to the justice model and to a large extent the text reflects the same ideals: those of an egalitarian version of liberal political theory where social justice and protection of the rights of individuals are primary concerns (Rawls, 1971, 1993).

The 'final' constitution also faces some of the same problems as the justice model. The domain of the 'final' constitution is wide and includes issues that go beyond what the domain of the constitution should include in a modern plural society, according to Rawls' criteria. Particularly in relation to social and economic rights, the scope for rational disagreement is wide. Rawls' main argument for excluding these from the constitution as such is that it renders the constitution vulnerable to excessive politicisation, and detracts from its basic rationale, to create a sufficient consensus for peaceful resolution of disputes. (Rawls 1989, see also discussion in chapter 4 above.)

Certain elements in the 'final' constitution reflect values of the communitarian tradition that seem at odds with this individualist and liberal approach. They seem to recognise the political relevance of deep social structures that are formative of individuals' identities, and the need to protect these through collective rights and acknowledgement of traditional practices. The recognition of traditional leaders and traditional structures of government, and the opening that is provided for acknowledging a collective right of communities to self-determination, can be seen to reflect such ideas.

## Restating the Argument

Is the 'final' constitution an ANC document? It depends on the perspective. The ANC won most of what was open for contest in the post-1994 constitutional negotiations. On the other hand, the constraints that the constitutional principles of the interim constitution placed on later negotiations amounted to significant concessions from the perspective of the ANC's negotiating position. The rejection by the Constitutional Court of the text adopted on 8 May 1996, highlights the relevance of these constraints.

Explicit power-sharing arrangements are out, at least with regard to the jewel in the crown, that of executive power. The system of the 'final' constitution is basically majoritarian, but one in which the opposition has considerably more impact than in a standard majoritarian democracy.

Throughout this chapter we have seen how many of the arrangements in the 'final' constitution are compromises between different conceptions of constitutionalism. There is a mixture of elements, some seeking to diffuse and share power between the parties and between layers of government, other elements facilitating a strong executive, yet other providing checks to tie the majority to the constitution. Some of the arrangements, most notably the 'parliamentary presidentialism' unique to South Africa, seem to be a result of the fact that the parties to the negotiations, most notably the NP and the ANC, steered towards different constitutional models and navigated on the basis of different conceptions of how political power should be constituted and limited. Is this an optimal balance given the particular social and political problems South Africa is facing, or a compromise that is inferior to the rivalling positions? This question will be addressed in the next, and last, chapter.

## Notes

1.  In the following the 'final' constitution is referred to by section number only, except where it is necessary to distinguish between the text that was adopted by the Constitutional Assembly on 8 May 1996 (NT) and the amended text (AT), adopted on 11 October 1996. The interim constitution is referred to as 1993 IC.
2.  That constitutionalism has increasingly been regarded by central actors within the ANC as an acceptable and even desirable path may also be seen as part of a world-wide trend. The focus on rights and constitutionalism was strengthened throughout the world from the late 1980s onwards, after the breakdown of the communist bloc in Eastern Europe.
3.  The core of the separation of powers' doctrine is the functional independence of branches of government. The principle of checks and balances is that the constitutional order will prevent the branches of government from usurping power from one another. This is not a fixed or rigid constitutional doctrine, it is given expression in many different forms. A strict form of the doctrine is implemented, in, among others, the USA and France, but even here it is not a matter of complete separation of powers (Constitutional Court judgement CCT 23/96 [109–12]).
4.  This was added later to accommodate conservative Afrikaners supporting the idea of an Afrikaner *Volkstaat*, and was instrumental in bringing the Freedom Front (FF) into the 1994 elections.
5.  The provincial powers were somewhat strengthened with the constitutional amendment of 3 April 1994, that brought the IFP into the elections. This extended the legislative competence of provincial legislature and granted them certain powers over financial and fiscal affairs, but as a whole the provinces remained relatively weak in relation to the centre.

6. Although the Constitutional Assembly is identical with the two chambers of Parliament in terms of members, the CA has its own administrative staff. Between these structures (and within each of them) coordination problems were evident. Representatives were frequently required to attend several meetings at the same time, often resulting in a lack of quorum.

7. Due to irregularities, the 1994 election results in KwaZulu-Natal have been widely regarded as unreliable and as an outcome of political horse-trading — 'a negotiated compromise designed to satisfy Inkatha' (Tjønneland, 1993: 45).

8. It is interesting to note that the FF with their relatively moderate rhetoric and amicable attitude towards President Mandela, succeeded in holding on to the main share of the conservative Afrikaner vote in the Local Government Elections in November 1995. The Conservative Party (CP), who boycotted the 1994 general elections, were all but wiped out.

9. The interim constitution prescribes that in case of a deadlock (i.e. less than two thirds majority in the CA) the constitutional proposal endorsed by the majority should be considered by the Constitutional Court to ensure that it is in line with the constitutional principles. The text should then be put before the public in a referendum. If it fails to win a 60 per cent majority, the President must dissolve Parliament and call a general election. The new constitutional assembly must adopt the new constitution within a year with a 60 per cent majority (1993 IC, Section 73).

10. The ANC won 68 per cent of the proportional vote in the November 1995 Local Government Elections (LGETG 1995). Elections in most of the Western Cape and KwaZulu-Natal, the bastions of the opposition, were not held at that stage. In real terms the ANC showing was thus somewhat down compared with the 1994 results of 62 per cent (Reynolds, 1994: 202), but the party continued to hold a comfortable majority in most provinces. In towns of the Western Cape where elections were held, the ANC even improved their standing somewhat, which was an important boost for the party. When the remaining local government elections in the Western Cape were held in late May 1996, shortly after the adoption of the 'final' constitution, the results were disappointing to the ANC. While improving marginally in terms of PR votes, the NP remain comfortably in the lead, and won decisive victories in Cape Town. The local elections in KwaZulu-Natal in June 1996 showed that the IFP continues to hold a firm grip on the rural areas, and remains the largest party in the province, while the ANC won in the cities and improved their standing relative to the 1994 results (LGETG 1996). The NP and the IFP consolidated their regional strongholds. When these are included, the ANC share of the proportional vote was down in the local elections compared to the 1994 national elections.

11. During the last days of the negotiations Cosatu (Congress of South African Trade Unions) launched a massive strike to protest inclusion in the constitution of the right of employers to lock out striking workers. The controversial strike was to some extent supported by the ANC leadership, prompting criticism that the party thus disregarded the democratic process in the CA.

12. In the following the judgement of the Constitutional Court will be referred to as CCT 23/97.

13. Cyril Ramaphosa, now Deputy Director of a private, black-owned, company (New Africa Investment Ltd) did, however, return for the final round of negotiations.

14. 84 private parties, mainly organisations, lodged objections. 27 of these, the Constitutional Assembly and the political parties, were invited to give oral statements to the Constitutional Court (CCT 23/96 [24]).

15. The parties that presented submissions were the National Party, Inkatha Freedom Party, the Democratic Party, the Christian Democratic Party, and the Conservative Party (the latter boycotted the 1994 elections and is not represented in Parliament or in the CA) (CCT 23/96 [24]).

16. Two of the other parties represented in Parliament, the Freedom Front and the Pan Africanist Congress, also did not make any submissions.

17. On 6 September, the same day that the Constitutional Court handed down judgement on the 8 May 1996 South African Constitution Bill, it also declined to certify the provincial KwaZulu-Natal constitution. Inkatha, who when boycott failed to produce results had tried to use the provincial constitution as a route to greater autonomy, may have seen a late re-entry as a last bid to get some of their demands through.

18. There is also a precedence for this in the South African constitution of 1983, where the State President is (indirectly) elected by Parliament. Also under this dispensation the President is both Head of State and Head of Government (1983 Constitution, Sections 6, 7, 19 and 20).

19. Under the 1993 interim constitution election and impeachment of the president required a majority both in the National Assembly and the Senate (IC Section 60) while in the 'final' constitution these powers lie solely with the National Assembly.

20. The argument was made by Jan-Erik Lane at the joined conference of the Southern African Sociological Association (SASA) and the International Committee on Political Sociology (CPS) in Durban, 7–11 July 1996.

21. According to the 'final' South African constitution, bills must be submitted to the President for assent. He or she may refer them back to the National Assembly for reconsideration, with reference to reservations about their constitutionality. If the reservations are not accommodated, the President may refer the bill to the Constitutional Court. If the Court finds the bill constitutional, the President must sign it (Section 79). While the President may delay the legislative process there is no actual veto power.

22. This was part of the argument made by Lane, referred to in note no. 20 above.

23. This has, however, not been the negotiating position of the ANC. Within the ANC, views have differed on this issue, and on the related question of a separation of the functions of head of government and head of state. To understand the position of the party it is necessary to take into account strategic considerations of party cohesion as well as the internal power-map of the ANC.

24. Another strategic consideration, at least for the short term, is that, with Mandela gone, the ANC as a party is likely to be more popular than its presidential candidate (set to be Thabo Mbeki).

25. A three quarters majority is needed to change the founding provisions (Section 1) and the provisions for constitutional amendments (Section 74).

26. Given the extensive tasks the Constitutional Court is to perform, the delay could be substantial.

27.     In a situation where a party controls two thirds of the seats in the National Assembly, the opposition have few powers. In that case the governing party could change the constitution more or less at will, at least with respect to issues outside the scope of the powers of the NCoP.

28.     Schedule 6, Section 6(3) with Schedule 6, Annexure A, Item 13. The regulation does not enjoy ordinary constitutional protection. It can be changed by the procedure that governs matters that fall under the area of concurrent national and provincial powers (76(1)). With respect to the NCoP the anti-defection clause is retained as an ordinary constitutional provision.

29.     The Senate of the interim constitution was composed of ten senators from each province, selected from party lists in proportion to party strength in provincial elections. The provinces differ in size, and the composition of the Senators in terms of parties could thus differ from that of MPs even with identical voting patterns for provincial and national elections. Voting patterns could also differ, particularly if provincial and national elections were held at different points in time (unlike in 1994). Still, the two chambers of parliament would be more similar under the IC, since Senators were party representatives. The NCoP seem to have more potential for representation of provincial interests.

30.     Among these are education; health and welfare services; population development; housing; cultural matters; language policy; traditional leadership; indigenous and customary law; agriculture; environment, nature and soil conservation; industrial promotion; tourism; trade, public transport and traffic regulation; urban and rural development; regional planning and development; as well as media and police services falling under provincial authorities and certain local government matters. Policing was added as an area of concurrent powers only during the amendment process in October 1996.

31.     The Mediation Committee is a novelty in the 'final' constitution and is to consist of one member of each provincial delegation and nine members of the National Assembly, in proportion to party strength. It operates on the basis of concurrent majority (a majority of the representatives from each chamber) (Section 78).

32.     The Senate reached decisions by a majority of individual votes. If a Bill was not passed, the matter was put before a joint sitting of the two chambers (1993 IC, Section 59). In cases affecting boundaries, powers or functions of provinces a Bill lapsed unless passed by the Senate. When affecting a particular province it also needed the approval of a majority of the senators from this province) (1993 IC, Section 67). Constitutional amendments required a two thirds majority of the total members of both houses in joint sitting. Provincial boundaries, legislative and executive competencies could only be changed if also consented to by the relevant provincial legislatures (1993 IC, Section 62).

33.     An 'equitable share' is to be determined by an Act of Parliament, on the recommendations of the Financial and Fiscal Commission and after consultation with the provincial governments. The provincial legislatures are also represented on the Financial and Fiscal Commission (Sections 214, 220 and 221).

34.     Ten representatives of organised local government may participate in the proceedings of the NCoP, but do not have voting powers.

35.    The first set of judges, appointed under the interim constitution were only appointed for 7 years (1993 IC, Section 99). In most countries with constitutional courts, terms are staggered to achieve continuity (O'Malley, 1996: 183). This is not done in the South African case, but with long terms and a requirement that judges retire at 70 years, there will be a 'natural' staggering.

36.    The Judicial Services Commission consists of the Chief Justice and the President of the Constitutional Court (both appointed by the president); the Minister of Justice; six persons designated by the National Assembly from among its members, of which at least three must come from the opposition; and four of the permanent delegates to the National Council of Provinces designated together by the Council and supported by a vote of at least six provinces (at present this could mean only ANC supporters, but is likely to include one or two from the opposition); four members are designated by the President as head of the national executive (after consulting with the leaders of the other parties). There are also a number of members from the legal profession: one Judge President designated by the Judges President; one teacher of law designated by teachers of law at South African universities; two practising advocates and two practising attorneys, each nominated from within the respective profession and appointed by the President.

37.    The composition of the present Constitutional Court has evoked criticism on such grounds. The president of the Court, Arthur Chaskalson, has had a long-standing affiliation with the ANC, and was their chief legal and constitutional adviser during the first phase of constitutional negotiations. Two other justices have been ANC members (Albie Sachs was even a member of the National Executive Committee). An additional three have known sympathies for the ANC while the rest are 'progressive'. Few candidates with known conservative views or sympathies for parties of the opposition were nominated, and none was appointed (O'Malley, 1996: 186). After two years of work both the Court and its president has, however, gained a reputation as a model of apolitical fairness' (*Mail & Guardian*, 27 March 1997).

38.    It is estimated that 33 per cent of the population is under 14 years, with an additional 9 per cent in the 14–17 age-group (Pillay, 1996: 21). The African population group is the largest (77 per cent of the total population), it is also the youngest (45 per cent children), and by far the poorest. The poverty rate among African children is estimated at 70 per cent (Pillay, 1996: 42).

39.    The public interest includes land reform and other reforms to bring about equitable access to the country's natural resources; and property is not limited to land (Section 25). At a late stage of the negotiations the ANC dropped their insistence that the State's ability to pay should be a factor in determining compensation for expropriating property (ANC Newswire Root, 5 April 1996).

40.    'Equality includes the full and equal enjoyment of all rights and freedoms. To promote the achievement of equality, legislative and other measures designed to protect or advance persons, or categories of persons, disadvantaged by unfair discrimination may be taken' (Section 9 (2)).

41.    Access to the Constitutional Court is comparatively easy. When the constitution is invoked a person may (when it is in the interest of justice and with leave of the Constitutional Court) bring the matter directly to the Constitutional Court or appeal directly to the Constitutional Court from any other court (Section 167 (6)). The requirements of *locus standi* are lenient.

42.   In full, Section 235 of the 'final' constitution states that 'The right of the South African people as a whole to self-determination, as manifested in this constitution, does not preclude, within the framework of this right, recognition of the notion of the right of self-determination of any community sharing a common cultural and language heritage, within a territorial entity in the Republic or in any other way, determined by national legislation'.

43.   In the interim constitution traditional leaders were *ex officio* entitled to a seat on local government bodies (1993 IC, Section 182). Provincial houses of traditional leaders and a national council of traditional leaders, were provided for, and entitled to be consulted in relation to relevant legislation (1993 IC, Sections 183 and 185). The 'final' constitution also recognise the 'institution, status and role of traditional leadership, according to customary law' (Section 211), but does not give the same protection to their political role. National legislation *may* provide for a role for traditional leadership as an institution at local level on matters 'relating to traditional leadership, the role of traditional leaders, customary law and the customs of communities observing a system of customary law', 'national or provincial legislation *may* provide for the establishment of houses of traditional leaders' while 'national legislation *may* establish a council of traditional leaders' (Section 212, my italics). Customary law is recognised 'subject to the constitution and any legislation that specifically deals with customary law' (Section 211).

44.   Fears have been expressed that these limitations might become useful instruments for suppressing legitimate expression of ideas. 'At face value these limitations make good sense — just as it made good sense, at face value, to prohibit the propagation of ideas that promoted or tended to promote racial hatred in the past. ... It will also be interesting to see how, for example, a piece of scientific information that could give rise to racial, religious or gender tensions will be handled under Section 16(2)' (Seleoane 1996).

45.   The 1993 interim constitution reflects the ideal of representation of group interests to a larger extent than the 'final' constitution. This is particularly visible in the requirements of coalition governments at national and provincial level, and in the provisions for local government, where wards to some extent are demarcated in terms of racial groups, and where special representation is given to traditional leaders and in some cases also to farmers.

# 10 Dynamics of Constitution-Making and Constitutionalism

There are full-fledged constitutions with little bearing on actual politics, not least in Africa. Are there reasons to expect the faith of the new South African constitution to be different? Having examined the new political framework in South Africa, this last chapter looks at how the dynamics of constitution-making — the character of the constitution-making process and the compromise that it produced — affect the prospects for constitutionalism.

Two discussions go into this examination. First, we look at the qualities of the constitution itself. How does it compare with the constitutional models advocated by the respective parties? Is it the best of the two worlds — or is it a compromise that is inferior to both?

The second discussion focus on the constitution-making process and its implications for the legitimacy of the constitution. A central premise throughout this book has been that the legitimacy of the constitution is crucial for constitutionalism and democratic consolidation. Constitutional legitimacy depend on the normative acceptability of the constitutional principles as well as on the ability of the system to function and produce results in terms of stability and economic development.

The normative acceptability of the constitution is also affected by the character of the process that brought it into being. As part of the South African constitution-making process, an impressive public participation programme was implemented. This effort is discussed in part two of this chapter, before concluding with a broader perspective on prospects for constitutionalism in South Africa.

## The 'Final' Constitution — the Best of Two Worlds?

This book juxtaposes the basically majoritarian justice model with the consensus-orientated consociational model in a manner indicating a dichotomy between them. The presentation of the interim constitution and the 'final' constitution in the previous chapter shows, however, that there is a

247

continuum of possibilities in between. In practical politics a mix — any mix — is possible as an outcome of negotiations. What is interesting from our point of view is whether a compromise can yield a better solution.

Both models diagnose important problems. Although it is still too early to draw firm conclusions about post-*apartheid* dynamics and cleavage structures. Consociationalists may well be right in assuming that ethnicity will become an important source of conflict in South African politics. So far voting patterns are open to various interpretations (Mattes, 1995). They may be seen to reflect structural conditions, but also race and ethnicity. For some of the parties, most notably the IFP and the FF, ethnic elements are clearly important in their rhetoric and mobilisation strategies, and coloured nationalism seem to be on the rise. Internationally, we find that ethnic conflict is manifest in countries with very different conditions and at various stages of 'modernisation'. This can be interpreted as an indication of a basic human need or desire for social structures providing a deeper sense of belonging and meaning. In light of this phenomenon, liberal tolerance is a difficult project.

At the same time, it is difficult to see how the political order of 'a new South Africa' could generate sufficient legitimacy to be stable without paying due respect to the idea of the moral equality of all individuals, and the ideals of democracy and human rights which it entails. Democracy, in the circumstances of South Africa, also leads to strong demands for governmental commitment to combat inequality, injustice and poverty, problems which also in and by themselves represent serious threats to stability. There is little doubt that poverty and inequality are important factors fuelling the spiralling crime rate, which currently poses a very serious threat to stability in South Africa. Inequality and battles over scarce resources also seem to add to ethnic tension and incite ethnic mobilisation.

The problems in South African society appear to require both types of solutions. And the balance of political power has produced a mixed solution. All is well — or is it? Is it possible, in theory, to combine promising elements from the two models into a constitutional structure with more potential for solving the problems of South Africa? Does the 'final' constitution represent such a fruitful synthesis? Does it give a convincing response to the challenges posed by politicised ethnicity while providing a framework with a potential for transformation of the social structure into a more just scheme of cooperation?

The constitutional models presented in Chapters 4 and 5 of this book are themselves products of convergence. Sachs' justice model includes a proportional electoral system in its basically majoritarian political structure. Lijphart's power-sharing proposal is more liberal than 'pure' consociationalism in that it relies on spontaneous group formation within a common political sphere and voluntary identification with ethnic (or other) parties. What are the limits to how a model can be modified without contradicting the logic underlying it, undermining its problem-solving potential and the mechanisms for keeping the government within the bounds of the constitution? In the following we consider the 'final' constitution in light of the concessions it represents from the perspective of each of the models.

## An Improved Justice Model?

Transformation and social justice are the core aims of the justice model. The main standard to judge the new constitution by is thus its potential for achieving redistribution and progressive change.

In the justice model, a strong executive is the most vital agent for achieving progressive social change. Separation of powers between a directly elected president, a uni-cameral parliament and an independent judiciary with powers of judicial review are, according to the logic of this model, the main mechanism for keeping the executive within the bounds of the constitution and prevent developments in reactionary or authoritarian directions, while providing for strong leadership. In this perspective the parliamentary form of government in the 'final' constitution is an improvement on the interim constitution's grand coalition requirements, but not an ideal arrangement. While it currently provides for a strong executive, it does so only as long as there is a majority party. And in a majority situation the checks on the executive may prove insufficient.

Given the political situation in South Africa, two scenarios are likely: either the ANC manages to keep the alliance together and retains an absolute majority of the votes for the foreseeable future, or there is a major split in the party, in which case no party is likely to win an overall majority of the votes. Both scenarios present problems for consolidation of democracy in South Africa from the perspective of the justice model.

If the situation develops into one in which no party has a secure majority, the executive will be too weak to sustain hopes of transforming the social structure in a manner consistent with the core ideals of the justice model. It will be restrained continuously by the need to forge compromises that can secure a majority in parliament. The heightened majority requirements, the procedures involving the NCoP, and the judicial review — designed to counter excesses of a strong majority — add greatly to the problems of a minority government. In this context progressive social change seems unlikely. And with a proportional electoral system there are few structural incentives that uphold a majority situation (particularly once the anti-defection clause is gone).

If the ANC should succeed in holding on to a secure majority other problems may arise. That the executive is chosen by and accountable to parliament renders the power-structure of the 'final' constitution more monolithic than it would have been with a clearer separation of powers, leaving long-term majority parties vulnerable to authoritarian developments. Complaints are already voiced from within the ANC over inadequate distinctions between the party and the government, lack of internal democracy, and a shrinking tolerance for dissent and internal critique (*Mail* and *Guardian*, 4 October 1996).

Another significant difference between the 'final' constitution and the justice model is the federal arrangements. Decentralisation and regional representation is not incompatible with the justice model, the crucial factor is the character of the relationship between the levels of government. Decentralisation, seen as favourable in terms of participation and increased sensitivity to local needs, is compatible with the logic of the justice model as long as it is organised according to the premises of the central government and subject to national control. Lower tiers of government must not be competing centres of power with the ability to resist implementation of policies aimed at redistribution and social change.

The 'cooperative government' arrangements set out in the 'final' constitution seem to articulate these concerns, specifying a relationship that utilises the capacity of lower tiers of government while facilitating a leading role for the central government in policy-making. On the other hand, the powers of the provinces are not negligible, neither individually nor collectively. If the majority party does not control a majority of the provinces, the provinces could exert substantial influence on national politics through National Council of Provinces.

The more the provinces' potential for countering the central state is actualised, the more it weakens the main dynamic that the justice model relies upon for social change, namely a strong central government. What are the prospects of such a development? Currently the ANC has a firm grip on five of the nine provinces. Eastern Cape, North West, Mpumalanga, Northern

Province and the Free State are all uncompetitive in the sense that the ANC won at least a three quarters majority in the 1994 elections (Mattes, 1995: 22). The ANC also control two of the remaining provinces, Gauteng and Northern Cape, but with a less secure majority. Unless support for the ANC declines dramatically, or the party is split, the ANC is likely to continue to control a majority of the provinces. This does, however, not necessarily imply that the government can rely on unwavering support from the NCoP. Much depends on the ability of the national party leadership to control their provincial counterparts. Candidates backed by the national ANC leadership, have been defeated in provincial leadership elections. Such challenges are likely to persist and increase. Interests of the provincial leadership may run counter to those of the national government, and distinct provincial identities are likely to develop also in ANC-led provinces (Davis, 1996).

To sum up, the redistributive potential of the 'final' constitution depends for a large part on whether or not there is a majority government. In the current context this means whether the ANC is able to prevent splits and retain an absolute majority of the seats in the National Assembly. How provincial politics develop is another factor. If the ANC continues to control both chambers of parliament as well as the executive, the new arrangement will function much like the justice model in terms of a strong executive. If there is no clear majority party, and/or the provinces develop their potential for resistance, the power-map will be more similar to that of the consociational model, which seems detrimental to a strong and active government.

*Consociationalism in Disguise?*

What is the potential of the 'final' constitution for management of ethnic conflict? From a consociational perspective this is the crucial question. Again, the federal arrangements are crucial, and in particular how they affect ethnic divisions.

South Africa's provincial boundaries do not run strictly along ethnic lines (which would also be impossible as any viable division of the country would result in ethnically heterogeneous provinces). At least three of the provinces — KwaZulu-Natal, the Western Cape and the Northern Cape — are, however, due to their demographic composition, 'natural' strongholds of existing, (partially) ethnically based, opposition parties. KwaZulu Natal has a predominantly Zulu population, which is favourable to the IFP, a majority of Afrikaans-speaking coloureds and a substantial proportion of whites in the Western and Northern Cape maximises the voter-potential of the National Party.[1] These provinces have a demographic profile where national (ethnic/linguistic/racial) minorities (Zulus, Afrikaans speakers, coloureds) have a fair chance of winning power at provincial level.

Also in other provinces, the ethnic composition differs from that of the country as a whole. If further political divisions should arise between ethnic groups within the African population, for instance along linguistic lines, the current provinces could provide several other groups with provincial strongholds (for instance Xhosa speakers in the Eastern Cape, Sotho speakers in the Free State and Pedi speakers in Northern Province) (DBSA, 1994). To the extent that the provinces provide (ethnic) groups with a regional power base, this could — from a consociational perspective — be favourable, as it provides minorities with a share in political power.

The 'final' constitution opens for cultural/ethnic associations and permits legislation to establish a *Volksstaat* Council and/or other Cultural Councils, and for these to be awarded a certain self-determination. What the status of such councils would be is not clear. To the extent that they provide self determination to cultural groups it implies that these to some extent are recognised as separate political spheres, protected from infringement by the majority, and that they provide alternative forms of inclusion into the political system. This echoes the central ideas of the consociational model, providing higher fences for the protection of minority interests. For the very same reason it is difficult to reconcile with the nature of the justice model. Equal representation of individuals in a common political sphere is fundamental to this model, both normatively and in limiting resistance to social change. The more the potential for (ethnic) group autonomy and representation is actualised, and the more the provinces become loci of ethnic or other opposition, the more unlikely it is that there will be a strong central government, capable of driving a process of redistribution and social change. To the extent that these features of the constitutional structure increase the potential for management of ethnic conflict, they seem to do so at the expense of the potential for redistribution and social justice.

The 'final' constitution also contain other elements that concur with the recommendations of the consociational model. Cultural rights and rights of free association are vital ingredients in the consociational framework recommended by Lijphart. The handling of linguistic, religious and cultural rights in the 'final' constitution should be compatible with consociation- alism, since they are placed within a context of freedom of association and organisation, including a right to form political parties. Combined with a proportional electoral system, these rights facilitate what to Lijphart is an important precondition for consociationalism in South Africa, namely 'spontaneous emergence of segments' (Lijphart, 1985, see also Chapter 5). The autonomy of the segments are limited, but the recognition of a right to self determination for groups of the population within the framework of the constitution is an important concession that, combined with federal arrangements, could provide minorities with a share in political power.

With regard to the form of state, 'parliamentary presidentialism' is not ideal from a consociational point of view. It is, however, superior to a directly elected president. Combined with a PR electoral system, parliamentarism lends itself to coalition governments and influence from opposition parties in executive decisions, at least when there is no clear majority party. PR is in itself conducive to party proliferation, which over time may remove the main obstacle to a government functioning roughly along the lines of the consociational model: namely the overwhelming voter support for the ANC.

From the perspective of consociationalism a main problem with the new constitution is the active role prescribed for the state in relation to social and economic rights. Some forms of redistribution and affirmative action are compatible with consociationalism, and may even be necessary, but only as long as this does not substantially widen the domain of the central state or threaten the vital interests of any group.

This discussion indicates that if the 'final' constitution operates so as to maximise the potential for accommodating (ethnic) groups within the system, it does so at the expense of a strong government with potential for redistribution. Conversely, if the system is effective in terms of maintaining its potential for transforming the social structure according to the logic of the justice model, there is little room for ethnic accommodation along the lines of the consociational model. The system contains both options to some extent, but does not seem able to do both at once.

## Is a Fruitful Synthesis Possible at All?

As is clear from the above analysis, the theoretical premises and the logic underlying the two models are incongruent. The constitutional frameworks are structured according to disparate world views, to achieve largely different goals and to overcome different obstacles, and they seek to bind the government to the constitution in different ways. Neither proposal is without problems, but each presents a coherent answer to the problems of South Africa as they emerge, from their own point of view. Not only do they have answers to the practical predicaments, they respond to what they see as the most important moral or normative challenges as well.

Incorporation of consociational elements into the justice model — such as institutionalisation of grand coalition governments, a shared executive, consensus-orientated decision-making procedures, and devolution of power in a way that creates alternative power-centres — while improving its potential to accommodate minority interests, will necessarily at the same time effectively reduce its capacity for redistribution.

Similarly, to change the consociational model into a workable instrument for redistribution in the South African context it is necessary to limit the scope of resistance for the rich — which implies relying on more majoritarian modes of decision-making and eliminating minority veto powers — thus destroying the central consociational idea of stabilising through reserving a protected area for each group.

A logical compromise — and a strategy pursued in the 'final' constitution — is to decentralise selectively and give special protection to domains of central importance to the maintenance of cultural distinctiveness and autonomy, while relying on centralised and majoritarian decisions in areas central to redistribution. A problem is that many policy areas, such as education and land, are central in both respects. A more fundamental problem is that consociational models regard political stability to result from the fact that the different segments of the population are 'left alone' and do not feel their ways of life threatened ('high fences make good neighbours'). It is obvious that differences in the ways of life of different segments of the South African population is a function of disparities in available resources and material well-being to a considerable extent. There is also little doubt that a radical redistribution of resources, and a 'lowering of standards' in areas such as education and health, is a widely feared threat to the way of life of the currently privileged. Establishment of lower-tier political bodies without economic leverage is — and will be perceived as — mere window dressing, and will hardly produce the 'fences' needed for stability.

Decentralisation that includes real economic and political power seem, on the other hand, likely to obstruct redistributive attempts. The obfuscation of the racial character of inequality would probably continue, as this is in the interests of all parties. The black elite would grow, as would the black middle class. There might also be a more visible element of poor whites. While this might be sufficient to make inequalities less offensive, it is unlikely to do much for the living conditions of the majority. The majority will still be overwhelmingly black and poor.

Whatever the mix of elements is, the central issue remains the same: Either the constitution produces a strong central government that — in theory — is capable of action and directed towards redistribution. Alternatively, there is a weak central government mainly mediating among groups, and a constitution safeguarding the constituent (ethnic) groups in society from domination and intrusion by others, leaving substantial matters to lower tiers of government (segmental autonomy). It is hard to see how any arrangement could do both at once. In this perspective a middle solution is likely to accomplish neither.

Theoretically it seems impossible to get 'the best of the two worlds'. The 'sequential' compromise of the 'final' constitution — where the constitutional structure changes character according to the political balance — is perhaps the more promising alternative after all.

If an overwhelming majority of South Africans continue to vote for one party and if that party also controls a majority of the provinces, the system is basically majoritarian, and functions more or less like the justice model, but with weaker separation of powers. In this case it may prove difficult to keep the government within the bounds of the constitution and prevent authoritarian developments in the majority party.

If, as seems likely in the long run, there is a split in the ANC, or its support declines below 50 per cent the 'final' constitution will function similar to the consociational model. Consociational traits may also be prominent if ethnic divisions become salient in South African politics, or for some other reason provincial identities develop in opposition to the centre. In this context the structure is conducive to coalition governments and there is a potential for group autonomy. The set-up seems conducive to such a development by meeting Lijphart's basic conditions for 'spontaneous group formation', namely freedom of association and PR elections. In this context the main problem is likely to be weak and unstable governments.

## Do Constitutions Matter?
## Constitutionalism, Legitimacy and Participation

The above discussion may give the impression of a deterministic relationship between the constitutional structure and politics, which of course is not the case. There are constitutions with very little impact whatsoever. And even if established and adhered to, a constitution only sets limits to and provides opportunities for political action. It may make certain forms of action more difficult, but the actual political development is always primarily a matter of how politics are conducted within this framework.

Constitutionalism has been defined as

> ... a commitment to limitations on ordinary political power; it revolves around a political process, one that overlaps with democracy in seeking to balance state power and individual and collective rights; it draws on particular cultural and historical contexts from which it emanates; and it resides in public consciousness (Greenberg *et al.*, 1993).

Constitutionalism is influenced by a number of factors (see Chapter 3). The legitimacy of the constitution is crucial, along with a strong civil society that can serve as a foundation for the constitution outside the realms of the state. Constitutional legitimacy is in turn influenced by the acceptability of the constitutional norms, as well as by governmental performance. The legitimacy of new constitutions also depend on the character of the process through which it was created. In the following sections the South African constitutional process is examined with a view to its effects on the legitimacy of the constitutional structure.

### 'For the People, by the People' — or Majoritarian Democracy through Elite Cartel?

The negotiation process at Kempton Park, leading up to the adoption of the interim constitution in 1993, was widely criticised for being undemocratic, restricted to a narrow elite, and lacking transparency.

It is often argued that it is difficult for political leaders to strike compromises if they have to announce each move and bring their constituency along every inch of the way. In this respect the secrecy of the process may have been conducive — but it was also a liability, particularly for the ANC, who campaigned on a ticket of making government accessible, transparent and responsible to ordinary people. For the sake of legitimacy (that of the ANC as well as of the constitution) the second phase of the constitution-making process — in the 'new South Africa' — had to be different. Or at least appear to be.

*'The new Constitution will be written by the most important person in the country: YOU.'*
*'You've Made your Mark, now Have your Say!'*
*'Now's your Chance to Tell the Authorities What to Do!'*

The public participation programme of the South African Constitutional Assembly calling for public submissions on the constitution, reads as an application of Albie Sachs' ideas about the participatory formulation of rights. The discussion in Chapter 5 show how Sachs' strategy rests on a conception of the relationship between the fairness of the process and the fairness of the product which parallels that of John Rawls' theory of justice. The rationale of implementing a process of participatory formulation of rights can be summed up in four points:

a) to create a better product — a better constitution — in harmony with the concerns and normative conceptions of the South African people;
b) to promote an understanding of 'the other' through dialogue and through principled thinking (the socratic element);
c) to stimulate the development and deepening of civil society by asking for formulations both from existing organisations and from less formalised groups; and
d) to create a sense of ownership of the product throughout society by means of opening up opportunities for participation.

The public participation programme of the Constitutional Assembly was even more extensive than that suggested by Sachs. In addition to asking organisations to formulate and comment on the constitutional text, the invitation was extended to the population at large. All were welcome to send in written submissions, make oral statements in public meetings, phone the Constitutional Assembly talk line, or use the Internet.

The response was amazing. The Constitutional Assembly received more than two million submissions and petitions. Fortunately for those who were asked to take them into consideration, the vast majority (1 990 354) were signatures on petitions. The petitions were concentrated around a limited number of issues: half of the total (1 001 246) petitioned for Afrikaans as official language, a further 650 000 to keep parliament in Cape Town. Other major issues were: in favour of the death penalty (186 376); against South Africa as a secular state (42 069); against legalisation of abortion (19 854); against including sexual orientation in the anti-discrimination clause (17 209);

for constitutional protection of animal rights (17 778); and the right to own firearms (14 475) (Constitutional Assembly, 1996a).

In addition to the petitions there were 13 443 individual submissions on a vast number of issues (some far outside the scope of the constitution-making process). Although less than seven per cent of the total, it is in itself a vast material. About ten per cent of the submissions (1 440) were from organisations. 235 were made by political parties, while the vast majority (11 768) came from individuals (Constitutional Assembly, 1996a). The submissions range in size from a few handwritten lines to more than a hundred pages of printed material. In addition to written submissions there were public hearings where key stakeholders from different sectors of society were consulted on a range of issues.[2]

In terms of information, the Constitutional Assembly published a popularised newsletter, *Constitutional Talk*, which was freely distributed. One of the issues (printed in four million copies) contained a full draft of the constitution, on which the public were asked to comment. It was a stated aim to write the constitution in plain language so that it as far as possible should be accessible to ordinary people.[3] Additional material popularising the process was also made available in all 11 official languages. Constitutional issues were debated in *Constitutional Talk* programmes on national television and phone-in programmes broadcast in different languages on eight radio stations. A face-to-face outreach programme with community workshops and public meetings, targeted areas that are hard to access by printed or electronic media (deep rural areas and communities with large numbers of illiterate or semi-literate people). A total of more than 1 000 workshops, briefings and meetings were held throughout the country, reaching approximately 95 000 people and involving local civil society organisations (Constitutional Assembly, 1996a). At the other end of the scale, the Constitutional Assembly developed an excellent Internet service where draft texts, reports and minutes of the proceedings were laid out, and where submissions from the public were made available in searchable databases.

The effort to involve the population at large is amazing, but did it have an impact on the constitution? What are the likely effects, if any, on the legitimacy of the constitution and the prospects for constitutionalism in South Africa? Before proceeding with these questions, I will pause to consider some paradoxes arising from the public participation efforts.

## Paradoxes of Public Participation

Was the content of the submissions of interest to the constitution-makers or only the fact that submissions were made?

Assuming it was mainly a matter of getting people involved in an attempt to create legitimacy for the end-product and the new regime — can it be justified to fool people into believing that their efforts are worthwhile in order to produce a 'by-product' (legitimacy)? And is it realistic to believe that a sufficient number of people can be fooled and that the 'by-product' will materialise?[4]

If we suppose that the call for submissions were made in good faith, other problems arise. On the practical side, the very magnitude of the material create problems: how can anyone — negotiating parties or experts — manage to take this enormous material into consideration? If this problem is overcome, and the public participation process constitutes a meaningful channel for influence into the constitution-making process, difficult normative questions arise. How should the submissions be treated? Should they be regarded as representative? What status should they have *vis-à-vis* the 'will of the people' as expressed in the election to the Constitutional Assembly? In a country with enormous disparities between population groups with regard to education, access to information and to means of communication (even literacy is a scarce commodity in the adult black population), the representativity of the process, or lack thereof, is particularity important to consider.

There are submissions written by hand by people in rural peripheries, but these are exceptions. A disproportionate share of the submissions seem to come from the well-educated, the middle class, former politicians, academics, professionals and political activists. (And people surfing the Internet and e-mailing the Constitutional Assembly, are hardly representative of the majority of South Africans.) Is it justified, on democratic grounds, to take into serious consideration the output of such a process? What status should it have in the process of negotiation between democratically elected parties?

The dilemma is thus: Either the submissions from the public are given weight, in which case it is generally the resourceful and privileged who are heard, shifting the emphasis away from 'the representatives of the people' elected to the Constitutional Assembly in democratic elections with a very high turnout. Alternatively, little notice is taken of the submissions, in which case it can be regarded as an insult to pour vast resources into fooling people to believe that their contribution can make a difference. And, on the practical side, can you have only the by-product? That is, can you reap the legitimacy of the participatory process without allowing a real impact for the participation?

### Did Public Participation Influence the Product?

It is impossible to establish the precise extent to which the submissions from the public influenced the negotiation process and the constitution itself. There are too many interacting factors, too many possible patterns of influence, and only tentative conclusions can be drawn.

When addressing the influence of the submissions it is useful to distinguish among the relatively few submissions from parties and organised civil society on the one hand, and the vast majority of submissions from the general public on the other. Representatives from organised civil society participated in the constitution-making process in several ways, directly, through the parties, and as organisers. Some organisations were explicitly asked to make submissions, either written or in sector hearings. Submissions from organisations — particularly from central stakeholder, organisations with links to political parties, and organisations with specialised knowledge of the matters under consideration — appear to have fed into the process in a meaningful way. These submissions can not be dismissed as mere window-dressing. However, the problem of representativity — which organised interests that are allowed to influence the negotiations — remains.

What about submissions from the public at large? An indication of whether the public submissions have had material impact, and, indeed, whether there was an intention to take them into consideration, is the status given to the submissions in the drafting-process. Did the process allow a meaningful space for this input?

There were two phases of submissions. The first and general phase started in December, 1994. After being copied and sorted by the secretariat the submissions were forwarded to the theme committees dealing with the relevant matters. The submissions were rather un-focused and spread over a vast number of issues. Consideration of the submissions was up to the technical experts and individual representatives in the various theme committees. Representatives were encouraged to look at the volumes of submissions, but at this point the magnitude of the proposals made serious consideration of individual submissions difficult, at least for the theme committees dealing with rights issues, which were the main 'targets' for submissions.

The impression gained by observing theme committee meetings, reading minutes, and conducting informal talks with some of the participants, was that at this stage of the process there was a (more or less explicit) understanding that the submissions from the general public were 'along for the ride'. There are few sign indicating that the material content of the submissions from the public were utilised or systematically and seriously considered by the drafters at this stage. On the other hand, a certain influence cannot be ruled out.

During December, 1995 and January, 1996 over four million copies of a working draft of the constitution (including explanatory articles and graphics to make it accessible to ordinary people) were printed. It was produced in all 11 official languages and distributed as inserts in various newspapers and directly to households.

In the second phase of the public participation programme the Constitutional Assembly asked for submissions on the working draft. These were more focused, and not as many (1 849 submissions and 248 504 petitions). The processing was also better. In addition to the procedure of copying the submissions for the theme committees, they were now summarised, organised according to the relevant section, and presented as end-notes to the fourth edition of the working draft. This more manageable form greatly increased the accessibility of the submissions and their probability of being taken into consideration.

From the Constitutional Assembly care was taken to point out that the submissions had made an impact:

> Two additions have been made to the state's duties in the Bill of Rights as a result of submissions from the public ... this concerned the opening sentence of the Bill of Rights: 'The state must respect, protect, promote and fulfil the rights in this Bill of Rights'. The clause did not originally contain the words promote and fulfil, but there were submissions that these be added to bring the state's duties into line with international precedents ... (Senator Yusuf Surtee (ANC) cited in *Constitutional Talk*, no. 2, 28 March 1996).

Two words, significant though they may be, are not much from over two million submissions... Constitutional law advisor Fink Haysom assures that many of the submissions have been incorporated in the constitution (*Mail & Guardian* 13 December 1996), but their impact is difficult to see. If we look at the petitions that make up the overwhelming majority of submissions, there are few signs of any impact. Of the major subjects of petitions there is only one that (with some goodwill) can be said to be consistent with the 'final' constitution, namely that in favour of Afrikaans as official language. Afrikaans is an official language, but only one of 11 languages of equal status. It does not have the preferential status it previously enjoyed (together with English). That the petitions should have made any difference with respect to this outcome is unlikely, as it has never been an option to exclude Afrikaans from the list of official languages. As for the other major subjects of petitions the constitution opposes all of them or does not take a stand, as in the cases of abortion and the location of Parliament, which were left for Parliament to decide.

It seems safe to conclude that the millions of submissions from the public had little direct influence on the outcome of the constitution-making process. There are also few signs indicating that the public participation programme was implemented out of concerns for the constitution as a product.

### Did the Public Participation Programme Create a Dialogue?

When Sachs recommends a process of 'participatory formulation of rights' part of the rationale is to create a dialogue to enhance the understanding of 'the other' (see discussion in Chapter 5).[5] To what extent can the public participation efforts be said to have achieved this?

With regard to dialogue between civil society and the state, non-governmental organisations (NGOs) involved in the process complained that while the Constitutional Assembly asked for input from the public, they were not prepared to engage in public dialogue on what were being submitted (*Mail & Guardian* 29 March 1996).

Internally, it seems that few organisations in civil society made serious attempts to draw their members into meetings or discussions about the Constitution-writing process. The notable exception is the trade unions. Survey results show that 37 per cent of trade union members had been informed about the Constitution by their union, and 29 per cent had the opportunity of attending meetings on the subject organised by the union (CASE 1996).

Still, it seems that the constitution-making process succeeded in generating discussion among South Africans. There was a significant debate on constitutional issues and the debate was not limited to the public sphere. Survey results indicate that a quarter of all adults had discussed the

Constitutional Assembly and constitution-related issues with friends or family (CASE, 1996).

Certain issues of great emotional value, such as the flag and the national anthem, were the subjects of huge numbers of submissions and much public debate. In both matters the compromises of the interim constitution — which no party initially wanted — has gained widespread support. This could be read as a fruit of the public dialogue around the issues, but may also be attributed to other factors, such as international triumphs on the rugby and soccer fields.

The significance of the constitutional debate for the understanding of 'the other' — for reconciliation — is difficult to establish. Acknowledgement of the value of public debate and of democratic processes as the legitimate approach to conflicts over the rules of politics, appear, however, to be widespread. This is indicated by surveys as well as by the marginalisation of the parties who chose to boycott parliamentary politics, such as the Conservative Party and ultra right-wing parties like the Afrikaner Weerstandsbewegig.

## Did the Public Participation Process Stimulate Civil Society?

'Civil society' is a wide term that includes organised interests outside of the state (organisations in the economic, cultural, religious and intellectual spheres of society) as well as formal and informal forums for public debate, the media and the channels that exist for articulation and distribution of opinions and critique. Constitutionalism requires that civil society is numerically and organisationally strong and active enough to be a political factor that the government and state apparatus needs to take into consideration. One of the objectives of pursuing a strategy of 'participatory formulation of rights' is to strengthen civil society both numerically and in terms of capacity-building.

Organised civil society were involved in the public participation process at various levels, and with different degrees of perceived impact. The process affected organisations differently and the precise positive and negative effects of the public participation process are difficult to establish.

Among the organisations most actively involved in the process have been the so-called human rights NGOs, a category which in South Africa covers a wide range of non-governmental organisations that grew out of the political resistance of the apartheid years. Most of these have struggled hard to reorient themselves and survive in the new South Africa. In many cases they have had to shift their focus and develop a new organisational identity. They have struggled to establish a working relationship with the new state, and a balance between constructive cooperation and critical distance *vis-à-vis* their former allies in the liberation movement. This has coincided with a loss of funds from international and local donors, and loss of key personnel who have moved into positions in government and the bureaucracy, as well as to business. In this sense the call for submissions for the constitutional process (as well as for other legislation and policy-formulation) has been a double-edged sword.

In a situation where organisations in civil society are declining in numbers and in size for reasons external to the constitution-making process, the public participation programme may have placed strains on the capacity of organisations that were already stretched to their limits. For others it provided a useful new focus — and even contracted work. Throughout civil society the process appears to have raised the awareness of constitutionalism and democracy.

## *Did the Public Participation Process Create a Sense of Ownership in the Product?*

Survey results indicate that the public participation efforts succeeded in creating a sense of ownership in the product. In the following section I will comment on the result of a survey conducted for the Constitutional Assembly by an independent agency (CASE) in mid-February 1996.[6] The results showed, first of all, that knowledge about the constitution is widespread. 60 per cent of the adult population had heard about the Constitutional Assembly and had a fair idea about its task. Almost as many knew how to take part in the process.

The survey found strong support for initiatives to involve the public in the constitution-making process. Half of the respondents believed that the Constitutional Assembly genuinely wanted them to participate, and more than 80 per cent felt that the public should be consulted. When asked whether they believed that the Constitutional Assembly would treat their submission seriously, 41 per cent responded positively. There are, however, significant differences across racial groups. 'The highest level of scepticism came from whites, of whom only 16 per cent believed their submission would be seriously treated, compared with 21 per cent of Indians, 29 per cent of

Coloureds and 48 per cent of African respondents' (CASE 1996).[7] The same antagonism towards the constitution-making process on the part of whites is found in an equivalent survey conducted a year before (CASE 1995, CASE 1996, Constitutional Assembly 1996a). Respondents were informed of the public participation campaign and its goals, and were asked whether they believed that ordinary people helped write the constitution. More than a third (35 per cent) of those asked believed that ordinary people made a positive contribution, while the rest were mostly unsure. Only 17 per cent were negative in their responses. Younger people were more likely to feel that the public had contributed (CASE 1996).

The widespread faith in the process was affirmed when respondents were asked whether they believed the final constitution could reflect everybody's views, and would reflect their own views. As many as 42 per cent were confident that it could, and only 25 per cent said it could not.

When asked to '(t)hink about South Africa in the future and please tell me how the new Constitution will affect the way South Africa is governed' a tenth of the sample answered that they believed constitution would either have no effect at all or would make things worse in South Africa, while three-quarters of the sample were positive, citing a range of improvements which they believed would result from the adoption of the Constitution (CASE 1996).

An amazing 57 per cent of the respondents believed that the constitution would guarantee freedom and equality for all South Africans. (Only 14 per cent replied negatively.) People from marginal areas expressed the greatest faith in the ability of the constitution to secure their future rights. 65 per cent of respondents in informal areas were optimistic in this respect. Rural dwellers were also more positive than formal urban dwellers, while those living in metropolitan areas were the least optimistic. Even among the latter, more than half (55 per cent) expressed belief in the ability of the constitution to guarantee freedom and equality for all South Africans.

While the results are impressive, there are also reasons for concern. One is the racial differences in the attitudes towards the constitution and the constitution-making process, indicating that whites, and to some extent Indians and Coloureds, are unsure about the political changes, and have significantly less faith in the constitution than the African majority. It should also be noted that 40 per cent of the adult population had not heard of the Constitutional Assembly and did not know what a constitution is. These are found predominantly among the most disadvantaged; people in deep rural areas, informal settlements, women and people over 50 years of age (CASE

266 The Battle over the Constitution

1996, Constitutional Assembly 1996a). The high confidence in the process, in the ability of the constitution to reflect everybody's views, and to guarantee freedom and equality, could also prove to be a double-edged sword, if expectations turn into disillusionment.

## Public Participation and the Legitimacy of the Constitution

The public participation strategy pursued by the South African Constitutional Assembly seems to have been successful in increasing the awareness of the constitution, and in making people feel part of the constitution-making process — at least in the short term.

There are, however, few signs indicating that the submissions from the public influenced the constitution as a product. It is also difficult to find indications of intentions to utilise their material content — or practical strategies to this effect. With six parties negotiating in the Constitutional Assembly, and the Inkatha Freedom Party as a major player outside the field, a host of constitutional experts, and formal and informal input from a wealth of pressure groups, little space seems left in the process for the submissions from the general public.

According to this line of reasoning, the public participation process was a case of going for the by-product, that is, to involve people primarily for the sake of enhancing the legitimacy of the product. This implies that people are fooled, which makes the apparent success of the strategy somewhat surprising.

It may, however, be that this entire perspective is misconstrued. It presumes that the motivation for those who participated is primarily linked to the instrumental value of participation, to expectations about the impact of their submissions on the constitution. If the intrinsic value of participation is seen as important — the expressive and symbolic value of taking part in the process whereby the 'birth certificate of a nation' is created — the link between the process and the outcome is less relevant.

Are there reasons to believe that the public participation process will increase the prospects for constitutionalism in South Africa? The stability of the new constitutional framework depend in part on the extent to which the constitution is able to generate its own support and develop authority. Given the lack of 'a religious trust in a sacred beginning', authority will have to be based on some form of 'constitutional patriotism'. The legitimacy provided by the character of the constitution-making process, and by rational acceptance of the principles of the constitution are here important elements. If the surveys have captured the sentiments, almost half the South African population felt part of the constitution-making process. Although this varies between gender, race and age groups, it is promising. The extent to which it develops into long-term legitimacy and 'constitutional patriotism' is difficult to predict at this stage. It depends on a host of factors, not least the ability of the sitting government to deliver, in the sense of producing tangible political output.

An acute aspect of this is security. The rampant crime rate, and in particular the very high levels of violent crime, seriously undermines the state's monopoly of violence. Combined with stringent provisions in the constitution for protection of the rights of detained and convicted criminals, and the Constitutional Court's decision to abolish the death penalty (CCT 3/94), this could seriously undermine the legitimacy of the constitution by creating the impression that the constitution does not adequately protect law abiding citizens, but on the contrary, operates so as to undermine an efficient protection of their most fundamental rights.

Legitimacy is not the only factor influencing the prospects for constitutionalism. For the political actors and the state bureaucracy to regard the constitution as binding, there must be a power-base for the constitution, both within the state, in the political opposition, and outside the state, in civil society. This book have highlighted the importance of the constitutional structure itself, but the character of civil society is also crucial for constitutionalism. There are strong and active organisations in South African civil society. It is, however, still an open question how these organisations, many of whom grew out of the resistance movement, will function under the new dispensation. Some have found a new working relationship with the state, a balance of cooperation and independence, loyalty and critique, others still struggle to find a new focus and mode of operation. Many experience declining resources, economically and in terms of membership. The role of the media, universities, churches and other institutions and forums for public debate, have also changed, along with their working conditions, and this transformation process is still ongoing.

## The New South Africa — a Constitutional Democracy?

The basic argument underlying this book is that constitutions matter. That the institutional set-up of constitutions, as well as their normative acceptability, have an impact on democratic stability.[8] It is vital that the constitution is designed so that it allows the most pressing and explosive problems of society to be meaningfully addressed within the structure, and that it is able to generate its own legitimacy. What is the most adequate constitutional structure for South Africa?

The analysis in Part Three of the book concludes that the normative adequacy of the rivalling constitutional models on the South African scene depends on which interpretation best fits South African society. In Chapter 9 we saw how the 'final' constitution seeks to combine rivalling positions, reflecting seemingly contradictory concerns and world views, and in this chapter we have looked at the potential for such a compromise to succeed, arguing that the more genuine the compromise between the two, the more likely it is to be deprived of the most promising mechanisms of both. Normatively as well as practically it is difficult to see how concerns arising from opposite methodological focuses and ontological assumptions, can be successfully combined. In this perspective the 'sequential' compromise of the 'final' constitution is interesting as it allows the dynamics of one or other model to operate, depending on the parliamentary balance.

In democratisation processes and transitions from authoritarian rule, the imperative of reaching agreements tends to overshadow the need to develop an adequate constitutional structure. The fact that it is possible to reach agreement on a certain 'solution' does not necessarily mean that it will work. It might even be argued on the contrary.

Sam Nolutshungu has made a useful distinction between two essential elements within the constitutional idea: that of a constitutional *moment* and that of the constitutional *function* (Nolutshungu, 1991: 92). The constitutional moment — the transition or 'new beginning' — is signified by the adoption of a new constitution. The debate is dominated by the need for a settlement between the parties to the conflict and the need for accommodation of all their interests. It is about securing a deal, striking a bargain. Focus is firmly on the *transfer* of power rather than its composition or limitation. It is a matter of negotiation between parties trading concessions rather than a confrontation of principles in a more open-ended deliberative process.

Solutions acknowledged to be second-best from any constitutionalist point of view will often be the most effective in letting parties off the hook and permitting peaceful change. 'Symbolic victories tend to matter more than the substance of what is agreed and its likely practical consequences' (Nolutshungu, 1991: 92). Thus the immediate needs of the transition — of the constitutional *moment* — may override the need of constitutional *function*, that is to construct a 'permanent' framework facilitating orderly political struggle.

An advantage of the unique two-stage process in South Africa is that it to some extent de-links the 'final' constitution from the transition proper. The process leading up to the adoption of the interim constitution, which laid the basis for the April, 1994 elections, has all the characteristics of a deal where parties trade concessions to facilitate peaceful change, and where the need for a well-functioning constitutional framework became secondary.

The second stage of the constitution-making process is a somewhat more open-ended deliberative process (at least until the last stage when bargaining and 'private' deals become more pronounced again). This should in theory be more conducive to an outcome taking into account the needs of 'constitutional function'.

A hinge is that so much of the original 'deal' was entrenched in the 34 constitutional principles, thus tying the 'final' constitution to the 'constitutional moment' and committing the constitution-makers to combine elements from both the constitutional models as described above. Given these restrictions the 'either/or' compromise in the 'final' constitution — that it does not combine the logic of the two constitutional models to the extent that the interim constitution did, but rather functions in terms of one or the other, depending on how the political scene develops — may prove fortunate. As long as the ANC controls an absolute majority of both chambers of Parliament the system will function more or less along the lines of what we have called Albie Sachs' 'justice model', representing the favoured constitutional option of the ANC. If there is no majority party in the National Assembly and/or provincial politics develop so that the collective power of the provinces against the National Government is activated, the elements of consociation or power-sharing as set forth by Arend Lijphart and favoured by the National Party, will be more prominent. Although theoretically problematic, the mixed solution of the 'final' constitution may function adequately in practical politics. The constitution is only a framework. Important though it is, neither redistribution nor management of ethnic conflict is achieved or prevented by constitutional design alone.

Is it likely that this 'final' constitution will take root in South Africa? That constitutionalism will be a regulative force?

When addressing the prospects for constitutionalism in South Africa under the new constitution, it is also relevant to take a look at the experience with constitutionalism in other parts of the continent.[9] 'Africa is full of beautiful constitutions that aren't worth the paper they are written on' (Fukuyama, 1991: 75). What is different in the South African case?

In many countries throughout Africa a seemingly paradoxical situation exist. While there are constitutions with bicameral legislatures, separation of powers provisions, bills of rights, judicial review etc., and the *idea* of the constitution appears fully established, constitutionalism is absent. The idea of the constitution is de-linked from what in liberal democratic theory is the most fundamental function of a constitution, namely to regulate the use of executive power. The classical notion that the purpose of constitutions is to limit and control political power, is replaced with an instrumental notion of constitutions as a way to facilitate the exercise of state power. The concern of African elites has been to preserve the integrity of the 'constituted polity' without being entangled in a maze of constitutional law, designed to control and supervise constitutionality (Okoth-Ogendo, 1991).

African elites have valued constitutions primarily for their constitutive value, their ability to provide the policy with a legitimate and sovereign existence. The notion of the constitution as the basic law of the state is also established, but does not involve any elements of sanctity (Okoth-Ogendo, 1991: 6). The relationship between law and power is thus conceived differently from the liberal theory, where constitutional government presupposes mechanisms within the constitution for the supervision of its provisions.

It is easier to understand why so many African countries have constitutions without constitutionalism if we concentrate on the functional element of constitutions — that is, regard them as 'power-maps' concerned with creation, distribution, exercise, legitimation and reproduction of power. Many African countries were left at independence with a fragmented political power-map, and considerable tension between the constitution and the rest of the legal order. The colonial powers themselves had favoured centralised power and direct rule, but left behind constitutions limiting the central political power through federalism, regionalism, bills of rights etc. (Okoth-Ogendo, 1991: 9). The constitutions reflected a novel concern for minority protection — in stark contrast with the rest of the legal order, characterised by a labyrinthine bureaucracy and coercive orientation, which constituted the basis for colonial policy and administration.

That the new regimes came to view the independence constitutions as liabilities should thus not surprise.They argued that the constitution frustrated the goals of equity that independence was expected to facilitate; that it failed to respond to people's expectations and aspirations; and that it was foreign to and incompatible with the African way of life. Since revision of the constitution according to its own terms was difficult, a lot of rhetoric went into exposing the absurdity of structuring the state apparatus around minority protection rather than majority expectations and developmental needs (Okoth-Ogendo, 1991; Shivji, 1991: 29).

Four main devices were used to re-centralise power: extension of the appointive and dismissal authority of the chief executive to all public offices; subjection of the process of political recruitment to strict party sponsorship; expansion of the coercive powers of the state by removing parliamentary supervision of emergency powers and redefining the conditions for invoking them, and thus for permitting derogation from the Bill of Rights; and revision of the entire constitution itself. The original (declared) intent of the changes was the need for *autochthony* — to redesign the state to a form appropriate to the social conditions of independent Africa. The result was politicised constitutions which functioned as instruments of political warfare and became crucial elements of the appropriation of power. The reconstituted African power maps were characterised by imperial presidentialism, a shrinkage of the political arena and the pre-eminence of discretion as the basis of 'constitutional' power (Okoth-Ogendo, 1991: 139).

Is the development — or decay — of constitutionalism in post-colonial African relevant when considering the prospects for constitutionalism in South Africa?

In several important respects the situation in South Africa differs from that of other African countries at their moment of independence. Contrary to its African neighbours, South Africa has a viable market economy coupled with a relatively highly developed industry. South Africa also has a much stronger civil society in terms of labour unions, professional organisations, media, civic organisations, human rights groups, churches cultural- and sports association etc.

The general international climate has changed as well. In the early 1990s a 'wave of democratisation' washed away many of the regimes described above. Multi-party systems are struggling to take hold on much of the African continent. Although the court is still out on whether they will succeed in consolidating democracy the general ideological climate is different, and more conducive to liberal democracy.

While the 'circumstances of justice' are different in South Africa than they were in the rest of post-colonial Africa at independence — there are also important and disturbing parallels. Although starting from a more fortuitous position, it would be naïve to regard South Africa as immune to a similar development.

Interestingly, an important reason for the 'derailing' of constitutions in post-colonialist Africa appears to be the inadequacy of the original constitutions. By imposing constraints on the new governments, they served to protect the privileged strata, and weaken the powers of the government to the extent that social transformation was inconceivable. They failed to echo the expectations and sense of justice of the 'liberated' majority and their rulers. In this perspective the subsequent lack of piety for the spirit of the constitution is quite understandable. There was little to hinder the elites from utilising the constitutions as means to further their own interests and otherwise circumvent or discard them. And little to prevent the replacement of the constitutional power-map with the alternative apparatus for rule inherited at independence: the coercively orientated legal body and administrative apparatus.

A new South African constitution could run the dangers of being perceived as primarily protecting the privileged and weakening the powers of the democratically elected government so as to prevent substantial change. In this case it is unlikely to be viewed as acceptable and legitimate by the majority. This in turn decreases the chances of constitutionalism taking root and developing into the civilising force it was designed to be. The role of civil society is crucial and compared with other African countries, the relative strength of civil society in South Africa is a reason for optimism. However, if the constitution does not reflect the prevailing moral sentiments and sense of justice in the politically active population, civil society is less likely to further constitutionalism. The dangers inherent in a democratic constitution that is out of step with the expectations of the majority, should not be ignored.

In South Africa, as was the case in other African countries at independence, there is an existing state apparatus directed at coercion, representing an alternative route of development if the constitution cripples the powers of the state. Therefore, while much of the essence of constitutionalism may lie in the limitation of arbitrary power, it is important to note that, in order to endure, the limiting of government should not be the weakening of it. The problem is to maintain a proper balance between power and law. In most African countries the issue was resolved in favour of power (Nwabueze, 1973).

In the light of the experience of many other African countries, no one can be assured that democratic manifestations that characterise the struggle will be carried over beyond the constitutional moment. But the process of democratisation in struggle is much further advanced in South Africa, and the diversity of forces engaged in struggle bids fair to keep it alive much longer. (Nolutshungu, 1991: 97)

There are several unfavourable factors to consitutionalism in South Africa, particularly related to the socioeconomic conditions. The widespread illiteracy is alarming, affecting the prospects for economic development. Lack of education significantly reduces the quality of 'human capital' in an industrialised economy. Widespread illiteracy also limits the alternatives with regard to political institutions, barring complex alternatives which otherwise might be of interest.[10]

The level of crime may undermine economic development as well as democratic stability and the legitimacy of the constitution. If crime cannot be brought under control this may also lead the state to develop in authoritarian direction.

In spite of the difficulties, South Africa has entered the democracy with advantages compared with other African countries, and also compared to many of the countries of Eastern Europe. There is an established tradition of multi-party politics, a relatively strong, functioning market-economy, a working banking system, a free press, universities with academic freedoms and standards, and a relatively impartial and independent judiciary. Perhaps most important, there is the organisational network. The importance of civil society as a social base for the constitution is as important as the technical qualities of the constitution. Since the legalisation of black trade unions in 1979, processes of collective bargaining has developed a relationship between employers and black trade unions, as well as valuable experience and skills. And, finally, there is a vibrant community of social, economic, cultural, religious, and sporting associations (Uys, 1991: 83). Considering the fragile state of civil society throughout Africa and in many Eastern European countries, South Africa enjoys important advantages.

The extensive public participation process that was part of the constitution-making process seems to have increased the awareness and legitimacy of the constitution in South African civil society. This may provide an initial legitimacy that could enhance the prospects for constitutionalism and consolidation of democracy.

It has been argued that the greatest problem for the future of the South African democracy will be if the electorate continues to vote overwhelmingly for one party, the ANC (Shrirer, 1996). There may be some truth in this. It is difficult in a democracy to check the powers of a strong and permanent majority, and to prevent a long-standing majority party from developing in an autocratic direction. But the 'final' constitution is in many ways tailored to fit a majority situation. Even though the majority is monolithic in the sense that it controls both the National Assembly and the executive, it is checked in several ways: the constitutional domain is wide and guarded by the Constitutional Court. The constitution is set to safeguard the fundamental rights of all — whether in minority or majority, and to protect the powers of the provinces. Special majority requirements prevent the majority from changing the rules, and the opposition may refer legislation to the Constitutional Court. The provinces could potentially also develop into centres of opposition, checking the central government through the National Council of Provinces.

There are fewer measures to safeguard the needs for efficient and stable government in a situation without a majority party. In a minority situation the executive would be weak. This is detrimental to attempts to implement policies aiming at distributive justice. In South Africa, failure to deliver in terms of social justice runs counter, not only to justice, but probably also to long-term political stability.

A final word of caution is appropriate after this preoccupation with the formal structures of the state. In constitutional democracies the basic rules of the political game are laid down in a formal constitution. That these rules are generally accepted and abided by are obviously vital for the basic norms to function as intended. However, even if (and this is an important if) South Africa becomes a well ordered society in the sense that the constitutional rules are complied with, this, in and by itself, does not imply realisation of 'the good society'.

Other factors are even more decisive. External economic conditions are crucial as is the outcome of the actual political process — the policy decisions that are made and the way they are implemented. Although the constitutional framework is directed towards certain goals, constitutional constraints will — in a democracy — only specify a range. The particular political output is primarily a product of politics, resources, political will and statesmanship.

The limited importance of constitutions *vis à vis* the role of politics is acknowledged in Chapter 3. Throughout the book, as the constitutional models are presented and evaluated, it may seem as if this basic insight is forgotten and too much is read into the constitution, or rather, out of the constitutional models. Given that the concern of this book has been to show why and how constitutions are important, the neglect of the role of politics may be justified. A final word of caution is, however, appropriate:

> What can be enacted in a constitutional process, are the formal structures, and this is not necessarily what in the end will seem important for the success or failure of democracy. (Hylland, 1991, my translation)

## Notes

1.  Despite this, the ANC won close to 50% of the votes in the Northern Cape in the 1994 elections and is currently the largest party.
2.  Among the issues discussed in public hearings were; the judiciary and legal system; business; children's rights; traditional authorities; youth; labour; women; socioeconomic rights; and land rights. A total of 596 organisations across the spectrum of civil society were involved as participants, speakers and in the organisation of events (Constitutional Assembly, 1996a).
3.  The aim was to create a constitution that people could easily read, understand and use to claim their basic rights. Many would say that this has not been achieved, although it may be simple compared with other such documents, it is too demanding for 'ordinary people', particularly in a country with a tradition of systematically poor education for the majority of the population. It has also been claimed that 'plain language' adds to the legal confusion over the interpretation of the constitution (Davis, 1996).
4.  I draw on Jon Elster's idea of states that are essentially by-products, i.e. that can be experienced as unintentional side-effects, but which will fail to materialise if that is what you intentionally are after (Elster, 1981).
5.  Belief in the 'socratic' element of public debate is central to much of contemporary normative political theory. John Rawls draws on this when discussing the ideas of overlapping consensus and reflective equilibrium (see discussion in Chapter 5 above). The emphasis on the value of public debate is, however, much more prominent to scholars within the deliberative democracy tradition, where Jürgen Habermas is the central figure (see for instance Habermas, 1996).
6.  The survey was conducted on a random household sample of 3800 South African citizens aged 18 and above. Being a household survey it excluded homeless people from the sample, otherwise it reflects the demographic profile of the country with respect to age, gender, race, level of education as well as with respect to type of dwelling, community and province. The respondents were interviewed face to face.
7.  Rural dwellers were more confident that their submissions would be taken seriously than urban and metropolitan dwellers, while those in informal areas were least inclined to believe so, but here the differences are smaller.
8.  The structure of the argument is visualised in Figure 3.1.
9.  In this section I draw mainly on the works of Okoth-Ogendo (1991) and Nolutshungu (1991).

10. It represents an obstacle to the possibilities for 'ethnic arithmetics' requiring complex voting procedures (such as the preferential electoral systems (the alternative vote or the single transferable vote) proposed by Horowitz), as well as non-territorial/personal federalism (as is found in Brussels).

# Appendix

**The 34 Constitutional Principles**
**as set out in Schedule 4 of the South African Interim Constitution of November 1993.**

I    The Constitution of South Africa shall provide for the establishment of one sovereign state, a common South African citizenship and a democratic system of government committed to achieving equality between men and women and people of all races.

II    Everyone shall enjoy all universally accepted fundamental rights, freedoms and civil liberties, which shall be provided for and protected by entrenched and justiciable provisions in the Constitution, which shall be drafted after having given due consideration to *inter alia* the fundamental rights contained in Chapter 3 of this Constitution.

III    The Constitution shall prohibit racial, gender and all other forms of discrimination and shall promote racial and gender equality and national unity.

IV    The Constitution shall be the supreme law of the land. It shall be binding on all organs of state at all levels of government.

V    The legal system shall ensure the equality of all before the law and an equitable legal process. Equality before the law includes laws, programmes or activities that have as their object the amelioration of the conditions of the disadvantaged, including those disadvantaged on the grounds of race, colour or gender.

VI    There shall be a separation of powers between the legislature, executive and judiciary, with appropriate checks and balances to ensure accountability, responsiveness and openness.

**VII** The judiciary shall be appropriately qualified, independent and impartial and shall have the power and jurisdiction to safeguard and enforce the Constitution and all fundamental rights.

**VIII** There shall be representative government embracing multi-party democracy, regular elections, universal adult suffrage, a common voters' roll, and, in general, proportional representation.

**IX** Provisions shall be made for freedom of information so that there can be open and accountable administration at all levels of government.

**X** Formal legislative procedures shall be adhered to by legislative organs at all levels of government.

**XI** The diversity of language and culture shall be acknowledged and protected, and conditions for their promotion shall be encouraged.

**XII** Collective rights of self-determination in forming, joining and maintaining organs of civil society, including linguistic, cultural and religious associations, shall, on the basis of non-discrimination and free association, be recognised and protected.

**XIII**
1. The institution, status and role of traditional leadership, according to indigenous law, shall be recognised and protected in the Constitution. Indigenous law, like common law, shall be recognised and applied by the courts, subject to the fundamental rights contained in the Constitution and to legislation dealing specifically therewith.
2. Provisions in a provincial constitution relating to the institution, role, authority and status of a traditional monarch shall be recognised and protected in the Constitution.

**XIV** Provision shall be made for participation of minority political parties in the legislative process in a manner consistent with democracy.

**XV** Amendments to the Constitution shall require special procedures involving special majorities.

**XVI** Government shall be structured at national, provincial and local levels.

**XVII** At each level of government there shall be democratic representation. This principle shall not derogate from the provisions of Principle XII.

## XVIII
1.     The powers, boundaries and functions of the national government and provincial governments shall be defined in the Constitution.
2.     The powers and functions of the provinces defined in the Constitution, including the competence of a provincial legislature to adopt a constitution for its province, shall not be substantially less than or substantially inferior to those provided for in this Constitution.
3.     The boundaries of the province shall be the same as those established in terms of this Constitution.
4.     Amendments to the Constitution which alter the powers, boundaries, functions, or institutions of provinces shall in addition to any other procedures specified in the Constitution for constitutional amendments, require the approval of a special majority of the legislatures of the provinces, alternatively, if there is such a chamber, a two-thirds majority of a chamber of Parliament composed of provincial representatives, and if the amendment concerned specific provinces only, the approval of the legislatures of such provinces will also be needed.
5.     Provision shall be made for obtaining the views of a provincial legislature concerning all constitutional amendments regarding its powers, boundaries and functions.

**XIX** The powers and functions at the national and provincial levels of government shall include exclusive and concurrent powers as well as the power to perform functions for other levels of government on an agency or delegation basis.

**XX** Each level of government shall have appropriate and adequate legislative and executive powers and functions that will enable each level to function effectively. The allocation of powers between different levels of government shall be made on a basis which is conducive to financial viability at each level of government and to effective public administration, and which recognises the need for and promotes national unity and legitimate provincial autonomy and acknowledges cultural diversity.

**XXI** The following criteria shall be applied in the allocation of powers to the national government and the provincial governments:

**1.** The level at which decisions can be taken most effectively in respect of the quality and rendering of services, shall be the level responsible and accountable for the quality and the rendering of the services, and such level shall accordingly be empowered by the Constitution to do so.

**2.** Where it is necessary for the maintenance of essential national standards, for the establishment of minimum standards required for the rendering of services, the maintenance of economic unity, the maintenance of national security or the prevention of unreasonable action taken by one province which is prejudicial to the interests of another province or the country as a whole, the Constitution shall empower the national government to intervene through legislation or such other steps as may be defined in the Constitution.

**3.** Where there is necessity for South Africa to speak with one voice, or to act as a single entity - in particular in relation to other states - powers should be allocated to the national government.

**4.** Where uniformity across the nation is required for a particular function, the legislative power over that function should be allocated predominantly, if not wholly, to the national government.

**5.** The determination of national economic policies, and the power to promote interprovincial commerce and to protect the common market in respect of the mobility of goods, services, capital and labour, should be allocated to the national government.

**6.** Provincial government shall have powers, either exclusively or concurrently with the national government, *inter alia* -

*(a)* for the purposes of provincial planning and development and the rendering of services; and

*(b)* in respect of aspects of government dealing with specific socio-economic and cultural needs and the general well-being of the inhabitants of the province.

**7.** Where mutual co-operation is essential or desirable or where it is required to guarantee equality of opportunity or access to a government service, the powers should be allocated concurrently to the national government and the provincial governments.

**8.** The Constitution shall specify how powers which are not specifically allocated in the Constitution to the national government or to a provincial government, shall be dealt with as necessary ancillary powers pertaining to the powers and functions allocated either to the national government or provincial governments.

**XXII** The national government shall not exercise its powers (exclusive or concurrent) so as to encroach upon the geographical, functional or institutional integrity of the provinces.

**XXIII** In the event of a dispute concerning the legislative powers allocated by the Constitution concurrently to the national government and provincial governments which cannot be resolved by a court on a construction of the Constitution, precedence shall be given to the legislative powers of the national government.

**XXIV** A framework for local government powers, functions and structures shall be set out in the Constitution. The comprehensive powers, functions and other features of local government shall be set out in parliamentary statutes or in provincial legislation or both.

**XXV** The national government and provincial governments shall have fiscal powers and functions which will be defined in the Constitution. The framework for local government referred to in Principle XXIV shall make provision for appropriate fiscal powers and functions for different categories of local government.

**XXVI** Each level of government shall have a constitutional right to an equitable share of revenue collected nationally so as to ensure that provinces and local governments are able to provide basic services and execute the functions allocated to them.

**XXVII** A Financial and Fiscal Commission, in which each province shall be represented, shall recommend equitable fiscal and financial allocations to the provincial and local governments from revenue collected nationally, after taking into account the national interest, economic disparities between the provinces as well as the population and developmental needs, administrative responsibilities and other legitimate interests of each of the provinces.

**XXVIII** Notwithstanding the provisions of Principle XII, the right of employers and employees to join and form employer organisations and trade unions and to engage in collective bargaining shall be recognised and protected. Provisions shall be made that every person shall have the right to fair labour practices.

**XXIX** The independence and impartiality of a Public Service Commission, a Reserve Bank, an Auditor-General and a Public Protector shall be provided for and safeguarded by the Constitution in the interests of the maintenance of effective public finance and administration and a high standard of professional ethics in the public service.

**XXX**
1.     There shall be an efficient, non-partisan, career-oriented public service broadly representative of the South African community, functioning on a basis of fairness and which shall serve all members of the public in an unbiased and impartial manner, and shall, in the exercise of its powers and in compliance with its duties, loyally execute the lawful policies of the government of the day in the performance of its administrative functions. The structures and functioning of the public service, as well as the terms and conditions of service of its members shall be regulated by law.
2.     Every member of the public service shall be entitled to a fair pension.

**XXXI**  Every member of the security forces (police, military and intelligence), and the security forces as a whole, shall be required to perform their functions and exercise their powers in the national interest and shall be prohibited from furthering or prejudicing party political interests.

**XXXII**  The Constitution shall provide that until 30 April 1999 the national executive shall be composed and shall function substantially in the manner provided for in Chapter 6 of this Constitution.

**XXXIII**  The Constitution shall provide that, unless Parliament is dissolved on account of its passing a vote of no-confidence in the Cabinet, no national election shall be held before 30 April 1999.

**XXXIV**
1.     This Schedule and the recognition therein of the right of the South African people as a whole to self-determination, shall not be construed as precluding, within the framework of the said right, constitutional provision for a notion of the right to self-determination by any community sharing a

common cultural and language heritage, whether in a territorial entity within the republic or in any other recognised way.

**2.** The Constitution may give expression to any form of self-determination provided there is substantial proven support within the community concerned for such a form of self-determination.

**3.** If a territorial entity referred to in paragraph 1 is established in terms of this Constitution before the new constitutional text is adopted the new Constitution shall entrench the continuation of such territorial entity including its structures, powers and functions.

# Bibliography

*Abolition of Influx Control Act* (1986), Pretoria, Government Printer.

Adam, H. (1983), 'The Manipulation of Ethnicity, South Africa in Comparative Perspective', in D. Rothchild and V.A. Olorunsola (eds), *State versus Ethnic Claims, African Policy Dilemmas*, Boulder, Colorado, Westview Press.

Adam, H. and Giliomee, H. (1979), *Ethnic Power Mobilised, Can South Africa Change?*, New Haven, Yale University Press.

Ake, C. (1967), *A Theory of Political Integration*, Homewood, Illinois, Dorsey Press.

Alexander, N. (1989a), *Language Policy and National Unity in South Africa/Azania*, Cape Town, Buchu Books.

Alexander, N. (1989b), 'The Language Question', *University of Cape Town, Institute of the Study of Public Policy, Critical Choices for South Africa*, No. 12.

Almond, G. (1956), 'Comparative Political Systems', *Journal of Politics*, vol. 18, no. 3.

Almond, G. and Verba, S. (1963), *The Civic Culture*, Boston, Little Brown and Company.

ANC (African National Congress) (1992), 'ANC Policy Guidelines for a Democratic South Africa', National Conference, 28–31 May.

ANC (African National Congress) (1994), *The Reconstruction and Development Programme, a Policy Framework*, Cape Town, ANC.

ANC (African National Congress) (1995), 'Building a United Nation, Policy Proposals for the Final Constitution', 31 March – 1 April, Johannesburg, mimeo.

ANC Constitutional Committee (1990), *A Bill of Rights for a New South Africa*, Working Document, Belville, Centre for Development Studies.

ANC, Constitutional Committee (1991), *Discussion Document, Constitutional Principles and Structures for a Democratic South Africa*, Centre for Development Studies, University of the Western Cape, Belville.

ANC Newswire Root, downloaded from the Internet at http://www.bibim.com/anc/.

Andreassen, B.A. and Swinehart T. (eds) (1991), *Human Rights in Developing Countries: 1990 Yearbook*, Kehl, Strasbourg, Arlington, N.P. Engel Publisher.

Andreassen, B.A. and Swinehart T. (eds) (1992), *Human Rights in Developing Countries, Yearbook on 1991*, Oslo, Universitetsforlaget.

Arendt, H. (1958), *The Human Condition*, Chicago and London, University of Chicago Press.

Arendt, H. (1969a), *Between Past and Future*, Cleveland and New York, Harcourt, Brace and World.

Arendt, H. (1969b), 'Truth and Politics', in P. Laslett, and W.G. Runciman (eds), *Philosophy, Politics and Society*, 3rd series, Oxford, Basil Blackwell, pp. 104–33.

Asmal, K. (1995), 'The Making of a Constitution', *South African Review of Books*, 36, March/April. pp. 11–15.

Barry, B. (1973) *The Liberal Theory of Justice: a Critical Examination of the Principal Doctrines in A Theory of Justice by John Rawls*, Oxford, Clarendon Press.

Barry, B. (1975a), 'Political Accommodation and Consociational Democracy', *British Journal of Political Science*, vol. 5, no. 4.

Barry, B. (1975b), 'The Consociational Model and its Dangers', *European Journal of Political Research*, vol. 3, pp. 393–412.

Barry, B. (1979), 'Is Democracy Special?' in P. Laslett and J. Fishkin (eds), *Philosophy, Politics and Society*, 5th series, New Haven, Yale University Press, pp. 155–96.

Barry, B. (1989), *A Treatise on Social Justice. Volume 1. Theories of Justice*, London, Sydney and Tokyo, Harvester-Wheatsheaf.

Basson, D. (1994), *South Africa's Interim Constitution. Text and Notes*, Kenwyn, RSA, Juta.

Bates, R.H. (1970), 'Approaches to the Study of Ethnicity', *Cahiers D'études Africaines*, vol. 10, pp. 546–61.

Bates, R.H. (1974), 'Ethnic Competition and Modernisation in Contemporary Africa', *Comparative Political Studies*, vol. 6, no. 4, pp. 457–84.

Beitz, C. (1989), *Political Equality*, Princeton, New Jersey, Princeton University Press.

Berger, P.L. and Godsell B. (eds) (1988), *A Future South Africa, Visions, Strategies and Realities,* Pretoria, Human and Rousseau; Cape Town, Tafelberg; and Boulder, San Francisco and London, Westview Press.

Berg-Schlosser, D. (1985), 'Elements of Consociational Democracy in Kenya', *European Journal of Political Research*, 1985, vol. 13, pp. 95–111.

Bindman, G. (ed.) (1988), *South Africa and the Rule of Law,* International Commission of Jurists, London and New York, Pinter.

Blaau, L.C. (1990), 'The Rechtsstaat Idea Compared with the Rule of Law as a Paradigm for Protecting Rights', *South African Law Journal*, vol. 107, no. 1, pp. 76–96.

Botha, S. (1996), 'South Africa's Party System', *Journal of Theoretical Politics,* vol. 8, no. 2, pp. 209–25.

Boynton, G.R. and Kwon, W.H. (1978), 'An Analysis of Consociational Democracy', *Legislative Studies Quarterly*, vol. 3, no. 1, pp. 11–25.

Brynard, D. J. (1995), 'Research Note, The Citizen and the State: Implications of the Interim Constitution of South Africa', *Journal of Theoretical Politics,* vol. 7, no. 4, pp. 511–16.

Buthelezi Commission. (1982), *The Requirements for Stability and Development in KwaZulu and Natal,* 2 vols, Durban, H and H Publications.

Butler, J., Elpic R. and Welsh D. (eds) (1987), *Democratic Liberalism in South Africa — Its History and Prospects,* Middletown, Conn., Wesleyan University Press and Cape Town and Johannesburg, David Philip Ltd.

Callaghy, T.M. (ed.) (1983), *South Africa in Southern Africa, the Intensifying Vortex of Violence,* New York, Praeger Publishers.

Cameron, R. (1996), 'The Reconstruction and Development Programme', *Journal of Theoretical Politics,* vol. 8, no. 2, pp. 283–94.

Carter, G.M. and O'Meara, P. (eds) (1985), *African Independence, the First Twenty Five Years,* Bloomington, Indiana, Indiana University Press; London, Hutchinson.

CASE (Community Agency for Social Enquiry) (1995), *Bringing the Constitution and the People Together: Assessing the Impact of the Media Campaign of the Constitutional Assembly,* Johannesburg, CASE.

CASE (Community Agency for Social Enquiry) (1996), *Evaluation Results,* loaded down from the Internet: http://www.constitution.org.za/12ca9596.htm.

Catholic Institute for International Relations and British Council of Churches (1989), *Rule of Fear, Human Rights in South Africa,* London.

Central Statistical Service (CSS) (1996), *Statistics in Brief. Demography,* loaded down from the Internet: http://www.css.gov.za/SABrief/table3.htm.

Central Statistical Service (CSS) (1997), *Census 96. Preliminary Results,* loaded down from the Internet: http://www.css.gov.za/CensRes/chapter2.htm.

Claassens, A. (1991), *Who Owns South Africa? Can the Repeal of the Land Acts De-racialise Land Ownership in South Africa,* Centre for Applied Legal Studies Occasional Papers 11, Johannesburg, University of the Witwatersrand.

Cock, J. (1990), 'The Role of Violence in Current State Security Strategies', in *Views on the South African State,* in M. Swilling (ed.), Pretoria, Human Sciences Research Council, 85–108.

Cohen, J. (1986), 'Book Review', Review of Michal Walzer, *Spheres of Justice, Journal of Philosophy,* vol. 83, no. 8.

Constant, B. (1820), *De la Liberté des Anciens Comparée à celle des Modernes.*

Connoly, W.E. (1996), 'Pluralism, Multiculturalism and the Nation-State: Rethinking the Connections, *Journal of Political Ideologies,* vol. 1, no. 1, pp. 53–74.

Constitutional Assembly (1996a), *Annual Report of the Constitutional Assembly,* loaded down from the Internet: http://www.constitution.org.za/11ca9596.htm.

Constitutional Assembly (1996b), *Constitutional Court of South Africa, Certification of the National Constitution, Submissions on behalf of the Constitutional Assembly,* loaded down from the Internet: http://www.constitution.org.za /ccourt/ca004066.htm.

Constitutional Court of South Africa (1995), *State v Makwanyane and Another,* case CCT 3/94, Johannesburg, Constitutional Court.

Constitutional Court of South Africa (1996a), *Certification of the Constitution of the Republic of South Africa.* Case CCT 23/96, Johannesburg, Constitutional Court.

Constitutional Court of South Africa (1996b), *Certification of the Amended text of the Constitution of the Republic of South Africa.* Case CCT 37/96, Johannesburg, Constitutional Court.

Constitutional Talk (1995), (Official Newsletter of the Constitutional Assembly) nos 1–13 and Working Draft Edition, 1996, nos 1–3.

*Constitutional Talk,* (1996), (Official Newsletter of the Constitutional Assembly) nos 1–3.

Corder, H. (ed.) (1988), *Essays on Law and Social Practice in South Africa,* Cape Town, Wetton, Johannesburg, Juta and Co. Ltd.

Corder, H. (ed.) (1992), 'Lessons from North America. Beware the "Legalisation of Politics" and the "Political Seduction of the Law"', *South African Law Journal,* vol. 109, no. 2.

Daalder, H. (1974), 'The Consociational Democracy Theme', *World Politics,* 26, 4, pp. 604–21.

Daalder, H. (1981), 'Consociationalism, Centre and Periphery in the Netherlands', in P. Torsvik (ed.) *Mobilisation. Centre-Periphery Structures and Nation Building,* Oslo, Universitetsforlaget.

Dahl, R.A. (1971), *Poliarchy, Participation and Opposition,* New Haven, Yale University Press.

Dahl, R.A. (1991), 'Democracy and Human Rights Under Different Conditions of Development', in A. Eide and B. Hagtvet (eds), *Towards a More Humane World, The Challenge of Global Human Rights after 40 Years,* Oxford, Blackwell.

Dahrendorf, R. (1991), 'Är det likheten som gør ett folk till ett folk?', *Dagen Nyheter,* 4 February.

Davenport, T.R.H. (1987), *South Africa — a Modern History,* third edn, Cambridge Commonwealth Series, Houndmills, Basingstoke, Hampshire and London, Macmillan Press.

Davis, D. (1996), 'Is Our New Constitution any Good?', *Mail and Guardian,* 10 May.

DBSA (Development Bank of Southern Africa), (1994), 'South Africa's Nine Provinces: a Human Development Profile' Midrand, DBSA.

de Kok, I. and Press, K. (eds) (1990), *Spring is Rebellious. Arguments about Cultural Freedom by Albie Sachs and Respondents,* Cape Town, Buchu Books.

de Villiers, B. (ed.) (1991), *An Electoral System for the New South Africa,* Pretoria, HSRC Centre for Constitutional Analysis, year 2, no. 2.

de Villiers, B. (ed.) (1994), *Birth of a Constitution,* Kenvyn, Juta.

Degenaar, J. (1992), *Nations and Nationalism. The Myth of a South African Nation,* IDASA, Occasional Papers No. 40.

Deng, L.A. and Tjønneland, E.N. (eds) (1996), *South Africa: Wealth, Poverty and Reconstruction*, Bergen, Chr. Michelsen Institute/Cape Town, Centre for Southern African Studies.

Diamond, L. (1987), 'Ethnicity and Ethnic Conflict', *Journal of Modern African Studies*, vol. 25, no. 1, pp. 117–28.

Diamond, L. (1994), 'Civil Society and Democratic Consolidation: Building a Culture of Democracy in a New South Africa, in H. Giliomee, L. Schlemmer and S. Haupthfeish (eds), *The Bold Experiment. South Africa's New Democracy*, Halfway House, Southern Books, pp. 48–80.

Diamond, L., Linz, J. and Lipset, S.M. (1988), *Democracy in Developing Countries, Vol. II, Africa*, Boulder, Co., Lynn Rienner.

Dick, W.G. (1974), 'Authoritarian versus Non-Authoritarian Approaches to Economic Development', *Journal of Political Economy*, vol. 82, no. 4.

Dlamini, C.R.M. (1988), 'A Court-Enforced Bill of Rights for South Africa?', *Journal of Contemporary African Studies*, vol. 7, no. 1/2, pp. 81–110.

Donnelly, J. and Howard, R.E. (1986), 'Human Dignity, Human Rights and Political Regimes', *American Political Science Review*, vol. 80, no. 3.

Dunk, H. von der (1982), 'Conservatism in the Netherlands', in Z. Layton-Henry (ed.), *Conservative Politics in Western Europe*, London, Macmillan.

du Toit, A. (1983), 'Afrikaner Political Thought: Analysis and Documents' *Perspectives on Southern Africa*, no. 22, Berkeley, University of California Press.

du Toit, A. (1988), 'Understanding Rights Discourses and Ideological Conflicts in South Africa', in H. Corder (ed.), *Essays on Law and Social Practice in South Africa*, Cape Town, Wetton, Johannesburg, Juta and Co. Ltd., pp. 237–66.

Dutter, L.E. (1978), 'The Netherlands as a Plural Society', *Comparative Political Studies*, 10, 4, pp. 555–88.

Duverger, M. (1964), 'The Development of Democracy in France', in H. Ehrmann (ed.), *Democracy in a Changing Society*, New York, Praeger.

Ehrmann, H. (ed.) (1964), *Democracy in a Changing Society*, New York, Praeger.

Eide, A. and Hagtvet B. (1992), *Towards a More Humane World, The Challenge of Global Human Rights after 40 Years*, Oxford, Basil Blackwell.

Elster, J. (1979) *Ulysses and the Sirens,* Cambridge, Cambridge University Press.

Elster, J. (1981), 'States that are Essentially By-Products', *Social Science Information*, vol. 29, no. 3, pp. 431–73.

Elster, J. (1986) *Rational Choice. Readings in Social and Political Theory,* Oxford, Basil Blackwells.

Elster, J. (1988), 'Introduction', in J. Elster and R. Slagstad (eds), *Constitutionalism and Democracy*, Cambridge University Press and Universitetsforlaget.

Elster, J. (1992), 'On Majoritarianism and Rights', *East European Constitutional Review*, vol. 1, no. 3, pp. 19–27.

Elster, J. and Slagstad, R. (eds) (1988), *Constitutionalism and Democracy*, Cambridge University Press and Universitetsforlaget.

Eriksen, T.H. (1991), 'Ethnicity versus Nationalism', *Journal of Peace Research*, vol. 28, no. 3.

Eriksen, T.H. (1992), 'Det flerkulturelle dilemma. Kulturrelativismens paradoks og menneskerettighetene', *Mennesker og rettigheter*, 10, no. 3, pp. 223–32.

Estman M.J. (ed.) (1997), *Ethnic Conflict in the Western World*, Ithaca, Cornell University Press.

Faaland, J., Parkinson, J.R. and Saniman, R. (eds) (1990), *Growth and Ethnic Inequality, Malaysia's New Economic Policy*, Kuala Lumpur/London, Dewan Bahasa Dan Pustaka/C. Hurst (in association with the Chr. Michelsen Institute, Bergen, Norway).

Faure, M. (1996), 'The Electoral System', *Journal of Theoretical Politics,* vol. 8, no. 2, pp. 193–208.

Finer, S.E. (1979), *Five Constitutions*, Sussex, Harvester Press.

Fink, E.C. (1995), 'Institutional Change as a Sophisticated Strategy, The Bill of Rights as a Political Solution', *Journal of Theoretical Politics,* vol. 7, no. 4, pp. 477–510.

Fourie, F. (1990), 'The Namibian Constitution and Economic Rights', *South African Journal on Human Rights*, vol. 6, part 3, pp. 363–71.

Frankel, P.H. (1980), 'Consensus, Consociation and Cooption in South African Politics', *Cahiers d'études africaines*, 20, 4, pp. 473–94.

Frederikse, J. (1990), *The Unbreakable Thread, Non-Racialism in South Africa.* London, Zed Books Ltd.

Fukuyama, F. (1991), 'The Next South Africa', *South Africa International*, October.

Furnival J.S. (1948), *Colonial Theory and Practice, a Comparative Study of Burma and Netherlands India*, London, Oxford University Press.

Giliomee, H. and Schlemmer, L. (eds) (1989a), *Negotiating South Africa's Future*, Basingstoke and London, Macmillan, in conjunction with the Centre for Policy Studies, University of the Witwatersrand, Johannesburg.

Giliomee, H. and Schlemmer L. (1989b), *From Apartheid to Nation-Building,* Cape Town, Oxford University Press.

Giliomee, H. (1991), Book Review of A. Sparks, *The Mind of South Africa — The Story of the Rise and Fall of Apartheid, South Africa International*, vol. 21, no. 3, pp. 183–90

Giliomee, H., Schlemmer L. and Haupthfeish, S. (eds) (1994), *The Bold Experiment. South Africa's New Democracy*, Halfway House, Southern Books.

Gilje, N. (1989), *Det naturrettslige kontraktparadigmet*, Bergen, Senter for Vitenskapsteori.

Gloppen, S. and Rakner, L. (1993), *Human Rights and Development. The Discourse in the Humanities and Social Sciences,* CMI Report no. 3, Bergen, Chr. Michelsen Institute.

Godsell, B. (1990), *Shaping a Future South Africa. A Citizens' Guide to Constitution-making*, Cape Town, Tafelberg and Human and Rousseau.

*Bibliography*

Goldman, A. and Kim, J. (eds) (1978), *Values and Morals,* Boston, Reidel.
Goodin, R.E. (1979), 'The Development-Rights Trade-Off, Some Unwarranted Economic and Political Assumptions', *Universal Human Rights*, vol. 1, no. 2.
Greenberg, D, Katz, S. N., Oliveiro, M. B. and Wheatley S. C. (eds.) (1993), *Constitutionalism and Democracy. Transitions in the Contemporary World*, New York, Oxford, Oxford University Press.
Gutman, A. (1985), 'Communitarian Critics of Liberalism', *Philosophy and Public Affairs*, vol. 74, no. 3.
Guy, J. (1989), 'Etnicitet og klassekamp i sydafrikansk arbeiderkultur, *Den ny verden* ('Kultur og udvikling i det sydlige Afrika'), vol. 22, no. 1, pp. 164–77.
Habermas, J. (1996) *Between Facts and Norms*, Cambridge, Polity Press.
Hadenius, A. (1992), *Democracy and Development*, Cambridge, Cambridge University Press
Halpern, S. M. (1986), 'The Disorderly Universe of Consociational Democracy', *West European Politics*, vol. 9, no. 2, pp. 181–97.
Harber, A. and Ludman, B. (ed.) (1994), *A-Z of South African Politics. The Essential Handbook,* Mail and Guardian.
Harber, A. and Ludman, B. (ed.) (1995), *A-Z of South African Politics. The Essential Handbook.* Mail and Guardian
Hardin, R. (1982), *Collective Action*, Baltimore, Johns Hopkins University Press.
Holmes, S. (1988a), 'Gag Rules and the Politics of Omission', in J. Elster and R. Slagstad, *Constitutionalism and Democracy*, Cambridge University Press and Universitetsforlaget, pp. 19–58.
Holmes, S. (1988b), 'Precommitment and the Paradox of Democracy', in J. Elster and R. Slagstad, *Constitutionalism and Democracy*, Cambridge University Press and Universitetsforlaget, pp. 195–240.
Horowitz, D.L. (1985), *Ethnic Groups in Conflict*, Berkeley, University of California Press.
Horowitz, D.L. (1989), 'A Democratic South Africa? Constitutional Engineering in a Divided Society', lecture delivered under the auspices of the Maurice Webb Memorial Trust in association with the University of Natal, Durban and Pietermaritzburg, July – August.
Horowitz, D.L. (1991), *A Democratic South Africa? Constitutional Engineering in a Divided Society,* Berkeley, Los Angeles, Oxford, University of California Press.
Howard, R.E. (1983), 'The Full Belly Thesis, Should Economic Rights Take Priority over Civil and Political Rights? Evidence from Sub-Saharan Africa', *Human Rights Quarterly*, vol. 4.
Huntington, S. (1968), *Political Order in Changing Societies*, New Haven, Yale University Press.
Huntington, S. (1991), *The Third Wave: Democratization in the Late Twentieth Century*, Norman, Okla, University of Oklahoma Press.

Hylland, A. (1991), 'What Type of Institution is a Constitution?' and 'On the Work on New Constitutions in the East-European Countries', lectures given at the Norwegian Political Scientists' Association conference on 'Constitutions — Symbols or Politics', Oslo, 6–8. November.

Jackson, R. H. and Rosenberg, C.G. (1984), 'Popular Legitimacy in African Multi-Ethnic States', *Journal of Modern African Studies*, vol. 22, no. 2, pp. 177–98.

Jeffrey, A. (1996) 'Do We Need to Change the Bill of Rights Before it's too Late?' in *The Sunday Independent*, 31 March.

Judicial Services Commission (1994), *Interviews by the Judicial Services Commission for Judges for the Constitutional Court of South Africa. Interview with Prof. Albert Louis Sachs*, loaded down from the Internet: http://www.law.wits.ac.za/court/sachs.html.

Kasfir, N. (1979), 'Explaining Ethnic Political Participation', *World Politics*, vol. 31, no. 3, pp. 365–88.

Katz, R. S. (1980), *A Theories of Parties and Electoral Systems*, Baltimore, Johns Hopkins University Press.

Kelsen, H. (1934/1967), *Reine Rechtslehre*, Wien, Verlag Franz Deuitishe.

Kendall, F. and Louw, L. (1987), *After Apartheid, the Solution for South Africa*, San Francisco, ICS Press.

Kendall, F. and Louw, L. (1989), *Let the People Govern*, Bisho Ciskei, Amagi Publications.

Kitchen, H. and Kitchen J.C. (ed.) (1994), *South Africa: Twelve Perspectives on the Transition*, Centre for Strategic and International Studies, Washington, DC, Westport, Connecticut, London, Praeger.

Kotzé, D. (1996), 'The New (Final) South African Constitution, *Journal of Theoretical Politics*, vol. 8, no. 2, pp. 133–57.

Kotzé, H. and Greyling, A. (1994), *Political Organisation in South Africa A-Z*, Cape Town, Tafelberg.

Krouse, R. and M. McPherson (1988), 'Capitalism, "Property-Owning Democracy", and the Welfare State', in A. Gutman (ed.), *Democracy and the Welfare State*. Princeton, New Jersey, Princeton University Press, pp. 79-106.

Kuhnle, S. (1987), 'Duvergers lov om to-partisystemet', in S.U. Larsen (ed.), *Lov og Struktur*, Bergen, Universitetsforlaget, pp. 78–86.

Kukathas, C. and Pettit, P. (1990), *Rawls — A Theory of Justice and its Critics*, Cambridge, Polity Press.

Kumado, K. and Busia N.K.A. Jr (1991), 'The Impact of Developments in Eastern Europe on the Democratisation Processes in Africa, An Exploratory Analysis', in B.A. Andreassen and T. Swinehart (eds), *Human-Rights in Developing Countries, 1990 Yearbook*, Kehl, Strasbourg, Arlington, N.P. Engel Publisher.

Kuznets, S. (1955), 'Economic Growth and Income Equality', *American Economic Review*, vol. 45.

Kymlicka, W. (1989), *Liberalism Community and Culture*, Oxford, Clarendon Press.

Kymlicka, W. (1990), *Contemporary Political Philosophy*, Oxford, Clarendon Press.

Lane, J.E., and Faure, M. (1996), 'Introduction', *Journal of Theoretical Politics*, vol. 8, no. 2, pp. 123–32.

Laslett, P. and Runciman, W.G. (eds) (1969), *Philosophy, Politics and Society*, 3rd series, 104–33, Oxford, Basil Blackwell.

Laslett P. and Fishkin J. (eds) (1979), *Philosophy, Politics and Society*, 5th Series, New Haven, Yale University Press.

Leatt, J., Kneifel, T. and Nürenberger, K. (eds) (1986), *Contending Ideologies in South Africa*, Cape Town and Johannesburg, David Philip.

Lehmbruch, G. (1967), *Proporzdemokratie, Politisches System und Politische Kultur in der Schweitz und in Österreich*, Tübingen, Mohr.

Leon, P. (1996), 'A Justifiable Bill of Rights', in *The Sunday Independent*, 31 March.

leRoux, P. (1990), 'The Case for a Social Democratic Compromise', in N. Natrass and E. Ardington, *The Political Economy of South Africa*, Cape Town, Cambridge University Press, pp. 24–42.

Lewis, W.A., (1965), *Politics in West Africa*, London, Allen and Unwin.

LGETG (Local Government Election Task Group), (1995), 'Local Elections Report: National and Provincial Summaries', Pretoria, LGETG, 20 November.

LGETG (Local Government Election Task Group), (1996), 'Consolidated results of Local Elections' (with national and provincial summaries, update of 12 July 1996), Pretoria, LGETG.

Licht, R.A. and de Villiers, B. (eds) (1994), *South Africa's Crisis of Constitutional Democracy. Can the U.S. Constitution Help?*, Cape Town, Wetton, Johannesburg, Juta and Co. Ltd., Washington, DC, The AEI Press.

Lijphart, A. (1968a), *The Politics of Accommodation: Pluralism and Democracy in the Netherlands*, Berkeley, University of California Press.

Lijphart, A. (1968b), 'Typologies of Democratic Systems', *Comparative Political Studies*, no. 1, 3–44.

Lijphart, A. (1971), 'Consociational Democracy', in R.J. Jackson and M.B. Stein, *Issues in Comparative Politics*, New York, St Martin's Press.

Lijphart, A. (1977a), *Democracies in Plural Societies, a Comparative Exploration*, New Haven, Yale University Press.

Lijphart A. (1977b), 'Political Theories and the Explanation of Ethnic Conflict in the Western World, Falsified Predictions and Plausible Postdictions', in M.J. Estman (ed.), *Ethnic Conflict in the Western World*, Ithaca, Cornell University Press.

Lijphart A. (1984), *Democracies — Patterns of Majoritarian and Consensus Government in Twenty-One Countries*, New Haven and London, Yale University Press.

Lijphart A. (1985), 'Power-Sharing in South Africa', *Policy Papers in International Affairs*, no. 24, Institute of International Studies, University of California, Berkeley.

Lijphart, A. (1987), 'Choosing an Electoral System for Democratic Elections in South Africa, an Evaluation of the Procipal Options', *Critical Choices for South Africa Series*, Institute for the Study of Public Policy, University of Cape Town, September.

Lijphart A. (1989a), 'The Ethnic Factor and Democratic Constitution-Making in South Africa' in E.S. Keller and L.A. Pricard (eds), *Domestic Change and International Conflict*, Boulder, Co, Lynne Rienner.

Lijphart, A. (1989), 'Democratic Political Systems, Types, Cases, Causes, and Consequences', *Journal of Theoretical Politics*, vol. 1, pp. 33–48.

Lijphart, A. (1990), 'Electoral Systems, Party Systems and Conflict Management in Segmented Societies', in R.A. Schire (ed.), *Critical Choices for South Africa, an Agenda for the 1990s*, Cape Town, Oxford University Press.

Lijphart, A. (1991a), 'Constitutional Choices for New Democracies', *Journal of Democracy*, vol. 2, no. 1, pp. 72–84.

Lijphart, A. (1991b), 'The Alternative Vote, a Realistic Alternative for South Africa?, *Politikon*, vol. 18, no. 2 (June), pp. 91–101.

Lijphart, A. (1992), *Parliamentary versus Presidential Government*, Oxford, Oxford University Press.

Linz, J.J. (1990), 'The Perils of Presidentialism', *Journal of Democracy*, vol. 1, no. 1, pp. 51–69.

Linz, J.J. (1992), 'Types of Political Regimes and Respect for Human Rights, Historical and Cross-Cultural Perspectives', in A. Eide and B. Hagtvet (eds), *Towards a More Humane World, the Challenge of Global Human Rights after 40 Years*, Oxford, Blackwell, pp. 177–222.

Lipset, S.M. (1959), 'Some Social Requisites of Democracy, Economic Development and Political Legitimacy', *American Political Science Review*, vol. 53.

Lipset, S.M. (1960), *Political Man*, London, Heinemann.

Lipset, S.M. (1981), *Political Man*, Baltimore: Johns Hopkins University Press.

Lipset, S.M. (1994), 'The Social Requisites of Democracy Revisited', *American Sociological Review*, vol. 59, pp. 1–22.

Lucardie, P. (1988), 'Conservatism in the Netherlands, Fragments and Fringe Groups in B. Girvin (ed.), *The Transformation of Contemporary Conservatism*, London, SAGE Publications.

Lustic, I. (1979), 'Stability in Deeply Divided Societies', in *World Politics*, Princeton.

MacMurrin, S. (ed.) (1982), *The Tanner Lectures on Human Values*, Cambridge, Cambridge University Press.

Mafeje, A. (1971), 'The Ideology of "Tribalism"', *Journal of Modern African Studies*, vol. 9, no. 2, pp. 253–61.

Malnes, R. (1987), 'Popular Sovereignty and Good Government, a Tension in Contract Theory and a Liberal Dilemma', in D. Anckar and M. Wiberg (eds), *Legitimacy and Democracy*, The Finnish Political Science Association.

Mamdani, M. (1990), 'The Social Basis of Constitutionalism in Africa', *The Journal of Modern African Studies*, vol. 28, no. 3, pp. 359–74.

Mandela, N.R. (1994/95), *The Long Walk to Freedom*, London, Abacus.

Maphai, V. (ed.) (1994), *The Challenge of Change*, Harare, Sapes Books.

March, J.G. and Olsen J.P. (1989), *Rediscovering Institutions, the Organisational Basis of Politics*, New York, The Free Press.

Marks, S. and Trapido, S. (eds) (1987), *The Politics of Race, Class and Nationalism in Twentieth Century South Africa*, Harlow, Longman.

Martin, R. (1985), *Rawls and Rights*, Kansas, University Press of Kansas.

Mathews, A. (1986), *Freedom, State Security and the Rule of Law, Dilemmas of the Apartheid Society*, Cape Town, Juta and Co. Ltd. Berkeley, L.A., London, University of California Press.

Mattes, R. (1995), *The Election Book. Judgement and Choice in South Africa's 1994 Election*, Cape Town, Idasa Public Information Center.

McGrath, M.D. (1990), 'Income Redistribution, the Economic Challenge of the 1990s', in R. Schrire (ed.), *Critical Choices for South Africa, an Agenda for the 1990s*, Cape Town, Oxford University Press, pp. 92–108.

Meli, F. (1989), *A History of the ANC. South Africa Belongs to Us*, Harare, Zimbabwe Publishing House, Bloomington and Indianapolis, Indiana University Press, London, James Currey.

Melson and Wolpe (1970) 'Modernization and the Politics of Communalism: A Theoretical Perspective', *American Political Science Review*, no. 4, p. 1127.

Minnaar, A. (ed.) (1992), *Patterns of Violence. Case Studies of Conflict in Natal*, Pretoria, HSRC.

Minnaar, A. (1993a), 'Hostels and Violent Conflict on the Reef', in A. Minnaar (ed.), *Communities in Isolation: Perspectives on Hostels in South Africa*, Pretoria: HSRC.

Minnaar, A. (1993b), *Communities in Isolation: Perspectives on Hostels in South Africa*, Pretoria: HSRC.

Minnaar, A. (1994), 'Research Note, Political Violence in South Africa', *Journal of Theoretical Politics*, vol. 6, no. 3, pp 389–99.

Moll, P., Nattrass, N. and Loots, L. (eds) (1991), *Redistribution, How Can it Work in South Africa?*, Cape Town, David Philip Publishers in association with the Economic Policy Research Project at the University of the Western Cape.

Mulhall, S. and Swift, A. (1996), *Liberals and Communitarians* (second edn), Oxford, Cambridge, Mass., Blackwell Publishers.

Mureinik, E. (1988), 'Dworkin and Apartheid', in H. Corder (ed.), *Essays on Law and Social Practice in South Africa*, Cape Town, Wetton, Johannesburg, Juta and Co. Ltd, pp. 181–217.

Nagata, J. (1979), 'Review of Lijphart', *International Journal*, vol. 34, no. 3, pp. 505–6.

National Party (1991), *Constitutional Rule in a Participatory Democracy* (the National Party's framework for a new democratic South Africa).

Nolutshungu, S.C. (1982), *Changing South Africa, Political Considerations*, Manchester, Manchester University Press.

Nolutshungu, S.C. (1991), 'The Constitutional Question in South Africa', in I. Shivji (ed.), *State and Constitutionalism, an African Debate on Democracy*, Harare, SAPES Books.

Nordlinger, E.A. (1972), *Conflict Regulation in Divided Societies*, Cambridge, Harvard University Centre for International Affairs, Occasional Paper No. 29.

Nowak, M. and Swinehart, T. (eds) (1990), *Human Rights in Developing Countries, 1989 Yearbook*, Kehl, Strasbourg, Arlington, N.P. Engel Publisher.

Nozick, R. (1974), *Anarchy, State and Utopia*, New York, Basic Books.

Nurmi, H. (1993), 'Problems in the Theory of Institutional Design, an Overview', *Journal of Theoretical Politics*, vol. 5, no. 4, pp. 523–40.

Nwabueze, B.O. (1973), *Constitutionalism in the Emergent States*, London, C. Hurst and Co.

Nyang'oro, J.E. (1993), 'Reform Politics and the Democratisation Process in Africa', mimeo, AAPS 20th Congress, Dar-es-Salaam.

Offe, C. (1985), 'Legitimation through Majority Rule?', in J. Keane (ed.) *Disorganised Capitalism, Contemporary Transformation of Works and Politics*, Cambridge, Mass., MIT Press, 259–99.

Okoth-Ogendo, H.W.O. (1991), 'Constitutions without Constitutionalism, Reflections on an African Political Paradox', in I. Shivji (ed.), *State and Constitutionalism, an African Debate on Democracy*, Harare, SAPES Books, pp. 27–54.

Olivier, N. (1991), 'ANC Constitutional Proposals and State Reaction', *South Africa International*, October.

O'Malley, K. (1996), 'The 1993 Constitution of the Republic of South Africa — The Constitutional Court', *Journal of Theoretical Politics*, vol. 8, no. 2, pp. 177–91.

Pateman, C. (1970), *Participation and Democratic Theory*, Cambridge, Cambridge University Press.

Peeters, Y.J.D. (1991), 'Specific Requirements for Genuine Democracy in Plural Societies', Lecture at Norwegian Institute for Human Rights, 9 November.

Pillay, P. (1996), 'An Overview of Poverty in South Africa', in L.A. Deng and E.N. Tjønneland (eds), *South Africa: Wealth, Poverty and Reconstruction*,

Bergen, Chr. Michelsen Institute/Cape Town, Centre for Southern African Studies, pp. 14–46.

Pretorius, L. (1996), 'Relations Between State, Capital and Labour in South Africa: Towards Corporatism?', *Journal of Theoretical Politics,* vol. 8, no. 2, pp. 255–82.

Putnam, R. (1993), *Making Democracy Work, Civic Traditions in Modern Italy,* Princeton, New Jersey, Princeton University Press.

Rabushka, A. and Shepsle, K.A. (1972), *Politics in Plural Societies, a Theory of Democratic Instability,* Columbus, Ohio, Merrill.

Rakner, L. (1992), *Trade Unions in Processes of Democratisation. A Study of Party Labour Relations in Zambia,* CMI Report No. 6, Bergen, Chr. Michelsen Institute.

Ramaphele, M. (1993), *A Bed Called Home: Life in the Migrant Labour Hostels of Cape Town,* Cape Town, David Phillip.

Rawls, J. (1971), *A Theory of Justice,* Oxford, Oxford University Press.

Rawls, J. (1978), 'The Basic Structure as Subject', in A. Goldman and J. Kim (eds), *Values and Morals,* Boston, Reidel, pp. 47–71.

Rawls, J. (1979), 'A Well-ordered Society', in P. Laslett and J. Fishkin (eds) *Philosophy, Politics and Society,* 5th series, pp. 6–20.

Rawls, J. (1980), 'Kantian Constructivism in Moral Theory', *The Journal of Philosophy,* vol. 88, pp. 515–72.

Rawls, J. (1982a), 'Social Unity and Primary Goods', in A. Sen and B. Williams (eds), *Utilitarianism and Beyond,* Cambridge, Cambridge University Press, pp. 159–85.

Rawls, J. (1982b), 'The Basic Liberties and their Priorities', in S. MacMurrin (ed.), *The Tanner Lectures on Human Values,* Cambridge, Cambridge University Press, pp. 1–89.

Rawls, J. (1985), 'Justice as Fairness, Political not Metaphysical', *Philosophy and Public Affairs,* vol. 14, pp. 223–51.

Rawls, J. (1987), 'The Idea of an Overlapping Consensus', *Oxford Journal of Legal Studies,* vol. 7, pp. 1–25.

Rawls, J. (1988), 'The Priority of Right and the Ideas of the Good', *Philosophy and Public Affairs,* 17, pp. 251–76.

Rawls, J. (1989), 'The Domain of the Political and Overlapping Consensus', *New York University Law Review,* vol. 64, pp. 233–55.

Rawls, J. (1993), *Political Liberalism,* New York, Chichester, West Sussex, Colombia University Press.

Raz, J. (1979), *The Authority of Law,* Oxford, Oxford University Press.

*Restoration of South African Citizenship Act,* Act No. 73 of 1986 (1986), Pretoria. Government Printer.

Reynolds, A. (ed.) (1994), *Election '94 South Africa: the Campaigns, Results and Future Prospects,* Claremont, RSA, David Phillip.

Riley, E. (1991), *Major Political Events in South Africa 1948–1990*, Oxford, New York, Facts on File.

RSA (Republic of South Africa) (1983), *Republic of South Africa Constitution Act, 1983*, Act 110.

RSA (Republic of South Africa) (1993), *Constitution of the Republic of South Africa, 1993*, Act 200.

RSA (Republic of South Africa) (1994), *White Paper on Reconstruction and Development. Government's Strategy for Fundamental Transformation*, Pretoria: Government Printer.

RSA (Republic of South Africa (1996), *Constitution of the Republic of South Africa 1996* (as adopted by the Constitutional Assembly on 8 May 1996), loaded down from the Internet: http://www.constitution.org.za/drafts/sacib96.htm.

RSA (Republic of South Africa) (1996b), *Growth, Employment and Redistribution. A Macroeconomic Strategy*, loaded down from the Internet: http://www.sacs.org.za/gov/finance/home/macroeco.htm.

Rustow, D. (1970), 'Transitions to Democracy. Towards a Dynamic Model', *Comparative Politics*, vol. 2, no. 3, pp. 337–63.

Rycroft, A.J. (1988), 'The Protection of Socioeconomic Rights', in H. Corder (ed.), *Essays on Law and Social Practice in South Africa*, Cape Town, Wetton, Johannesburg, Juta and Co. Ltd, pp. 267–83

Sachs, A. (1986), 'Towards the Constitutional Reconstruction of South Africa', *Lesotho Law Journal* vol. 2.

Sachs, A. (1989), 'Post-Apartheid South Africa, a Constitutional Framework', *World Policy Journal*, vol. 6, no. 3, pp. 503–29.

Sachs, A. (1990a), *Protecting Human Rights in a New South Africa*, Cape Town, Oxford University Press.

Sachs, A. (1990b), 'The Future Constitutional Position of White South Africans in a Democratic South Africa', *African Studies Seminar Paper No. 281*, African Studies Institute, University of the Witwatersrand.

Sachs, A. (1992a), *Advancing Human Rights in South Africa*, Oxford, Oxford University Press.

Sachs, A. (1992b), 'Affirmative Action and Good Government', in P. Hugo (ed.), *Redistribution and Affirmative Action. Working on the South African Political Economy*, Southern Book Publishers, Pretoria.

Sachs, A. and Welch, G.H. (1990b), *Liberating the Law, Creating Popular Justice in Mozambique*, London and New Jersey, Zed Books.

Sandel, M. (1982), *Liberalism and the Limits of Justice*, Cambridge, Cambridge University Press.

Sandel, M. (1988), 'The Political Theory of the Procedural Republic', *Revue de Metaphysique et de Morale*, vol. 93, pp. 57–68.

Sartori, G. (1987), *The Theory of Democracy Revisited*, New Jersey, Catham House.

Sartori, G. (1994), *Comparative Constitutional Engineering: an Inquiry into Stuctures, Incentive and Outcomes,* Basingstoke, Macmillan.

Scanlon, T.M. (1982), 'Utilitarianism and Contractualism', in A. Sen and B. Williams (eds), *Utilitarianism and Beyond,* Cambridge, Cambridge University Press.

Schrire, R.A. (ed.) (1990), *Critical Choices for South Africa. An Agenda for the 1990s,* Cape Town, Oxford University Press.

Schrire, R.A. (1992), *Wealth or Poverty? Critical Choices for South Africa,* Cape Town, Oxford University Press.

Schrire, R.A. (ed.) (1994), *Leadership in the Apartheid State,* Cape Town, Oxford University Press.

Schrire, R.A. (ed.) (1996), 'The President and the Executive', *Journal of Theoretical Politics,* vol. 8, no. 2, pp. 159–75.

Shivji, I. (ed.) (1991), *State and Constitutionalism, an African Debate on Democracy,* Harare, SAPES Books.

Schlemmer, L. (1978) 'The Devolution of Power in South Africa: Problems and Prospects', in N. Rhoodie (ed.) *The Road to a Just Society,* Johannesburg, South African Institute of Race Relations.

Schlemmer, L. (1991), 'The National Party Constitutional Proposals — Stable Democracy or Minority Imperialism?', *South Africa International,* October.

Schlemmer, L. (1994), 'South Africa's first open election and the future of its new democracy' in H. Giliomee *et al.* (eds) (1994), *The Bold Experiment. South Africa's New Democracy,* Halfway House, Southern Books, pp. 149-167.

Schumpeter, J.A. (1940/1976), *Capitalism, Socialism and Democracy,* 5th edition, London, George Allen and Unwin.

Seleoane, M. (1996) 'Freedom of Expression: the Challenges Ahead', in *HSRC Centre for Constitutional Analysis,* vol. 7, no. 4.

Semb, A.J. (1992), 'Liberalism, Communitarianism, and Individualism', unpublished paper, Institute for Political Science, Oslo.

Sen A.K. (1970/1979), *Collective Choice and Social Welfare,* Amsterdam, New York, Oxford, North-Holland Publishing Company.

Simkins, C. (1986), *Reconstructing South African Liberalism,* Johannesburg, South African Institute of Race Relations.

Simkins, C (1987), 'Democratic Liberalism and the Dilemmas of Equality', in Butler, J. (ed.), *Democratic Liberalism in South Africa,* Cape Town, David Phillip.

Simkins, C. (1988), *The Prisoners of Tradition and the Politics of Nation Building,* Johannesburg, South African Institute of Race Relations.

Sisk, T.D. (1993), 'Choosing an Electoral System: South Africa Seeks New Ground Rules', *Journal of Democracy,* vol. 4, no. 1, pp. 79–91.

Sklar, R.L. (1967), 'Political Science and National Integration — a Radical Approach', *Journal of Modern African Studies,* vol. 5, no. 1, pp. 1–11.

South Africa Foundation (1992), *South Africa 1993*, Johannesburg, South Africa Foundation.

South African Ministry for Welfare and Population Development (1995), *Population Policy for South Africa. A Green Paper for Public Discussion.* Pretoria, The Ministery for Welfare and Population Development.

South African Institute of Race Relations (1993), *Race Relations Survey 1992/1993*, Johannesburg, SAIRR.

South African Institute of Race Relations (1994), *Race Relations Survey 1993/1994*, Johannesburg, SAIRR.

South African Institute of Race Relations (1995), *Race Relations Survey 1994/1995*, Johannesburg, SAIRR.

South African Law Commission (1989), 'Project 58, Group and Human Rights', Working Paper 25, Pretoria, S.A. Law Commission.

Southall, R.J. (1983), 'Consociationalism in South Africa, the Buthelezi Commission and Beyond', *Journal of Modern Africa Studies*, vol. 21, no. 1, pp. 77–112.

Southall, R.J. (1990), 'Negotiations and Social Democracy in South Africa', *The Journal of Modern African Studies,* vol. 28, no. 3, pp. 487–509.

Sparks, A. (1990), *The Mind of South Africa — the Story of the Rise and Fall of Apartheid*, London, Heinemann.

Steiner, J. (1974), *Amicable Agreement versus Majority Rule, Conflict Resolution in Switzerland*, Chapel Hill, University of North Carolina Press.

Steiner, J. (1986), *European Democracies*, New York, Longman Inc.

Steiner, J. and Obler J. (1977), 'Does the Consociational Theory Really Hold for Switzerland?', in M. Esman (ed.), *Ethnic Conflict in the Western World*, Ithaca, Cornell University Press.

Stokke, L. (1991), 'The Consociational Model, Neither a Valid Generalisation nor a Healthy Recommendation?', unpublished paper, Department of Comparative Politics, University of Bergen.

Suckling, J. and White, L. (eds) (1988), *After Apartheid, Renewal of the South African Economy*, York and London, Centre for Southern African Studies, University of York in association with James Currey and Africa World Press.

Sunstein, C,R. (1988), 'Constitutions and Democracies, an Epilogue', in J. Elster and R. Slagstad, *Constitutionalism and Democracy*, Cambridge University Press and Universitetsforlaget, pp. 327–53.

Swensen, I.A. (1990), *Konservatismen i Nederland og Norge*, Cand Polit Thesis, Department of Political Science, University of Oslo.

Swilling, M. (1990), *Views on the South African State*, Pretoria, HSRC.

Taylor, R. (1991a), 'Looking Behind the "FACT" of Ethnic Conflict', *Democracy in Action*, IDASA, 15 October, pp. 7–8.

Taylor, R. (1991b), 'The Myth of Ethnic Division, Township Conflict on the Reef', *Race and Class*, vol. 32, no. 2, pp. 1–14.

Tjønneland, E.N. (1990), 'Negotiating Apartheid Away', *PRIO Report*, no. 2.

Tjønneland, E.N. (1992a), *Southern Africa after Apartheid, an Analysis with Implications for Norwegian Development Assistance,* Draft Report April/May, Bergen, Chr. Michelsen Institute.

Tjønneland, E.N. (1992b), 'The Politics of Poverty Reduction and Development in the Rainbow Nation — an Overview', in L.A. Deng and E.N. Tjønneland (eds), *South Africa: Wealth, Poverty and Reconstruction,* Bergen, Chr. Michelsen Institute/Cape Town, Centre for Southern African Studies, pp. 1–13.

Tjønneland, E.N. (1993), *South Africa's 1994 Elections,* Human Rights Report No. 3, Oslo, Norwegian Institute of Human Rights.

Tocqueville, A. (1835–1840/1981), *Democracy in America,* abridged with an introduction by Thomas Bender, New York, The Modern Library.

Tomasevski, K. (1990), 'The World Bank and Human Rights', in M. Nowak and T. Swinehart (eds), *Human Rights in Developing Countries, 1989 Yearbook,* Kehl, Strasbourg, Arlington, N.P. Engel Publisher.

Tørres, L. (1995), *South African Workers Speak,* Common Security Forum Studies, Oslo, FAFO.

United Nations (1987), 'The Limburg Principles on the Implementation of the International Covenant on Economic, Social and Cultural Rights', UN Document E/CN.4/1987/17.

Uys, S. (1991), 'Can a Democratic Constitution take Root in South Africa?', *South Africa International,* October.

van den Berghe, P.L. (1981), 'Protection of Ethnic Minorities, a Critical Appraisal', in R.G. Wirsing (ed.), *Protection of Ethnic Minorities. Comparative Perspectives,* Pergamon Press.

van der Merwe, H.W. (1989), *Pursuing Justice and Peace in South Africa,* London and New York, Routlege.

van der Merwe, H.W. and Schire R. (1980), *Race and Ethnicity. South African and International Perspectives,* Cape Town and London, David Philip.

Van Diepen, M. (ed.) (1988), *The National Question in South Africa,* London and New Jersey, Zed Books Ltd.

van Huyssteen, E.F. (1996), 'By the people, for the people? The South African Constitutional Assembly and the writing of the new Constitution', paper presented at the SASA conference, July 1996, Durban, South Africa.

Van Schendlen, M.P.C.M. (1983), 'Critical Comments on Lijphart's Theory of Consociational Democracy, *Politicon,* vol. 10, no. 1, pp. 6–32.

Van Schendlen, M.P.C.M. (1984), 'The Views of Arendt Lijphart and Collected Criticisms', *Acta Politica,* vol. 19, no. 1, pp. 19–55.

van Vuuren, D.J. and Kriek, D.J. (eds) (1983), *Political Alternatives for Southern Africa, Principles and Perspectives,* Durban, Butterworths.

van Vuuren, D.J., Wiehahn N.E., Lombard, J.A., Rhoodie (1985), *South Africa — A Plural Society in Transition,* Durban, Butterworths.

van Zyl Slabbert, F. (1992), *The Quest for Democracy, South Africa in Transition,* Harmondsworth, Penguin.

Venter, A.J. (1983), 'Consociational Democracy', in D.J. van Vuuren and D.J. Kriek (eds), *Political Alternatives for Southern Africa, Principles and Perspectives,* Durban, Butterworths.

Waltzer, M. (1981), 'Philosophy and Democracy', *Political Theory,* vol. 9, pp. 379–99.

Walzer, M. (1982), 'Pluralism in Political Perspective', in M. Walzer *et al.* (eds), *The Politics of Ethnicity,* Cambridge, Mass., The Belknap Press of Harvard University Press, pp. 1–28.

Walzer, M. (1983), *Spheres of Justice. A Defence of Pluralism and Equality,* Oxford, Blackwell.

Walzer, M. *et al.* (eds) (1982), *The Politics of Ethnicity,* Cambridge, Mass., The Belknap Press of Harvard University Press.

Weber, M. (1968), 'Ethnic Groups', in G. Roth and C. Wittich (eds), *Max Weber, Economy and Society, an Outline for Interpretative Sociology,* New York, Bedminister Press.

Whiteside, A. (1991), 'Labour Migration in Southern Africa to the Year 2000 and Beyond', unpublished paper, Economic Research Unit, University of Natal, Durban.

Young, C. (1982), 'Patterns of Social Conflict, State, Class, and Ethnicity, *Daedalus,* vol. III, no. 2, pp. 71–98.

Zolberg, A.R. (1977), 'Splitting the Difference, Federalisation Without Federalism in Belgium', in M. Esman (ed.), *Ethnic Conflict in the Western World,* Ithaca, Cornell University Press.

# Index

precommitment 47-50, 54, 61, 95, 118, 173, 206, 214
presidentialism 50, 61, 95, 102, 118, 206, 214, 216, 218, 241, 254, 272
principles of justice 71, 74-77, 84-86, 115
procedural justice 72, 73, 114
property rights 87, 231, 236, 239
proportional representation (PR) 44, 62, 100-103, 108, 154, 202, 205, 215, 236, 238
provinces 26, 201-204, 209, 213-219, 222-227, 236, 238, 251-253, 256, 270, 274
public participation 11, 248, 258-267, 274
Public Service Commission 202, 213
Public Protector 202, 213, 228

quasi-presidentialism 206, 214, 216

Ramaphosa, C. 211
Rawls, J. 8, 41, 58, 61, 65, 70-77, 81-89, 112-118, 128-130, 144, 147, 152, 184, 240, 258, 263
rechtsstaat 45-47, 50, 54, 61, 66, 67, 88, 95, 109, 110, 118, 206, 214
redistribution 28, 66, 99, 119, 130, 141, 145, 153, 159, 161, 170-183, 192, 250, 251, 253-256, 270

rule of law 45-47, 50, 54, 61, 67, 82, 95, 109, 110, 152, 206, 214

Sachs, A. 5, 8, 9, 20, 42, 45, 58-74, 77-89, 92, 93, 96, 100, 105, 106, 110-119, 128, 144, 148-154, 157-163, 166, 167 171, 174, 175, 180, 183-187, 200, 215, 225, 227, 230-233, 249, 258, 263, 270
Senate 12, 119, 201, 202, 215, 216, 219, 222, 223

separation of powers 47, 62, 63, 68, 69, 202, 209, 217-219, 226, 250, 251, 256, 270
social and economic rights 8, 47, 68, 69, 88, 152, 158-161, 168, 174, 230- 234, 239, 240, 254
social justice 8, 69, 160, 200, 232, 235, 236, 240, 250, 253, 275
Sotho 18, 253
special procedures for constitutional amendment 43, 203, 213, 219-221, 225
spontaneous formation of groups 98, 166
stability 5-14, 17, 28, 36-42, 48-52, 55, 58, 61, 64, 80, 88, 92-95, 99-106, 109, 118, 119, 127, 128, 133-137, 144, 145, 154, 155, 167-171, 176-182, 188-193, 206, 214, 235, 236, 248, 249, 255, 267, 268, 273, 275

third force 15, 143
traditional leaders 216, 225, 235-238, 240
Truth and Reconciliation Commission (TRC) 14, 16

violence 6, 12-17, 21-28, 94, 96, 99, 111, 133, 143, 157, 192, 201, 207, 237
Volkstaat 201, 203, 208, 215, 235

Wessels, L. 211
Western Cape 15, 139, 187, 209, 211, 252
Westminster model of democracy 44, 69, 136, 142, 200, 217

Xhosa 18, 22, 23, 131, 178, 253

Zulu 14, 18, 22, 23, 178, 188, 202, 207, 235, 252